Beyond (Straight and Gay) Marriage

Beyond (Straight and Gay) Marriage

Valuing All Families under the Law

Nancy D. Polikoff

Beacon Press
Boston

Beacon Press
25 Beacon Street
Boston, Massachusetts 02108-2892
www.beacon.org

Beacon Press books
are published under the auspices of
the Unitarian Universalist Association of Congregations.

Printed in the United States of America

11 10 09 08 8 7 6 5 4 3 2 1

This book is printed on acid-free paper that meets
the uncoated paper ANSI/NISO specifications
for permanence as revised in 1992.

Text design and composition by Tag Savage
at Wilsted & Taylor Publishing Services

Polikoff, Nancy D.
Beyond (straight and gay) marriage : valuing all families under the law / Nancy D. Polikoff.
p. cm.
Includes bibliographical references and index.
ISBN 978-0-8070-4432-2
1. Unmarried couples—Legal status, laws, etc.—United States. 2. Domestic partner benefits—Law and legislation—United States. 3. Same-sex marriage—Law and legislation—United States. 4. Civil unions—Law and legislation—United States. 5. Gay couples—Legal status, laws, etc.—United States. 6. Lesbian couples—Legal status, laws, etc.—United States. I. Title.

KF538.P65 2007
346.7301'6—dc22 2007021330

To my teachers, especially

Horace Ports (in memoriam)

Judith Fetterley

Judith Areen

Contents

A Note from the Series Editor

The history of the LGBT movement has been a serpentine series of crusades to identify and combat the myriad legal discriminations, oppressions, and social proscriptions that faced its constituents. Choosing what battles to fight—for any group—is always a complicated historical and cultural process, and the choices made depend on a wide range of factors. In recent years the battle for marriage equality has become, for many activists, the central struggle of the fight for lesbian and gay rights. This is understandable since marriage equality deals with relationships, legal rights, medical and economic benefits, and sustaining family units. But in the midst of any conflict it is often difficult to see the broader picture—and other options.

Nancy Polikoff's *Beyond (Straight and Gay) Marriage: Valuing All Families under the Law* is one of the first books to examine, in detail and with a plethora of real-life as well as legal examples, what all families need to survive in a world that is becoming, socially and economically, increasingly harsh and complicated. Polikoff's brilliant and incisive legal analysis cuts through the arguments for and against same-sex marriage recognition to show us that both sides are arguing from a place that misses the larger picture of what all families—of whatever configuration—need to continue to support themselves and flourish. Drawing on cutting-edge family law, feminist theory, and plain old common sense, Polikoff brings us a vision of how we, as a society, can legally and ethically value everyone's desire for family, stability, and security. In many ways *Beyond (Straight and Gay) Marriage* offers us a vision of the LGBT movement as it grows up to become as mature, inclusive, and progressive as its potential has always indicated it could be.

MICHAEL BRONSKI
Series Editor

Introduction

Karen Thompson had a problem. Her lover of four years, Sharon Kowalski, lay in a hospital bed, having suffered a brain injury caused when a car operated by a drunk driver collided with her car on a stormy Minnesota night. Because Karen wasn't a family member, the nursing staff would not let her see Sharon; this would be the beginning of a decade-long struggle pitting Karen against Sharon's parents over control of Sharon's treatment.[1]

Susan Burns had a problem. The divorce decree awarding custody of her three children to their father stated that the children could not visit her if at any time during their stay she was living with or spending overnights with a person to whom she was not legally married. More than four years later, on July 1, 2000, Vermont instituted civil unions for same-sex couples. Susan entered into a civil union with her partner on July 3. When the children spent the night in the home Susan shared with her partner, a judge found her in contempt of court.[2]

Larry Courtney had a problem. His partner of fourteen years, Eugene Clark, did not come home from his job on the 102nd floor of the south tower of the World Trade Center on September 11, 2001. When Larry filed a workers' compensation claim, the reviewing agency replied that he did not qualify for benefits, which might instead be paid to Eugene's father, from whom Eugene had been estranged for twenty years.[3]

Lisa Stewart had a problem. At thirty-three, and with a five-year-old daughter, Emily, she was diagnosed with breast cancer, which became terminal. She was unable to continue working as a real estate appraiser and lost her income and her health insurance. Her partner of ten years, Lynn, had insurance through her job, but it did not cover Lisa and Emily. Lisa and Lynn live in South Carolina, which does not allow "second-parent" adoption, so Lisa is Emily's only legally recognized parent. When Lisa dies, Emily will receive Social Security survivors' benefits, but Lynn will not.[4]

A consumer of current news might imagine that access to same-sex marriage is the most contested issue in contemporary family policy, and that marriage is the only cure for the disadvantages faced by lesbian and gay families. Both of these observations would be wrong. The most contested issue in contemporary family policy is whether married-couple families should have "special rights" not available to other family forms. Excluded families include unmarried couples of any sexual orientation, single-parent households, extended-family units, and any other constellation of individuals who form relationships of emotional and economic interdependence that do not conform to the one-size-fits-all marriage model. No other Western country, including those that allow same-sex couples to marry, creates the rigid dividing line between the law for the married and the law for the unmarried that exists in the United States.

Consider the situations of the people above. Some may see them as evidence that same-sex couples must be allowed to marry. If Karen and Sharon had been married, no one would have questioned Karen's right to be Sharon's guardian. If Susan and her partner were married, she would not have been in violation of the court order when her children visited. If Larry and Eugene had been married, Larry would have received Eugene's workers' compensation benefit. If Lisa and Lynn could marry, Lisa would be covered on Lynn's health insurance, Lynn could adopt Emily, and Lisa and Emily would both receive Social Security survivors' benefits when Lisa died.

I see these stories differently. Karen was the right choice to be Sharon's guardian because she knew Sharon best and was indisputably committed to her, because Sharon progressed when Karen worked with her while she was institutionalized, and because Karen was willing to take Sharon out of an institution and care for her in their home. Susan and her children were entitled to regular visitation to sustain and support their mother-child relationship, and unless her partner was harming the children, the fact that Susan lived with a partner should not have concerned a family court judge. Larry and Eugene were an economic unit; Eugene's death hurt Larry, not Eugene's father. Lisa needed healthcare; her daughter needed legal recognition of the two parents she had; and on Lisa's death, Lynn needs survivors' benefits to help her continue raising Emily.

I propose family law reform that would recognize all families' worth. Marriage as a family form is not more important or valuable than other forms of family, so the law should not give it more value. Couples should have the choice to marry based on the spiritual, cultural, or religious meaning of marriage in their lives; they should never *have to* marry to reap specific and unique legal benefits. I support the right to marry for same-sex couples as a matter of civil rights law. But I oppose discrimination against couples who do not marry, and I advocate solutions to the needs all families have for economic well-being, legal recognition, emotional peace of mind, and community respect.

Consider the following:

Bonnie Cord graduated from law school and began working at a government agency. She bought a home with her male partner in the foothills of the Blue Ridge Mountains in Virginia. When she applied to take the Virginia bar exam—a test necessary to obtain the right to practice law in the state—a judge ruled that her unmarried cohabitation made her morally unfit to do so.[5]

Catrina Graves was driving her car behind a motorcycle driven by Brett Ennis, the man with whom she had been living for seven years. A car failed to stop at a stop sign and hit Brett's motorcycle; Brett was thrown onto the pavement. Catrina saw the accident, stopped her car, and ran to Brett, who had suffered trauma to his head and was bleeding from the mouth. He died the next day. When Catrina sued the driver for negligent infliction of emotional distress, the court dismissed her lawsuit because she was not related to Brett by blood or marriage.[6]

Olivia Shelltrack and Fondray Loving had lived together for thirteen years when they bought a five-bedroom home in Black Jack, Missouri. They moved in with their two children and a third child from Olivia's previous relationship. The city denied them an occupancy permit because its zoning laws prohibit three persons unrelated by blood or marriage from living together.[7]

These are heterosexual couples and they *could* marry. But they shouldn't *have* to. Bonnie's choice to live with an unmarried partner bore no relationship to her ability to practice law. Catrina's anguish would have been no different had Brett been her spouse. The proper zoning concerns of Black Jack, Missouri, do not turn on whether Olivia and Fondray marry.

Extending legal rights and obligations to unmarried couples, as many Western countries do, is a start, but it is not enough. "Couples," meaning two people with a commitment grounded on a sexual affiliation, should not be the only unit that counts as family.

Consider these examples:

As a foster child, Jason was placed with married parents, Daniel and Mary Lou, who divorced two years later. Jason then lived with Mary Lou and visited Daniel, who also paid child support. When Mary Lou and Daniel petitioned to adopt Jason, the court ruled that unmarried adults could not adopt a child together.[8]

Two sisters in England, Joyce, eighty-eight, and Sybil, eighty, have lived together all their lives. They grew up on a thirty-acre farm and worked on the land. They moved away for about fifteen years but returned in 1965, built a home on the land, and leased the farm. They live off the rental income. They each have wills naming the other as their beneficiary. When the first sister dies, the 40 percent inheritance tax will make it necessary for the survivor to sell the land and move. The survivor of a heterosexual married couple or a registered same-sex civil partnership would not have to pay this tax.[9]

Fifty-nine-year-old Maria Sierotowicz had been living in the same one-bedroom, subsidized housing unit in Brooklyn since 1984. Her mother, who lived with her, passed away in 1990. Ten years later, her eighty-one-year-old father returned to the United States from Poland and moved in with her so that she could care for him. Maria followed procedures and requested that he receive permission to join her Section 8 household. Her request was denied because he wasn't her spouse and his presence would make her unit "overcrowded." Maria received a notice terminating her Section 8 subsidy.[10]

Marriage cannot be the solution to these problems. Jason's parents tried marriage; it didn't work for them. They need to be able to adopt Jason as two unmarried parents, if a judge finds that such an adoption is in Jason's best interests. Sybil and Joyce are a family, but not a family based on marriage or even on a marriage-like relationship. They are a long-term, interdependent unit, and they need—

perhaps more than many spouses do—the financial advantages now extended only to spouses. If Maria had married, her husband would have automatically received permission to live with her. Instead she wants to care for someone unable to care for himself. She needs occupancy rules that do not stand in her way.

It is possible to envision family law and policy without marriage being the rigid dividing line between who is in and who is out. Keeping the state out of marriage entirely, making marriage only a religious, cultural, and spiritual matter, would be one way to accomplish this. But the law would still have to determine how to allocate rights and responsibilities in families and when relationships among people would create entitlements or obligations. This necessity, coupled with the disruption of expectations that ending the state's involvement in marriage would produce, suggests another approach.

I call this approach valuing all families. The most important element in implementing this approach is identifying the purpose of a law that now grants marriage unique legal consequences. By understanding a law's purpose, we can identify the relationships that would further that purpose without creating a special status for married couples.

Sweeping legal changes in the late 1960s and early 1970s altered the significance of marriage and laid the groundwork for this pluralistic vision. Those changes grew out of cultural and political shifts, including feminism and other social-change movements, greater access to birth control and acceptance of sex outside marriage, and increased dissatisfaction with marriage. The legal changes included decreased penalties on nonmarital sex, especially an end to discrimination against children born to unmarried mothers; equality between women and men; and no-fault divorce.

Early gay and lesbian rights advocates forged alliances with others who challenged the primacy of marriage: divorced and never-married mothers, including those receiving welfare benefits; unmarried heterosexuals, both those consciously rejecting the baggage associated with marriage and those who simply did not marry; and nonnuclear units, such as communal living groups and extended families. The gay rights movement was part of broader social movements challenging the political, economic, and social status quo and seeking to transform society into one in which sex, race, class, sexual orientation, and marital status no longer determined one's place in the nation's hierarchy. Marriage was in the process of losing its ironclad grip on the organization of family life, and lesbians and gay men benefited overwhelmingly from the prospect of a more pluralistic vision of relationships.

There were setbacks. A backlash resulted in restrictions on women's reproductive freedom, repeal of gay rights laws, and less support for welfare mothers. Conservatives employed the rhetoric of "traditional family values" to fight any proposal advancing recognition and acceptance of lesbian, gay, bisexual, and transgender (LGBT) people, and used antigay propaganda to raise money and garner votes for a wide-ranging conservative agenda.

I seek to reclaim and build on the principle that law should support the diverse families and relationships in which children and adults flourish.

Since the mid-1990s, two movements have placed marriage in the public policy spotlight. The "marriage movement"—with both religious and secular components—opposes not only recognition of LGBT families but also easily obtained divorce, childbearing and sex outside marriage, and sex education that teaches anything other than abstinence. It advocates government funding of "marriage promotion" efforts. Its most prominent religion-based groups are Focus on the Family and the Family Research Council. They speak of a "God-ordained family."

David Blankenhorn of the Institute for American Values and Maggie Gallagher of the Institute for Marriage and Public Policy are leading spokespeople for the secular claim that supporting any family form other than heterosexual marriage endangers the social fabric. By blaming poverty, crime, drug abuse, and education failure on family diversity, they point the finger at unmarried mothers and absolve government of the responsibility for wage stagnation, income inequality, poor schools, sex and race discrimination, and inadequate childcare and healthcare. Legal groups such as the Alliance Defense Fund and Liberty Counsel represent these positions in litigation. The mission of Liberty Counsel is "restoring the culture one case at a time by advancing religious freedom, the sanctity of human life, and the traditional family."

The "marriage equality" movement advocates for gay and lesbian couples to be able to marry. Attorney Evan Wolfson heads a national organization, Freedom to Marry, which has the support of numerous partner organizations, gay and nongay, at the national, state, and local levels. Two national groups, the Human Rights Campaign and the National Gay and Lesbian Task Force, work to advance many LGBT rights issues and devote some of their resources to marriage-related organizing and advocacy. Four legal groups that challenge discrimination against LGBT people in all areas, including employment, schools, immigration, the military, and family law, have had primary responsibility for the litigation contesting restrictions on access to marriage: Lambda Legal (formerly known as Lambda Legal Defense and Education Fund); Gay & Lesbian Advocates & Defenders, the Boston-based group that won the right to marriage equality in Massachusetts; the American Civil Liberties Union Lesbian Gay Bisexual Transgender Project; and the National Center for Lesbian Rights.

Both these movements focus on marriage. Neither starts by identifying what all families need and then seeking just laws and policies to meet those needs. The marriage movement does not want to meet the needs of all families. Its leading spokespeople argue that the intrinsic purpose of marriage is uniting a man and a woman to raise their biological children. They oppose marriage for same-sex couples, and want marriage to have a special legal status.

The marriage-equality movement wants the benefits of marriage granted to a larger group: same-sex partners. With few exceptions, advocates for gay and lesbian access to marriage do *not* say that "special rights" should be reserved for those who marry. But the marriage-equality movement is a movement for gay civil rights, not for valuing all families. As a civil rights movement, it seeks access to marriage as it now exists.

The movement's most consistent claim is that exclusion from marriage harms same-sex couples in tangible ways. But people in any relationship other than marriage suffer, sometimes to a level of economic or emotional devastation. The law is not uniquely unfair for gay and lesbian couples. Access to marriage will provide some gay men and lesbians with the economic support and peace of mind that come from knowing that all your family members have adequate health insurance, that a loved one can make medical decisions for you if you are ill, that your economic interdependence will be recognized at retirement or death, and that your children can be proud of the family they have. But other LGBT people, and all whose family form, for whatever reason, is not marriage, will still be without those supports that every family deserves.

The focus on access to marriage may be constricting the imagination of advocates for LGBT families who attribute every problem a same-sex couple experiences to marriage discrimination. Consider this:

Openly gay San Francisco supervisor Harvey Milk was assassinated on November 27, 1978, by a former supervisor, who also murdered the city's mayor, George Moscone. Milk was a community leader, dubbed the Mayor of Castro Street, and the first openly gay elected official in a major U.S. city. A film about his life won the Academy Award for best documentary in 1985. San Francisco named a plaza in his honor, and numerous gay community organizations and alternative schools across the country bear his name.

His surviving partner, Scott Smith, received death benefits from the state Workman's Compensation Appeals Board.[11]

When gay surviving partners of those who died on September 11, 2001, did not receive workers' comp death benefits, gay rights advocates attributed it to marriage discrimination. But solutions to this problem and others are available or more achievable using a valuing-all-families approach, and they will help more people. Scott Smith was successful because California does not base entitlement to workers' comp death benefits on marriage. Its law is one model other states could adopt.

Laws that distinguish between married couples and everyone else need to be reexamined. They stem from the days when a husband was the head of his household with a dependent wife at home, when a child born to an unmarried woman was a social outcast, and when virtually every marriage was for life regardless of the relationship's quality. It was a very different time.

When the Supreme Court declared the laws differentiating between men/husbands and women/wives unconstitutional, the laws became gender-neutral. This created a new problem. It left distinctions between married couples and everyone else without assessing the justness of that approach. It's time to make that assessment. Today more people live alone, more people live with unmarried partners, and more parents have minor children who live neither with them nor with their current spouse. The laws that affect families need to be evaluated in light of contemporary realities. A valuing-all-families approach does this by demanding a good fit between a law's purpose and the relationships subject to its reach.

Karen Thompson was the right choice to be Sharon Kowalski's guardian. Susan Burns and her children needed regular visits with each other. Larry Courtney deserved compensation for Eugene's death. Lisa Stewart needed health insurance and the ability to provide for her family when she dies, and her daughter needed two legal parents.

Many of these results could be secured right now by looking for solutions other than marriage. In every area of law that matters to same-sex couples, such as healthcare decision making, government and employee benefits, and the right to raise children, laws already exist in some places that could form the basis for just family policies for those who can't marry or enter civil unions or register their domestic partnerships, as well as for those who don't want to or who simply don't, and whose most important relationship is not with a sexual partner. These laws will help many families, not just LGBT ones, and not just couples.

Successful reform that values all families may not come in the name of gay rights. It may come under the banner of, for example, patients' autonomy, family pluralism, and the needs of children. Some lawmakers will support important reforms precisely *because* they help many people in many families and do not appear to be "gay rights" issues. In recent years, that motivation has produced a policy in Salt Lake City that extends health insurance to any one adult member of an employee's household and that person's children, a law in Virginia requiring hospitals to allow patients to select their own visitors, and a change in federal pension law that allows any beneficiary to inherit retirement assets without paying a tax penalty. After such laws change, gay rights leaders rightly trumpet that they will help LGBT families.

A strategy in the name of gay rights toward recognition of same-sex partnerships, where successful, is a civil rights triumph. It may, however, have unfortunate consequences for family policy. Same-sex couples will have the right to a formal legal status for their relationships; those who exercise that right will have the array of consequences that married spouses now receive. This will disregard the needs of LGBT couples who don't marry or register, LGBT singles and households not organized around sexual intimacy, LGBT parents without partners, and the families and relationships of vast numbers of heterosexuals.

Where a gay rights strategy loses and does not result in marriage, civil unions, or partnership registration, the "special rights" given marriage will continue to harm same-sex couples. Where a losing gay rights strategy results in a constitutional amendment barring recognition of unmarried same- and different-sex couples, as more than a dozen states have, those couples may be worse off than they are now. That's what happened in Michigan, where public employees lost domestic partner benefits.

A valuing-all-families strategy achieves good results, for good reasons, and makes marriage matter less. That was the direction in which U.S. law and policy was headed before the right-wing backlash against feminism, LGBT rights, and other progressive social change. That backlash today includes the religious and secular marriage movement. *Its* emphasis on marriage should not lead gay rights activists away from advocacy that will meet the needs of diverse families and relationships in a pluralistic society.

CHAPTER ONE

The Changing Meaning of Marriage

Out of the radical and reform movements of the 1960s and 1970s, and the changes in social norms that accompanied those movements, came a transformation in the legal significance of marriage. The constitutional principles of equality and liberty toppled ancient rules about families that were based on hierarchy and conformity. The seeds of valuing all families were planted.

When the movement for gay and lesbian rights and liberation emerged during that time, marriage was considered part of the problem, not part of the solution. Marriage was a problem because it regulated the lives of men and women along gender lines—both within and outside of marriage—and because it policed the boundary between acceptable and unacceptable sexual expression. By themselves, the small number of those willing to live openly, proudly, even defiantly as gay men and lesbians could have made little headway against this institution that sought to channel them into, and keep them within, acceptable heterosexual norms.

But they didn't have to do it themselves. They had heterosexuals who were increasingly open about rejecting the sexuality-channeling function of marriage, and they had feminism. Feminism had the support and the momentum to demand an end to the limits on women's life choices attributable to the expectations of women's roles within marriage. For many women, these demands included the right *not* to marry. The contemporary movement for the rights of lesbian, gay, bisexual, and transgender people owes a great debt to the feminist movement of the 1960s and early 1970s, including its critique of marriage and the family.

In an astonishingly short period of time, feminist agitation and the social and cultural changes of this era produced a seismic transformation of the law of marriage. The old set of laws punished sex outside of marriage, imposed catastrophic consequences for bearing children outside of marriage, assumed and fostered "separate spheres" for men and women, and denied the ability to exit a marriage except under penalty. These laws had endured for hundreds of years. In less than a decade, a completely revised set of laws emerged. The new laws discarded the gender script, made entry into marriage more optional, and made exit from marriage more ordinary. In doing so, they made marriage a different institution and opened avenues for recognition of new family forms, including those of gay men and lesbians.

The History of Gender and Marriage

Feminists had much to complain about in the law of marriage. English common law, adopted by the United States, understood a husband and wife as one person, and that person was the husband.[1] Under the doctrine of coverture, a wife had no independent legal identity. She could not sign a contract, own property or money, or bring a lawsuit. She was required to provide services and labor for her husband and to obey him, and in return he was required to support her. Since any property a woman owned while single became her husband's upon marriage, and since her earnings and any other property she acquired while married belonged to him, his support obligation was crucial; by marrying, she lost the ability to support herself. The husband had the right to the labor and earnings of his children as well, and, with that, the right to keep custody of the children if the couple separated.

Because of the legal unity of husband and wife, spouses could not testify against each other in court; be guilty of conspiracy to commit a crime; or recover money damages for wrongs committed against each other. Upon marriage a woman acquired her husband's surname. She also lost control over her body; a husband was not subject to the charge of rape with respect to his wife, because her consent to marry him included consent to sexual intercourse on his terms. A husband had the right to determine where the couple lived. Because a husband had a right to his wife's services, any injury to his wife caused by a third party was also an injury to him; he could sue and recover for the loss of these services, called loss of consortium.

In July 1848, the first women's rights convention was held in Seneca Falls, New York. The Declaration of Sentiments that emerged, which focused largely on women's inability to vote, also decried the status of women in marriage.[2]

The legal disabilities of wives carried over into laws affecting all women. Women could not vote, nor could they serve on juries. In 1873, when Myra Bradwell sought admission to the bar of Illinois and was denied, the U.S. Supreme Court affirmed with the following:

> The civil law, as well as nature herself, has always recognized a wide difference in the respective spheres and destinies of man and woman. Man is, or should be, woman's protector and defender. The natural and proper timidity and delicacy which belongs to the female sex evidently unfits it for many of the occupations of civil life. The constitution of the family organization, which is founded in the divine ordinance, as well as in the nature of things, indicates the domestic sphere as that which properly belongs to the domain and functions of womanhood. The harmony, not to say the identity, of interests and views which belong, or should belong, to the family institution is repugnant to the idea of a woman adopting a distinct and independent career from that of her husband.[3]

Although the Court recognized that there were unmarried women, it considered them "exceptions to the rule."

The first changes to the legally prescribed roles of husband and wife occurred in the mid-nineteenth century with the passage of the Married Women's Property Acts. These laws at first permitted women to keep property they owned at the time of the marriage. Later, after feminist advocacy, the laws were expanded to allow married women to enter into contracts and to control money they earned, although this change did not occur in some states until well into the twentieth century. Some legislators who resisted these changes as against God's law declared them certain to lead to adultery and divorce.[4]

In the eight states (Arizona, California, Idaho, Louisiana, Nevada, New Mexico, Texas, and Washington) whose laws derived from continental European law rather than English common law, spouses owned together as "community property" anything acquired by either during the marriage, except through gift or inheritance. Although appearing more generous than common law rules, an inherent feature of this system was that the husband had absolute control over the community property, including his wife's earnings.

The law refused to recognize any agreement a married couple made that altered the gender-based rights and obligations of marriage. Although the abolitionist and feminist Lucy Stone and her like-minded husband Henry Blackwell made a contract when they married in 1855 in which they rejected gender-based laws and agreed, among other things, that she would keep her own name, no court would have enforced this agreement, as any terms altering marriage's gender-based rules were against public policy.

To contemporary young people, these consequences of marriage may seem like ancient history. They are not. In *Women and the Law: The Unfinished Revolution,* law professor Leo Kanowitz, writing in 1969, described the legal status of married women. Surprisingly little had changed since the nineteenth-century Married Women's Property Acts. Although women gained the right to vote in 1920, they could still be excused from jury service solely because they were considered "the center of home and family life." In 1966 the U.S. Supreme Court upheld a Texas law that allowed a wife to avoid repaying a loan from the Small Business Administration because she had not received court permission to sign the note as required of married women under state law. Married women could still be required to use their husband's surnames, and, for the most part, a wife's legal residence followed that of her husband, affecting her ability to vote, hold public office, receive government benefits, qualify for free or reduced college tuition, serve on a jury, pay taxes, or probate a will.[5]

Giving the husband the right to determine the couple's legal residence meant also that if he moved and the wife refused to move with him, she would be guilty of desertion and could be divorced based on her fault. An Arizona court writing in 1953 upheld the husband's right to decide where the couple lived, because he had the duty of financial support and "there can be no decision by majority rule as to where the family home shall be maintained."[6]

The right of a wife to support—what she got in exchange for acceding to the husband as the head of the household—was not a right she could enforce during a marriage. In a 1953 Nebraska case, the wife asked a court to order her husband to pay for indoor plumbing, a new furnace, and money she could use for clothing, furniture, and other expenses. She testified that her husband had not given her any money for four years, that he would not allow any charge accounts, and that he did not permit her to make any long-distance telephone calls. The trial judge ordered the husband to buy some items and to provide a monthly allowance to his wife. The state supreme court reversed that decision, holding that a wife could proceed against her husband for support only if they were separated. "As long as the home is maintained," the court wrote, "it may be said that the husband is legally supporting his wife."[7]

Gendered roles within marriage had always affected women's opportunities in public life. Until 1963, it was legal to pay women less than men for doing the same job. That year, the Presidential Commission on the Status of Women spearheaded passage of a federal law guaranteeing equal pay for men and women. The following year, Congress enacted the Civil Rights Act, with Title VII prohibiting discrimination in hiring, promotion, and other areas of employment on the basis of sex as well as race. Even after the mandate of equal opportunity for women, employers were slow to change their practices; into the early 1970s, newspapers routinely divided job advertisements into "Help Wanted: Male" and "Help Wanted: Female."

Second-Wave Feminism—Liberals, Radicals, and Lesbians

Liberal Feminism

Betty Friedan's groundbreaking book, *The Feminine Mystique*, appeared in 1963, naming the malaise of the white, educated, stay-at-home suburban housewife as "the problem that has no name." In 1966, at a conference on employment discrimination, Friedan, Pauli Murray, and others concerned that the Equal Employment Opportunity Commission was not serious about enforcing the anti–sex discrimination provisions of Title VII, founded the National Organization for Women (NOW). Gloria Steinem helped found the National Women's Political Caucus (NWPC) in 1971 and *Ms.* magazine in 1972. The goal of NWPC was increasing women's participation in government. *Ms.* was the first feminist publication targeting a national mainstream audience.

NOW sought legal equality between men and women. Its political agenda centered on enacting the equal rights amendment (ERA), an amendment to the U.S. Constitution stating that "equality of rights under the law shall not be denied or abridged by the United States or any state on account of sex." The amendment passed the House of Representatives in 1971 and the Senate in 1972, and it had been ratified by thirty-three of the required thirty-eight states by 1974.

Simultaneously, NOW and other liberal feminists who focused on legal equality between men and women pursued litigation rooted in the equal protection clause of the Fourteenth Amendment to the Constitution. Lawyers in previous generations had made constitutional arguments without success. In 1948, for example, the Supreme Court upheld a law prohibiting a woman from working as a bartender unless her husband or father owned the establishment in which she worked.[8] But the civil rights movement had achieved significant victories using the equal protection clause. An analogous strategy for women sought to make sex a classification that could not be used in the law without a compelling need to do so. Attacking the radically gendered law of marriage, and other laws based on gender roles within marriage, proved fertile grounds for advancing women's equality.

Radical Feminism

During this same period, another form of feminism developed out of the dramatic social movements of the 1960s. These movements protested the white, wealthy, elite power structure of U.S. society and demanded profound political, social, cultural, and economic changes, which many referred to as revolution. They included free speech, student, and welfare rights movements; civil rights and black power groups; the "New Left," an appellation designed to distinguish anticapitalist groups from earlier left-wing organizations aligned with Soviet Communism; and a growing movement against America's war in Vietnam. These movements asserted their demands through marches, mass demonstrations, sit-ins, and grassroots organizing.

Women in these movements grew angry at their second-class status and began demanding changes. In 1964 Ruby Doris Smith-Robinson challenged the Student Nonviolent Coordinating Committee on the inferior status of women. This led to Stokely Carmichael's infamous rejoinder that "the only position for women in SNCC is prone." Women in Students for a Democratic Society (SDS) raised concerns at the organization's 1965 convention, resulting in a resolution at the group's 1967 national conference calling for full participation of women in the group.[9]

The women in these organizations challenged both the roles male leaders assigned them and the content of the demands made on the larger society. Women in SDS, for example, urged the organization to work on issues of childcare, dissemination of birth control, availability of abortion, and equal sharing of housework. Ultimately, many of these women, and others with similar experiences in male-dominated political groups, formed their own organizations.

Radical feminists stressed consciousness-raising and spread these ideas through "A Program for Feminist Consciousness Raising," first circulated at a Chicago conference in 1968. Consciousness-raising led to the conclusion that "the personal is political." By sharing their stories, women discovered that their relationships with men were not the product of individual and unique dynamics but were rather the collective manifestations of sexism and patriarchy. It was not simply that an individual man expected his wife or girlfriend to perform sexual services geared to his pleasure alone or do housework and care for children while he operated in the public sphere. Housework, childcare, and sex became subjects of political action rather than personal complaint. In consciousness-raising groups, each woman learned that her individual experience of male domination within the family was not a private matter; it was part of a systemic problem—male supremacy—for which the collective action of feminists was the antidote.

Radical feminists wrote articles condemning social structures that perpetuated male domination of women. They started women's centers, law collectives, health projects, battered-women's shelters, publishing enterprises, artists workshops, and other endeavors that enabled women to control the delivery of services and the accumulation and dissemination of knowledge.

Radical feminists organized dramatic direct actions to call attention to their points. They demonstrated against the images of women at the 1968 Miss America pageant and protested the legal status of wives outside the New York marriage license bureau in 1969, where they distributed a leaflet that read:

> Do you know that rape is legal in marriage? Do you know that love and affection are not required in marriage? Do you know that you are your husband's prisoner? Do you know that, according to the United Nations, marriage is "slavery-like practice"? So, why aren't you getting paid? Do you resent this fraud?[10]

Radical feminists held a sit-in at the office of *Ladies' Home Journal* in 1970, demanding that the magazine be run by women and that it establish an on-site childcare center, hire women of color for the staff in proportion to their numbers in the population, and publish articles addressing the real needs of readers. When the editor agreed to allow the demonstrators to write an eight-page insert for an issue, the group wrote a "Housewives' Bill of Rights," demanding paid maternity leave and vacations, free twenty-four-hour childcare centers, Social Security benefits for housework, and health insurance.[11]

Radical feminists also recognized that women's equality depended on control over their reproductive lives. One of their major goals was repeal of laws criminalizing abortion. A Chicago-based organization, Jane, facilitated over eleven thousand illegal, but safe, abortions between 1969 and 1973.[12] In California, women held classes on abortion, inviting arrest so that they could challenge the restrictions in court. In 1969, women in New York demonstrated at legislative hearings on abortion reform and then organized speak-outs at which women told the stories of their illegal abortions. Subsequently, women of color led feminist efforts to end forced sterilization, a phenomenon primarily affecting black, Puerto Rican, and Native American women.

Radical feminists challenged male dominance of women in the family. They often drew links between the oppression of women and the oppression of workers and people of color in a capitalist, racist society. As liberal feminists mounted law reform efforts to eliminate legally sanctioned distinctions between husbands and wives, radical feminists addressed issues of power and hierarchy that could not be fixed by replacing "husband" and "wife" with gender-neutral terminology.

Lesbians and Feminism

In their earliest years, both liberal and radical groups making up the second wave of feminism were silent about lesbian issues, and there was no visible lesbian presence. By the end of the 1960s, there was a shift. The rise of feminism made some women who had worked in the gay rights movement more aware of their differences with the male leaders of that movement. Some of the women in both the national women's rights organizations and the smaller feminist consciousness-raising and direct action groups came out as lesbians. In 1969 and 1970, NOW's leadership, headed by Betty Friedan, opposed adding lesbian rights to the group's agenda and tried to purge what Friedan labeled the "lavender menace" from the organization.

In 1971 Del Martin and Phyllis Lyon, the founders of an early gay rights (then called "homophile") group called Daughters of Bilitis, spoke to the Los Angeles NOW conference about the problems lesbians faced. Later that year, at the NOW national conference, delegates passed a resolution stating that it was unjust to force lesbian mothers to stay in marriages or to keep their sexuality secret in order to keep their children. The organization committed to offering legal and moral support in cases involving the child custody rights of lesbian mothers. This soon became the driving legal issue for gay and lesbian families.

During this same period, lesbians raised issues inside radical feminist organizations. In 1970 a group called Radicalesbians took over the microphone at a women's liberation conference and issued a statement called "The Woman-Identified Woman." While radical feminism challenged the power structure within marriage and heterosexual relationships, lesbian feminism challenged the institution of heterosexuality itself, the assumption that women needed men for sexual and emotional fulfillment. "The Woman-Identified Woman" argued that

> as long as woman's liberation tries to free women without facing the basic heterosexual structure that binds us in one-to-one relationship with our oppressors, tremendous energies will continue to flow into trying to straighten up each particular relationship with a man, into finding how to get better sex, how to turn his head around, into trying to make the "new man" out of him, in the delusion that this will allow us to be the "new woman." This obviously splits our energies and commitments, leaving us unable to be committed to the construction of the new patterns which will liberate us. It is the primacy of women relating to women, of women creating a new consciousness of and with each other, which is at the heart of women's liberation, and the basis for the cultural revolution.[13]

The statement also encouraged women to recognize that as long as "lesbian" and the slang term "dyke" were pejorative words, men would use these labels against assertive feminists who resisted men's sexual and housekeeping demands.

Common Ground

Despite different analyses and priorities, liberal feminists, radical feminists, and lesbian feminists engaged in joint actions. On August 26, 1970, the fiftieth anniversary of the passage of the constitutional amendment giving women the right to vote, all parts of the feminist movement participated in the first mass women's march since the suffrage struggle. Some fifty thousand women marched to Central Park in New York demanding passage of the equal rights amendment, equal employment and educational opportunity, twenty-four-hour community-controlled childcare, and free abortion on demand.

Liberal, radical, and lesbian feminists also came together for the National Women's Conference. Early in 1975, President Gerald Ford had established the National Commission on the Observance of International Women's Year to make recommendations on promoting equality between men and women. Representative Bella Abzug, after returning from the 1975 United Nations International Women's Year Conference in Mexico City, wrote legislation that allocated $5 million to fund a national women's conference to be held in Houston in 1977. The conference would follow meetings in all states and territories that would elect delegates, consider platform issues, and prepare for the national conference. State conventions were open to all females over sixteen; racial, religious, ethnic, economic, and age diversity was required. About 130,000 people attended state conferences between February and July 1977.[14] The national conference was attended by, among other notables, Rosalynn Carter, Lady Bird Johnson, Betty Ford, and Coretta Scott King.

The twenty-six planks that emerged in the Plan of Action and that won the support of 80 percent of the delegates reflected a broad feminist vision extending beyond formal legal equality in marriage and the workplace. Women raising children on welfare were portrayed as deserving; Abzug stated that "just as with other workers, homemakers receiving income transfer payments should be afforded the dignity of having that payment called a wage, not welfare."[15] Other planks addressed the feminist issues of ending rape and woman battering and the availability of abortion and childcare, as well as other issues such as affirmative action for racial minorities and an end to deportation of mothers of American-born children.

Lesbian feminist delegates supported this wide-reaching feminist agenda and persuaded the delegates to include a "sexual preference" plank in the plan. It called for antidiscrimination statutes, repeal of antisodomy laws, and legislation that would prohibit consideration of sexual or affectional orientation as a factor in any judicial determination of child custody or visitation rights. The background paper noted that lesbians suffer double discrimination and deplored judicial decisions labeling lesbian mothers "unfit."

The Sexual and Divorce Revolutions

Until the 1960s, social and legal consequences of nonmarital birth demonstrated strong condemnation of sex outside marriage. Pregnancy and childbirth were hard-to-avoid consequences of sex, as abortion was illegal and effective contraception was either illegal or difficult to obtain. Teenage pregnancy rates peaked in the 1950s, but half of those pregnancies resulted in shotgun weddings, pressed by the woman's family to preserve a daughter's honor and avert shame and disgrace. Of those who did not marry, over twenty-five thousand a year were sent to more than two hundred "unwed mother" homes where they gave birth secretly and almost always relinquished their children for adoption. Women who gave birth and kept their children, including the black women who were excluded from most of the unwed-mother homes, faced harsh state policies, including eviction from public housing and denial of public assistance. Doctors sometimes sterilized them without their knowledge or consent.[16]

The cultural changes that accompanied the social and political movements of the 1960s included a revolution in sexual mores. The birth control pill, introduced in 1960, for the first time provided women a reliable means of being sexually active and avoiding pregnancy. "Make love, not war" was a refrain for a generation that questioned the authority of its elders. A sexual double standard lingered for women and men, but this was decried by second-wave feminism. The groundbreaking studies of sexuality researchers William Masters and Virginia Johnson identified women's sources of sexual satisfaction, demonstrating, among other things, that women could achieve sexual fulfillment without men. As hostility to nonmarital sex decreased, legal doctrine reflecting condemnation of such sex became less tenable.

Demand for divorce also increased. U.S. courts had granted divorces since the late eighteenth century, but only on specified grounds requiring that one party be at "fault." The idea behind fault-based divorce was that divorce should be the exception, not the rule, and should be available at the option of the "innocent" party only.

One spouse's fault not only gave the other grounds for divorce, it also to a large extent determined the consequences of divorce. Adultery was a ground for divorce everywhere. Although in the mid-twentieth century a "tender years presumption" meant that mothers of young children would be awarded custody if there was a divorce, this only held true if they were without fault. Sex outside marriage rendered a mother "unfit" and cost her not only her marriage but her children as well. A woman's fault also relieved her husband of any obligation to support her. Even though a divorced woman could keep property she owned in her own name or had purchased with her own money, the rigid gender roles assigned husbands and wives made it unlikely that she had such assets. With no access to property in her husband's name, no entitlement to spousal support or child custody if she committed marital fault, and limited options for economic self-sufficiency in a marketplace rampant with sex discrimination, the consequences of extramarital sex for a woman were severe.

By the 1960s, social practice was out of step with divorce law. Cohabitation became more accepted and more common as "desertion" occurred, and without divorce there could be no remarriage. The divorce rate rose, in part due to liberal divorce laws in Nevada and in other countries, where the wealthy could travel to dissolve their unions. Many couples who wanted to end their marriages manufactured grounds—such as physical cruelty or adultery—to get divorced. This was particularly rampant in New York, where adultery remained the only ground for divorce until 1966.[17]

Legal Transformations Involving Marriage and Family

Women's Equality

The law reform strategy of liberal feminists achieved extraordinary success in a series of cases in the 1970s. The first Supreme Court case to strike down a distinction between men and women as unconstitutional arose out of an Idaho statute that presumed men more capable than women of administering the estate of a person who died without a will. When a child named Richard Reed died, his mother and father, who were separated, each sought to administer his estate. The judge appointed Richard's father. The Idaho Supreme Court held that "nature itself" created the distinction between men and women and the legislature could conclude that in general men were better qualified than women to administer estates. When this case reached the U.S. Supreme Court in 1971, the Court ruled for the first time that a sex-based statute was "arbitrary" in a way that violated the equal protection clause. The Court required the judge to hold a hearing to determine who was better suited to administer the estate.[18]

This case was not about "family law" narrowly defined as the obligations of a husband and wife toward one another. But the law at issue was the explicit product of the gendered view of men and women under the doctrine of coverture. Writing the brief for Sally Reed, future Supreme Court Justice Ruth Bader Ginsburg protested the "subordination of women" inherent in preferring men without regard to the ability of the applicants.

Reed v. Reed, decided as the demands of second-wave feminism became audible across the country, signaled the beginning of the end of legalized, formal inequality between women and men. Notably, most of the cases in the decade following concerned either sex-based classifications in family law or notions of gender with their origins in the laws of coverture. For example, two years later, the Supreme Court declared unconstitutional a law that extended benefits to married male members of the armed forces but gave those benefits to a married female service member only if she could prove that her husband depended on her for more than one-half of his support. The scheme dated back to the 1940s and 1950s and reflected the legal reality that a husband was obliged to support his wife and the corresponding factual reality, as found by the trial court that heard the case, that husbands were typically breadwinners and wives typically dependent.

The government argued in favor of retaining the distinction between men and women because of "administrative convenience." It said that because most wives were dependent on their husbands, it was cheaper and easier to presume dependence and automatically award the benefits. But because few husbands were dependent on their wives, it was appropriate to require proof of the husband's dependence before spending government funds. The Supreme Court eliminated the sex discrimination by allowing all married service members additional benefits.[19]

In 1975 the Supreme Court heard the case of Stephen Wiesenfeld, whose wife, Paula, had died in childbirth. Their child was entitled to receive Social Security survivors' benefits as a result of Paula's death, but Stephen was not; a surviving mother could receive benefits after the father's death, but a surviving father could not receive benefits after the mother's death. This sex-based classification had been included in amendments to Social Security enacted in 1939 when it was a "generally accepted presumption that a man is responsible for the support of his wife and children." The Court found that the purpose of the benefit was to allow women to forgo paid employment and stay home with their children. By focusing on the interest in providing a child with a stay-at-home parent after the other parent died, the Supreme Court concluded that it was irrational, and therefore unconstitutional, to provide the benefit only to surviving mothers.[20] In

1977 the Supreme Court found sex discrimination in another Social Security regulation, this one providing survivors' benefits to all elderly widows, but to elderly widowers only if they had been receiving more than one-half of their support from their wives.[21]

Some Supreme Court cases decided in the decade after *Reed* lay within the realm of family law. In a Utah case, the law eliminated a parent's obligation to support his daughter at eighteen, and his son at twenty-one. The state supreme court upheld the law based on the belief that "the man's primary responsibility [is] to provide a home and its essentials for the family," and the extra education or training enabled by the requirement of parental support until twenty-one would facilitate that.[22] The U.S. Supreme Court reversed. In 1979, the Court invalidated the sex-based classification in an alimony statute that denied husbands the opportunity to get alimony from their wives,[23] and in 1981 it invalidated a Louisiana law that made the husband the "head and master" of the household and thus gave him the power to dispose of all community property without his wife's consent.[24]

These cases made progress in achieving formal equality through elimination of sex-based classifications. Although the law today does allow some sex-based distinctions, it permits none of the distinctions once linked to the gendered nature of marriage. As a result of the Supreme Court decisions, all benefits and obligations once tied to the legally mandated dependency of women upon their husbands have been eliminated or expanded to include both spouses. *Both* have a right to request alimony; *both* have the right to manage community property; *both* are entitled to survivors' benefits under Social Security and workers' compensation laws.

Feminist efforts resulted in gender neutrality superimposed on a set of laws grounded in the gendered nature of marriage. The resulting regime singles out marriage for special treatment, but only as a byproduct of the remedy for ending gender inequality, not as a reasoned conclusion that marriage entitles people to special treatment that other relationships cannot claim. In other words, the special treatment accorded marriage in family law, Social Security, employee benefits, and other critical areas masks the original purpose of those areas of law.

Alimony is a good example. Alimony enforced a husband's obligation to provide lifelong support to his wife. He had to assume this obligation at marriage because she lost the ability to support herself. He could be relieved of this obligation only if she died or, in the rare circumstance of divorce, if she married another man who assumed responsibility for her support. Feminist success in achieving formal equality eliminated the gender component, and now, where appropriate, either a husband or wife may seek alimony, even though neither spouse loses the ability to support himself or herself when marrying and easy divorce means that whatever obligations spouses have toward one another are not inherently lifelong.

Formal equality for women made alimony gender-neutral, but did not detach it from marriage. Yet the justifications for alimony today are completely different from those of the earlier, gendered era. Contemporary justification for ongoing support after a relationship dissolves rests on the economic consequences of one person forgoing individual financial stability while making uncompensated contributions to a family. This may occur whether the couple is married or not married, and there is no principled basis for restricting support awards today only to husbands and wives.

The End of "Illegitimacy"

The long-standing social stigma of illegitimacy was accompanied by harsh legal consequences. The law permitted and endorsed discrimination against children born outside marriage as a means of expressing condemnation of nonmarital sex. For centuries such children were *fillius nullius,* the child of no one, meaning they had no legally recognized relationship with, including no right to support from, their mother or father.[25]

The distinction between children born to a married mother and those born to an unmarried mother seemed out of step with the social and political changes of the 1960s. In 1966, Illinois law professor Harry Krause published an article voicing the idea, revolutionary at its time, that U.S. law should reduce this distinction. Krause argued that the disadvantaged status of nonmarital children came from "ancient prejudice based on religious and moral taboos that properly are losing their taboo status."[26] Krause supported his call for the equal treatment of all children by invoking the statutes and constitutions of dozens of other countries.

Krause took his ideas to the U.S. Supreme Court, where children and parents harmed by the different status given marital and nonmarital children invoked the equal protection clause to argue that the distinctions were unconstitutional. In 1968, in *Levy v. Louisiana*, surviving nonmarital children challenged a Louisiana statute that denied them the ability to recover for the wrongful death of their mother. The state court upheld the statute because it "properly" discouraged nonmarital childbearing. Using language that would resonate with today's marriage movement, Louisiana defended its laws by arguing that it was not trying to punish or discriminate. Rather, it was trying to encourage marriage. The state's brief read:

> Louisiana's purposes . . . are positive ones: the *encouragement* of marriage as one of the most important institutions known to law, the preservation of the legitimate family as the preferred environment for socializing the child. . . .
>
> Since marriage as an institution is fundamental to our existence as a free nation, it is the duty of . . . Louisiana to encourage it. One method of encouraging marriage is granting greater rights to legitimate offspring than those born of extra-marital unions. Superior rights of legitimate offspring are inducements or incentives to parties to contract marriage, which is preferred by Louisiana as the setting for producing offspring.[27]

The Supreme Court rejected this reasoning, simultaneously striking down a statute denying a mother the right to recover for the wrongful death of her nonmarital child.[28] Illegitimate children were human beings, "persons" within the Constitution's equal protection clause. In the *Levy* case, they had been dependent on their mother, who had died as a result of medical malpractice. The Court refused to allow the wrongdoers to escape responsibility for their negligence simply because the children were born outside of marriage. Encouraging marriage and expressing disapproval of nonmarital sex were no longer constitutionally sufficient reasons to deny rights to children and their parents.

In 1972 the Court found unconstitutional a state scheme that awarded workers' compensation death benefits to a father's four legitimate children but not his two illegitimate ones, even though he lived in one household with all of them.[29] By now Associate Justice (and future Chief Justice) William Rehnquist had joined the Court. He alone dissented, accepting the state's interest in discouraging "illicit family relationships."

That same year the Supreme Court further reduced the legal significance of marriage. In *Stanley v. Illinois,* Peter Stanley challenged an Illinois law that automatically made his children wards of the state when their mother died.[30] The state would not have stepped in if he and their mother had been married. The Court ruled that the state could not presume Stanley unfit simply because he was never married to the children's mother, with whom he had lived intermittently for eighteen years. Stanley had a constitutional right to raise his children; marriage was irrelevant. With this case, the Court overturned centuries of law that created a father-child relationship only for a man married to a child's mother. The next year the Court ruled that children's right to support payments from their father could not turn on whether their father had been married to their mother.[31]

A 1973 decision limited the government's ability to deny benefits to households with unmarried parents. *New Jersey Welfare Rights Organization v. Cahill* challenged a New Jersey program that extended benefits to financially needy households consisting of "two adults of the opposite sex ceremonially married to each other" who also had at least one biological or jointly adopted child, or one child born to one spouse and adopted by the other.[32]

The trial court ruled in favor of the state. It determined that the state could favor married families because such families provided norms, preventing a breakdown in social control. The court described marriage as a "permanent, or at least semi-permanent institution." It noted that "a living arrangement which does not have the aura of permanence that is concomitant with a ceremonial marriage, often does not provide the stability necessary for the instillment of those norms with the individual necessary for proper behavior." It concluded that it was proper for the state to refuse to subsidize a living unit that violated its laws against fornication and adultery and that New Jersey could use its program to discourage immorality and illegitimacy. According to the trial court, the program did not unconstitutionally discriminate against nonmarital children, because their parents could cure the problem by getting married, and this was a proper incentive for the state to offer.

The Supreme Court reversed the lower court. It found "no doubt that the benefits extended under the challenged program are as indispensable to the health and well-being of illegitimate children as to those who are legitimate." Therefore the program violated the equal protection rights of nonmarital children. Justice Rehnquist was again the lone dissenter. He argued that the state could require marriage as an essential ingredient of a deserving family unit and said that, "the Constitution does not require that special financial assistance designed by the legislature to help poor families be extended to 'communes' as well."

Harry Krause influenced the National Conference of Commissioners on Uniform State Laws, the body that proposes model uniform laws to state legislatures, to address the issue of nonmarital children. His work led to the Uniform Parentage Act, written between 1969 and 1972. It was adopted in some form in nineteen states, and it greatly influenced new laws in every state. In less than a decade, the legal doctrine of illegitimacy had all but disappeared.

Acceptance of Sex outside Marriage

During this same period, another series of Supreme Court cases directly addressed nonmarital sex. In a 1968 case, *King v. Smith*, Alabama claimed that, in order to discourage illicit sex and nonmarital births, it could deny public assistance to a sexually active unmarried mother and her children.[33] The Supreme Court noted that moral fitness had once been a requirement of receiving aid. Social workers made unannounced visits to the homes of welfare recipients and removed them from the rolls if there was evidence of a "man in the house." The Supreme Court ruled that the Alabama law ran afoul of changes Congress had made prohibiting such disqualification. Justice William Douglas wrote separately that denying assistance to needy children based on the mother's "immorality" was unconstitutional.

A few years later, the Court found unconstitutional a law making it illegal to distribute birth control to unmarried people. In the 1965 case of *Griswold v. Connecticut*, the Court had struck down a statute prohibiting the sale of contraceptives to married couples, articulating a right of privacy within a marriage.[34] In 1972, in *Eisenstadt v. Baird,* the Court ruled that distinguishing between married and unmarried people violated the Constitution's equal protection clause. The majority reasoned as follows:

> If under *Griswold* the distribution of contraceptives to married persons cannot be prohibited, a ban on distribution to unmarried persons would be equally impermissible. It is true that in *Griswold* the right of privacy in question inhered in the marital relationship. Yet the marital couple is not an independent entity with a mind and heart of its own, but an association of two individuals each with a separate intellectual and emotional makeup. If the right of privacy means anything, it is the right of the *individual,* married or single, to be free from unwarranted governmental intrusion into matters so fundamentally affecting a person as the decision whether to bear or beget a child.[35]

Although not directly at issue in the case, the Court's reasoning that a married couple consisted of two *separate* individuals was a repudiation of the long-standing common law concept that the husband and wife were one—the husband.

The next year, the Supreme Court decided *U.S. Department of Agriculture v. Moreno,* a challenge to a federal law denying food stamps to financially eligible households whose residents were unrelated.[36] The law excluded households with poor people who lived together for all sorts of reasons, but the express congressional intent of the restriction had been to prevent "communal 'families' of unrelated individuals" and "hippie communes" from receiving food stamps.

Although the government first argued that the law's purpose was to foster morality, it abandoned that argument and asserted that the restriction would reduce fraud. The Supreme Court recognized that the true motivation was a "bare congressional desire to harm a politically unpopular group" and held that, under the equal protection clause, this could not be a legitimate reason to deny otherwise eligible poor people food stamps. Justice Rehnquist again dissented, arguing that it was reasonable for Congress to allocate food stamps to "some variation on the family as we know it."

In these three cases, *King v. Smith, Eisenstadt v. Baird,* and *U.S. Department of Agriculture v. Moreno,* the Supreme Court refused to implement laws reflecting disapproval of sex outside marriage. Rather, it sided with the enormous social and cultural changes of the time. Thus, birth control became a matter of constitutional right for unmarried as well as married people, and the government was denied the ability to condition financial assistance to the poor on conformity to the sexual morality of earlier decades. The landmark 1973 decision in *Roe v. Wade,* which followed several years of feminist agitation for legal and safe abortion on demand, declared a woman's constitutional right to decide in consultation with her doctor whether to terminate a pregnancy. *Roe* built on the right of privacy articulated in both *Griswold* and *Eisenstadt,* ensuring that abortions for single as well as married women could not be criminalized.

No-Fault Divorce

Marriage was no longer necessary to create legally recognized relationships with children. Marriage was no longer necessary to stave off moral judgments enforced by law. People could be sexually active and remain unmarried. The final seismic shift of this period transformed the law of divorce, enabling people who did marry to leave those marriages for reasons unheard of in previous centuries.

In 1964 the California legislature held hearings on the state's divorce laws. Professor Herma Hill Kay, among others, testified about eliminating fault as the basis for divorce. Two years later, the governor appointed a Commission on the Family, and the commission's report became the basis for the nation's first pure no-fault divorce law, enacted in 1969. During this period, the National Conference of Commissioners on Uniform State Laws studied marriage and divorce law, culminating in a draft in 1970 of the Uniform Marriage and Divorce Act, which recommended no-fault divorce.[37]

The impetus toward no-fault divorce did not come from the women's movement. To the contrary, some men wanted a way out of marriage that removed the leverage that wives had over husbands who wanted divorces but could not get them without their wives' collusion, obtained in return for generous financial packages. But once women began considering law reform from a feminist perspective, they supported a range of divorce-reform issues, including the grounds for divorce. New York NOW, for example, called for no-fault divorce in 1971. Feminism turned the private and personal dissatisfaction that some women experienced in their marriages into a socially acceptable reason to leave a marriage to escape rigid sex roles and male domination. It also helped open the employment opportunities that made it financially feasible for women to live independently from men. These accomplishments were consistent with new laws approving easy exit from marriage.

No-fault divorce brought with it new thinking about the role of fault in determining child custody. The rule that a parent who has sex outside marriage was automatically unfit to have custody was out of step with increased acceptance of nonmarital sex. Responding to changing sexual mores, when the drafters of the Uniform Marriage and Divorce Act considered a model statute on child custody, they included the provision that "the court shall not consider conduct of a proposed custodian that does not affect his relationship to the child." This constituted a rejection of the rule automatically linking sex outside marriage to unfitness. While it is unlikely the drafters had lesbian and gay parents in mind, the idea that parents' sexual behavior should not automatically keep them from having custody was an enormous boon to those who would soon advocate that lesbian mothers leaving marriages should be able to keep custody of their children. Combined with the removal of homosexuality from the American Psychiatric Association's list of mental disorders in 1973, this became the backbone of the legal strategy in support of lesbian mothers.

The Family Redefined

Looked at together, these changes in the law of gender, sex, relationships, households, and families were adjustments to the dramatic social changes and political demands of the 1960s and early 1970s. Some of these developments, most notably in divorce laws, occurred through enactment of new statutes, reflecting a political consensus to conform law to modern life. As important, however, is the role that the Supreme Court played in constraining both federal and state legislators unwilling to adapt to a society in which people organized their lives less and less around marriage.

In 1973, the American Home Economics Association defined a family as

> two or more people who share resources, share responsibility for decisions, share values and goals, and have commitments to one another over time. The family is that climate that one "comes home to" and it is this network of sharing and commitments that most accurately describes the family unit, regardless of blood, legal ties, adoption or marriage.[38]

At the time, there was every reason to believe that the law would continue to develop in the direction of such a definition, encompassing lesbian and gay families as well as those of the heterosexuals who had toppled the rigid, dichotomized, hierarchal family structures of old.

CHAPTER TWO

Gay Rights and the Conservative Backlash

In 1970 Sandy Schuster, a psychiatric nurse, met Madeleine Isaacson, a Sunday school teacher, at the Pentecostal church in Seattle where Isaacson taught one of Schuster's sons. They were both married and between them they had six children. They fell in love, and their husbands filed for divorce in a joint proceeding and requested custody of the children. The judge permitted the mothers to keep custody, but ordered them not to live together. Sandy and Madeleine set up apartments across the hall from one another, and embarked on a public campaign to undo the restriction placed on them. They interested a doctor at the University of Washington in their family, and he helped the university get a grant to make a documentary, *Sandy & Madeleine's Family,* which included Margaret Mead articulating a supportive position.[1] In 1974, their ex-husbands took the women back to court, but the judge allowed the couple to keep their children and lifted all restrictions on their custody.[2]

In 1973 Marilyn Koop, another Washington mother, was not so lucky. She had three children, ages fifteen, twelve, and ten, all of whom wanted to live with her and her partner, Nancy Driber, rather than with their father. The judge permitted the eldest to live where she wished, but gave custody of the younger two to their father. When these children ran away from their father's home and later told the judge they would not live with him, the judge ordered them placed in a juvenile detention center, where they spent three months. They were later placed with their married half sister. The judge called the mother's living arrangement "abnormal" and said it would be "highly detrimental to the girls." Even after the half sister, plus a court social worker and a psychiatrist, testified that the court should return the children to their mother, the judge refused.[3]

These cases of mothers in the early 1970s, coming out as lesbians while married or after divorce and seeking to keep custody of their children, are examples of the first family law issue addressed by the burgeoning gay rights movement. Lesbian lawyers, grounded in feminism and aware of the cultural and legal developments concerning family structure and the status of women, developed the theories and strategies that made plausible—and often successful—the claim that lesbian mothers were suitable parents.

Lesbians asserted the right to divorce without paying a penalty for their freedom; they had sex outside of marriage; they built lives outside a patriarchal family structure; they defied entrenched breadwinner/homemaker gender roles. For these reasons, their fate was intertwined with that of heterosexual mothers who divorced dominating husbands, lived with unmarried partners or in communal households, or bore children without being married, including welfare mothers who sought adequate public assistance.

By the time openly lesbian mothers argued in court for their right to raise children, a social and political movement for gay rights and liberation had joined the other movements of the 1960s. While that movement was a necessary part of the climate that allowed lesbian mothers to come out, it worked in tandem with the legal changes accompanying feminism and the sexual revolution.

The Homophile Movement

The patrons of New York City's Stonewall bar rioted on June 27–29, 1969, and that is generally understood as the dawn of the gay rights movement. But almost two decades of "homophile" organizing preceded that night and helped ensure that the sexual revolution of the 1960s would encompass gay men and lesbians as well as heterosexuals.[4] Harry Hay and others founded the Mattachine Society in Los Angeles in 1951. Their greatest legal concern was use of criminal law to arrest gay men and close gay bars. In 1955 in San Francisco, Phyllis Lyon and Del Martin founded the women's homophile group Daughters of Bilitis (DOB), primarily as a social alternative to lesbian bars. They published a magazine, *The Ladder.* Barbara Gittings started a New York chapter in 1958. DOB had members who were mothers, and *The Ladder* included articles about them. In 1957 Lyon and Martin arranged a meeting between members with children and three professionals in mental health and education.

Mattachine and DOB hoped to educate professionals who could sway public opinion. For the most part, they stressed assimilation and restraint, counseling members to wear gender-appropriate clothing and asserting that homosexuals were no different from heterosexuals except for their choice of sexual partners. In 1961 Franklin Kameny formed a Mattachine group in Washington, D.C., after spending four years fighting the federal government for its decision to fire him because he had been arrested for lewd conduct. Breaking with decisions by previous groups, Kameny advocated a direct action strategy modeled on the civil rights movement. He and fellow Mattachine members wrote letters to those in the legislative, judicial, and executive branches, seeking meetings to discuss discrimination in the government and armed services. He also was a founding member of the local affiliate of the American Civil Liberties Union, which challenged in court the exclusion of gay men and lesbians from federal employment, winning a small step in the direction of ending the ban. In 1963 the local ACLU joined Mattachine in opposing police harassment, and in 1964 it persuaded the national ACLU to resolve that no private sexual behavior between consenting adults should be a crime.[5]

Subsequently, the national ACLU adopted gay rights positions on sodomy laws, police harassment, immigration, government employment, security clearances, and the right to assemble in bars. By the time of the Stonewall Rebellion, the ACLU was litigating to further those positions in several states.

Stonewall and Beyond

Although it was not the beginning of the movement, Stonewall was certainly a turning point; on the second night of the rioting, "gay power" appeared as New York graffiti. The Gay Liberation Front was founded the next month, and within a year gay liberation groups had formed on college campuses and in cities across the country. They tapped into the movements against the war in Vietnam and for black and women's liberation; they became a part of the New Left. The new gay activists differed from their earlier homophile counterparts in both their rhetoric of revolution and their willingness to challenge gender conformity. As Allen Young, coeditor of a gay liberation anthology, described:

> Gay liberation, on the surface, is a struggle by homosexuals for dignity and respect—a struggle for civil rights. Of course, we want to "come out" . . . to hold down jobs without having to play straight, and to change or abolish those laws which restrict and denigrate us.
>
> But the movement for a new definition of sexuality does not, and cannot, end there. The definition of sexism, as developed by women's liberation and gay liberation, presupposes a struggle against the main perpetrators of sexism—straight white men—and against the manifestations of sexism as they appear in all people. The revolutionary goals of gay liberation, including the elimination of capitalism, imperialism and racism, are premised on the termination of the system of male supremacy.[6]

The link between this new movement and the existing radical movements was demonstrated by the presence of a representative of New York's Gay Liberation Front as a speaker at the massive Washington, D.C., march against the war in Vietnam in November 1969.

The gay and lesbian movement grew exponentially. On the one-year anniversary of the Stonewall riots, thousands commemorated the event in a march from Greenwich Village to Central Park. More lesbians and gay men lived openly and proudly. Their lives converged with those of heterosexuals who divorced, lived together without marrying, or bore children outside marriage. Their challenge to gender norms converged with the demands of feminists.

The homophile movement's emphasis on reforming the mental health profession's assessment of sexual orientation gave it common cause with feminists, who wanted the profession to stop pathologizing women who resisted traditional, subservient roles. Post-Stonewall gay activists adopted the tactics of direct action common to radical feminism. Thus, in 1970, gay and feminist demonstrators together interrupted the national convention of the American Psychiatric Association in San Francisco. They stormed the stage during the delivery of a paper on "aversion therapy," a treatment designed to change sexual orientation using electric shock or nausea drugs in conjunction with sexually provocative same-sex visuals. They demanded that the profession end its part in perpetuating both rigid sex roles for women and the view that homosexuals were sick.

At the 1972 convention, Kameny and Gittings, some heterosexual psychiatrists, and one gay psychiatrist who would only appear if he could disguise his identity and use a voice-distorting microphone, spoke to a packed house on a panel titled "Psychiatry, Friend or Foe to Homosexuals?" This spurred the beginning of an official gay group within the APA. Just one year later, in 1973, the board of trustees voted to remove homosexuality from the list of mental disorders.[7] This development was critical to any legal strategy supporting the custody rights of lesbian mothers.

Phyllis Lyon and Del Martin pushed feminist groups to embrace the concerns of lesbians. They spoke about lesbian mothers and inspired the formation of a Lesbian Mothers Union in California in 1971. Their 1972 book, *Lesbian/Woman*, included a chapter on lesbian mothers.[8] The next year, they authored an article on lesbian mothers in *Ms.* magazine,[9] and articles discussing lesbian mothers appeared in the *New York Times* and *Newsweek*. In 1974 the custody case of Sandy and Madeleine spawned the Lesbian Mothers National Defense Fund, a volunteer-run, Seattle-based national clearinghouse for legal and psychological materials; the organization published a newsletter, maintained a referral service, and raised money to help lesbian mothers with legal bills.

The lawyers in the women's movement—most of them heterosexual—were working primarily on the equal rights amendment and other issues of sex equality. Lawyers in the gay rights movement—most of them men—were working primarily on sodomy law reform and employment discrimination. The National Gay Task Force (now the National Gay and Lesbian Task Force) and Lambda Legal Defense and Education Fund (now Lambda Legal) were both started in 1973, but neither initially addressed lesbian mothers.

Lesbian lawyers developed a strategy to protect the custody rights of openly lesbian mothers. In 1974, child custody became the first lesbian issue addressed at the National Conference on Women and the Law, an annual gathering of feminist lawyers that began in 1970. Each year thereafter, this feminist conference was the place at which lawyers were trained to represent lesbian mothers. In 1977, San Francisco lawyer Donna Hitchens founded the Lesbian Rights Project as an offshoot of the feminist Equal Rights Advocates. Although the project addressed a range of issues, such as employment, immigration, and discharge of lesbians from the military, its focus was parenting. Pushed by lesbian activists, nondiscrimination in custody decisions became a plank of the feminist Plan of Action adopted at the 1977 National Women's Conference in Houston.

The victories in the early and mid-1970s, including that of Sandy and Madeleine, were made possible because of the convergence of social and legal changes, and the efforts of lesbian feminist lawyers who were able to channel those changes into a legal strategy. Other successful cases in the mid-1970s occurred in California, Maine, Ohio, Oregon, and South Carolina. In the first—and still one of the few—victories for transsexual parents, in 1973 a Colorado appeals court told a trial court that it was wrong to remove custody of four children from a mother simply because she had undergone a sex-change operation and become a man.[10]

Cases in which lesbian mothers, like Marilyn Koop, lost custody of their children, were more numerous, and many mothers gave up custody without going to court; the backward-looking forces of the status quo, resistant to both the changing status of women and the increased visibility and acceptance of homosexuality, controlled most of the judiciary. But forward-looking judges and lawyers accepted the basic tenets of feminism and the other progressive social movements of the time and the sexual revolution that accompanied them.

Beginning in 1972 in Ann Arbor, Michigan, counties and cities passed ordinances outlawing discrimination against gay men and lesbians in employment, housing, and public accommodations. In 1976 the District of Columbia City Council extended its antidiscrimination law to prohibit judges from using sexual orientation as a basis for denying custody or visitation. That year, the American Psychological Association resolved that sexual orientation should not be a primary component in decisions on custody, adoption, or foster parenting. The civil rights paradigm that offered equality to previously oppressed groups seemed broad enough to encompass an end to discrimination based on sexual orientation. The recognition of family ties based on shared resources and commitments, not blood, legal formalities, or marriage, indicated the likelihood of increasing success for the custody claims of lesbian mothers and increased recognition of the varied households in which gay men and lesbians lived. It was just a matter of time.

The Backlash Begins

When the backlash came, it hit both feminism and gay rights. Phyllis Schlafly, author of a book extolling the conservatism of Barry Goldwater, formed the Eagle Forum to oppose the equal rights amendment. She used the specter of gay marriage to rally voters to defeat the ERA. Abortion opponents formed a "right to life" movement to protest the Supreme Court's *Roe v. Wade* decision. As the gay rights movement experienced successes, it too incurred the wrath of those who wanted to turn back the clock.

In 1977, five years after the first law prohibiting discrimination based on sexual orientation, Dade County, Florida, passed such an ordinance. Anita Bryant—a singer, former beauty queen, and spokesperson for the Florida orange juice industry—spearheaded an effort to repeal it by popular vote. Her "Save the Children" campaign capitalized on fears of "homosexual recruitment" of children and child molestation; she called gay men and lesbians "human garbage." On June 7, 1977, the referendum was held and the ordinance repealed. The next day the governor signed legislation banning adoption by lesbians and gay men.[11]

The forward trajectory of feminism and gay and lesbian rights and the backlash these movements inspired met at the National Women's Conference that summer in Houston. Phyllis Schlafly's Eagle Forum joined the John Birch Society, the Ku Klux Klan, the Mormon Church, and other conservative organizations to oppose the state-level conferences that preceded the national gathering. Schlafly predicted that the Houston conference would finish off the women's movement by showing feminists to be "the radical, antifamily, prolesbian people they are." At the national conference Schlafly led a vocal minority of about 20 percent of the delegates.

The delegates who sided with Schlafly produced a minority report that read as a blueprint for the conservative agenda. It advocated limits on taxation and nonessential government spending, and it identified national defense as the primary role of the federal government. It called for libraries to stock materials portraying traditional wives, mothers, and homemakers in a positive light, "instead of the predominance of material of the feminist viewpoint"; it opposed battered-women's shelters and federally funded childcare and early-childhood-development programs; it recommended that teachers, counselors, school administrators, and psychologists "research studies which prove that sexually differentiated behavior is firmly rooted in the biological phenomenon of hormonal action on the fetal brain so they can understand the ultimate damage to the student that can result from unisex conformity and/or role reversal." Although it approved of equal employment opportunities, it stated that women working outside the home still considered their families their primary careers and were working because of the need to keep pace with the wage-price spiral caused by inflationary deficit spending.[12]

The report's "sexual preference" plank affirmed: "We oppose giving lesbians or homosexuals privileges of adopting children, of teaching in schools, of acting as role models, or otherwise promoting their way of life. We believe that the definition of a family should never be extended to in any way include homosexuals or biologically unrelated, unmarried couples or otherwise accord to them the dignity which properly belongs to husbands and wives."

The positions in the minority report might have seemed an anomaly had the signs of successful backlash not appeared elsewhere. President Jimmy Carter did not back the progressive Plan of Action that emerged from Houston. When Bella Abzug continued to push for its implementation, Carter fired her as chair of the National Advisory Committee on Women; other committee members quit in protest. The antiabortion movement gained a political victory in 1976 when Congress passed the Hyde Amendment denying federal funding of abortion for Medicaid recipients.[13] In 1977 the Supreme Court upheld an analogous state law, the first decision by the Court approving a limit on abortion.[14] In 1979 the Supreme Court upheld the Social Security law that granted survivors' benefits to a deceased worker's wife if she was raising his children but not to an unmarried partner raising his children; the Court ruled that this was not unlawful discrimination against nonmarital children.[15]

Schlafly's anti-ERA movement succeeded. In 1977 Indiana was the thirty-fifth state to ratify the amendment (out of thirty-eight needed). In spite of legislation extending the deadline from 1979 to 1982, not a single additional state ratified it, and some attempted to rescind their ratifications.

Bryant took her antigay crusade around the country. She was successful in Saint Paul, Minnesota, Eugene, Oregon, and Wichita, Kansas. After the Wichita vote, she announced, "It is now obvious that the will of the American people is to return this country to pro-family, Bible morality."[16]

Defining the family divided advocates into two camps, exemplified when President Carter fulfilled his 1976 campaign pledge to convene a White House Conference on the Family. In early 1979, the official name was changed to the White House Conference on Families. Some delegates demanded restoration of the original name to recognize that "our nation was founded on a strong traditional family, meaning a married heterosexual couple with or without natural children."[17]

The group urging a return to the original name was the National Pro-Family Coalition. It worked hard to elect delegates and obtain platform positions opposing feminism, abortion, the ERA, homosexuality, and big government. It argued against unmarried partners, mothers with nonmarital children, and gay and lesbian relationships.

Opposing this limited vision was the Coalition for Families, made up of almost fifty moderate and liberal organizations. It endorsed the ERA, the right to choose abortion, and the "elimination of discrimination and encouragement of respect for differences based on sex, race, ethnic origin, creed, socioeconomic status, age, disability, diversity of family type, sexual preference, or biological ties."[18]

The opposing camps looked at the variety of family structures in U.S. society and perceived them differently. Where the Coalition for Families saw family pluralism, the National Pro-Family Coalition saw family breakdown. Family pluralism encompassed everyone who benefited from the demise of legally mandated gender norms and the reduced imperative of marriage that characterized the late 1960s and early- to mid-1970s. Expanded options for women and new family structures constituted family breakdown for those who imposed the "traditional" married heterosexual couple as the ideal and labeled other forms deviant.

Also in 1979, Reverend Jerry Falwell founded the Moral Majority, an organization that became so pervasive its name was applied to Christian right-wing groups in general. Its strategy was to create a conservative movement using social issues including abortion, homosexuality, the ERA, busing, and affirmative action. The decline of the "God-ordained institution of the family," to use the words of James Dobson's Focus on the Family, was one of its battle cries.

This coalition proved critical to Ronald Reagan's 1980 election. The day after Reagan's success, conservative activists held a news conference to announce their agenda. In addition to support of both a constitutional amendment to ban abortion and an antigay and antifeminist "family protection act," they called for increased defense spending, massive tax cuts, and cuts in health and human services programs.

Feminists and Gay Rights Advocates Fight Back

The backlash against feminism and gay rights dwelled on *family*, invoking the language of "traditional family" and "family values." It was an attack on the changes in law and culture that facilitated family pluralism, sexuality beyond that simply for procreation, and liberation from rigid gender norms. Feminists resisted. In November 1979, NOW Legal Defense and Education Fund held a National Assembly on the Future of the Family, which drew two thousand participants. The scope of the assembly was vast; in addition to covering issues typically associated with families, such as marriage, domestic violence, childcare, and divorce, it made recommendations on education, housing, community organizing, and government benefits.[19]

The panel on nontraditional families addressed heterosexual unmarried couples, with or without children; gay and lesbian couples, with or without children; adults who may or may not share an intimate relationship raising children in a shared household; and single adults raising children. The panel's recommendations dealt with the issues relevant to lesbian and gay families in a larger context. Thus, it advocated that parents seeking custody of their children not be penalized because their "family style" was not traditional. The report also noted that

> the rights of children to education, support, care and nurturing must be protected regardless of the choices made by the parents.... An example of such benefits would be the availability of health insurance coverage for dependents within family units.... A single wage earner supporting an extended family should be permitted to include dependents—regardless of blood relationship—in a health insurance plan.

The panel recommended that tax laws be revised to avoid rewarding certain types of families and penalizing others; that survivors' rights should be determined by functional—not legal—relationships; and that Social Security should recognize services rendered in the home.

Lesbians and gay men also resisted. Some one hundred thousand people turned out for the first National March on Washington for Lesbian and Gay Rights in 1979. One of the three principal demands of the march was an end to discrimination against lesbian and gay parents. Court cases continued to produce victories as well as defeats. In what remains one of the most eloquent expressions of the positive aspects of having a lesbian mother, a 1979 New Jersey appellate court reasoned:

> [These children may] emerge better equipped to search out their own standards of right and wrong, better able to perceive that the majority is not always correct in its moral judgments, and better able to understand the importance of conforming their beliefs to the requirements of reason and tested knowledge, not the constraints of currently popular sentiment or prejudice.[20]

Throughout the 1970s, advocates for lesbian and gay parents and relationships benefited from their common ground with bigger, better-established social justice movements. Organizing for the 1979 march reflected a commitment to ending racism and sexism by requiring 50 percent of the leaders to be women and at least 20 percent to be people of color. NOW, the National Lawyers Guild, and the antiwar and antinuclear group Mobilization for Survival all endorsed the march. These groups shared a commitment to racial, economic, and gender justice and to peace. The right-wing backlash, in its relentless support for the male-dominated, heterosexual family, opposed both gay rights and the feminist movement. Anita Bryant's crusade was part of a larger conservative movement that rejoiced in the election of Ronald Reagan and presented new challenges for all progressive movements.

CHAPTER THREE

Redefining Family

In 1975 Miguel Braschi and Leslie Blanchard began living together in a New York City apartment leased in Blanchard's name alone. Blanchard contracted AIDS, and he died in September 1986. Two months later, the landlord sought to evict Braschi from the home he had shared with Blanchard for eleven years. The law allowed an occupant whose name was not on the lease to remain in the apartment only if he was a surviving spouse or some other member of the deceased tenant's "family." The first appeals court to hear the case ruled that the law included only "traditional," legally recognized, family relationships. The state's highest court, however, ruled in 1989 that "the intended protection against sudden eviction should not rest on fictitious legal distinctions or genetic history, but instead should find its foundation in the reality of family life." Miguel Braschi won the right to keep his home.[1]

In December 1979 Karen Thompson and Sharon Kowalski exchanged rings. They lived in Saint Cloud, Minnesota, far from the post-Stonewall climate of New York and San Francisco. They loved each other, but they did not use the word "lesbian"; they told almost no one the nature of their relationship. Soon thereafter they moved in together.

The car accident on November 13, 1983, in which Sharon sustained severe physical and neurological injuries, changed everything. First it was the hospital that denied Karen access to her partner of four years; then it was Sharon's family. Relations were initially cordial between Sharon's parents and Karen, but they grew strained as Sharon's father questioned how much time Karen spent assisting with Sharon's care and therapy. After about three months, Karen told Sharon's parents about the relationship she had with their daughter; they did not believe her, and they were revolted. As court-appointed guardian, Sharon's father stopped Karen's visits with Sharon. He moved her to a distant nursing home where she did not get rehabilitative treatment, and her condition deteriorated. Although Sharon showed some ability to express a preference to be with Karen, the courts upheld the decisions Sharon's father made for eight years; for three and a half years Karen did not see Sharon at all.

Around the country, feminist, lesbian, and disability rights groups organized on Karen and Sharon's behalf. Among their activities were demonstrations in twenty-one cities on August 8, 1998, Sharon's thirty-second birthday, a day activists named "National Free Sharon Kowalski Day." Karen's book about the ordeal, *Why Can't Sharon Kowalski Come Home?* was published that year. In 1992, after three attempts in the Minnesota Court of Appeals, Karen was named Sharon's guardian. Sharon has been living ever since with Karen and Karen's new partner, Patty.[2]

Couples and Others outside Marriage

Even before the tragedies that changed forever the lives of Miguel Braschi, Leslie Blanchard, Karen Thompson, and Sharon Kowalski, it was apparent that unmarried couples could suffer from the absence of legal recognition. When "illegitimate" children had suffered because they lacked access to the benefits given children born to married couples, the solution had been to reduce the legal significance of marriage—to make something other than marriage the dividing line between who was included and who was excluded from particular benefits. Redefining family, including recognizing unmarried couples, was an extension of the developments of the 1970s that made marriage matter less. Redefining family, rather than achieving marriage for same-sex couples, was also the driving vision of the coalitions in which advocates for gay and lesbian families participated.

That is not to say that same-sex couples never considered marriage. Shortly after Stonewall, a few had tried to marry and had failed. In 1970 two gay activists at the University of Minnesota had called a press conference to draw attention to their application for a marriage license. When the city clerk denied the application, television and newspapers around the country carried the story. That same year, two Seattle men, who lived in a commune, ran a gay community center, and were friends who sometimes had sex but were not romantic partners, sought a marriage license in order to generate public discussion about gay relationships. When both these couples brought court challenges, judges rebuffed the claims that same-sex couples should be allowed to marry, finding them inconsistent with the definition of marriage.[3]

Those cases were not part of, nor were they followed by, any organized political or legal effort to legalize same-sex marriage. Well into the 1980s, the legal arm of the gay rights movement was staffed almost entirely by volunteers. With scarce resources, lawyers focused on issues most likely to be successful; same-sex marriage was not one.

The feminist critique of marriage also steered advocates for lesbian and gay families away from marriage. Marriage came with a patriarchal script. The legal and political developments of the 1970s had chipped away at that script, but the Christian Right was trying to hammer it back into place. Women were voting on marriage with their feet; 1979 and 1981 saw the highest divorce rates in the history of the country. Heterosexual feminists were eschewing marriage in the hopes of building more egalitarian relationships. The lesbian lawyers debating movement priorities, and a few of the gay male lawyers as well, were as committed to feminism as they were to gay rights and saw the two as intertwined. The overarching goal was facilitating social, legal, and economic support for diverse family forms outside the patriarchal family; *less marriage*, not *marriage*, was consistent with that vision.

What's more, the Christian Right lumped together same-sex couples and unmarried heterosexual couples for the threat they posed to "traditional" marriage, and their template for traditional marriage included rigid gender roles. The Christian Right also lumped homosexual sex with nonprocreative and nonmarital heterosexual sex as immoral affronts to God's law. The Christian Right opposed government spending on antipoverty and civil rights programs, linking such spending to family decline. Speaking in 1982 at a Family Forum conference cosponsored by the Moral Majority Foundation, Pat Robertson, the founder and president of the Christian Broadcasting Network, who would run for president of the United States later in the decade, expressed the connections:

> Deficit spending, from the 1940's through the 1970's, put an intolerable burden on the American people... So it became necessary for women to enter the work force not because they wanted to but because they had to. Twenty-five million children under school age are dumped into day care centers by their mothers. Teenagers come home and there's no one there, so they think, "How about a little marijuana and a little sex." When mother gets home she's tired, and squabbles with her husband. They get divorced, the children lose their role models, there is more rebellion in the schools and homosexuality and the children of divorce get divorced themselves.[4]

Robertson's solution was "a Christian marriage." "Being a housewife," he said, "is a noble profession. My father was a Senator, but my mother stayed home to tell me about Jesus Christ."[5] Thus, whether on the offensive seeking recognition or on the defensive in response to the backlash, gay and lesbian advocacy was intertwined with advocacy for diverse family and relationship forms, freedom of sexual expression, and elimination of male supremacy.

An Alternative to Marriage

The push for a status called "domestic partnership" began in the early 1980s as an alternative to marriage. It was a status available to both same-sex and different-sex couples. Although heterosexuals *could* marry, domestic partnership recognition was consistent with the proposition that they should not have to. The need for recognition of those who *could not* and those who *chose not to* marry was two sides of the same coin.

Private employers, colleges and universities, and cities and counties all contributed to the development of domestic partnership. In 1982 the *Village Voice* newspaper became the first employer to provide health, disability, and life insurance to the "spousal equivalent" of any gay or straight employee who had lived with the employee for at least a year.

Ben & Jerry's, a small company based in Waterbury, Vermont, began to offer health insurance coverage to unmarried partners in 1989. Human resources manager Liz Lonergan explained the company's reasoning: "We really believe the family is who you love and who you live with," and that "the families of all [Ben & Jerry's'] workers deserve as a basic human right to live free of the fear that a catastrophic illness or accident could destroy them financially."[6]

In 1990 the National Gay and Lesbian Task Force surveyed benefit policies at colleges and universities. Out of 500 questionnaires sent out, 110 were returned; over 20 percent of the responding institutions recognized nontraditional families and/or domestic partners in some fashion.[7]

Some policies extended beyond couples to an even broader definition of family. Mission College permitted paid bereavement leave for immediate family or "any other significant person who was living in the . . . employee's household." Bowdoin, Georgia State, Michigan, and North Dakota authorized leave to tend to a sick family member as defined by the employee. Oberlin had a broad nondiscrimination policy that extended equal access to services, facilities, housing, and employee benefits to those meeting the criteria of "cohabitation, long term emotional commitment, and financial interdependence."

In 1985 Berkeley and West Hollywood passed the first municipal domestic partner ordinances, with Santa Cruz following in 1986. In 1988 Los Angeles extended to city employees the ability to use sick or bereavement leave for the illness or death of a domestic partner if the couple registered with the city after living together for at least a year. San Francisco enacted a domestic partner ordinance in 1989, extending health insurance coverage to partners of city employees and bereavement leave identical to that given spouses. It also gave all who registered, not just city employees, the right to hospital visitation.

The Madison Example

Some communities sought to expand the relationships entitled to legal recognition beyond couples. In Madison, Wisconsin, in 1983, the Alternative Family Rights Task Force of the Madison Equal Opportunities Commission (MEOC) began a study of community needs. The task force considered the testimony of two Hispanic women who described the prevalence in minority cultures of close ties with extended alternative families. It heard from lesbian couples and unmarried heterosexual couples who could not protect their families through employer-provided health insurance and sick leave. One couple could not obtain a family membership in the YWCA. A hospital refused to allow a stepmother to visit her seriously ill stepson whom she had helped raise for eight years. The task force reviewed a newspaper article about three women over sixty living as a family in a group home provided by their church.

Ultimately, the city chose to define domestic partners as those in a "relationship of mutual support, caring, and commitment [who] intend to remain in such a relationship in the immediate future.... Mutual support means that the domestic partners contribute mutually to the maintenance and support of the domestic partnership throughout its existence."[8] They must live together as a "single, nonprofit housekeeping unit, whose relationship is of permanent and distinct domestic character" and their relationship must not be "merely temporary, social, political, commercial, or economic in nature."

The history of the Madison definition is almost unique.[9] The Alternative Family Rights Task Force sought equal respect for and recognition of a wide variety of family forms. It was not driven by a desire either to compensate same-sex couples for the inability to marry or to recognize unmarried couples. The ordinance covers any two adults who meet the criteria.

The District of Columbia, which enacted its domestic partner registration in 1992 as part of a coalition effort to recognize the city's diverse families, also uses an atypical definition. Its eligibility criteria extends to two individuals in "a familial relationship... characterized by mutual caring and the sharing of a mutual residence." Madison and D.C. thus open registration to same-sex couples, different-sex couples, and those in nonconjugal relationships. Because the definitions do not bar those who are related closely enough that they cannot marry, registration is also available to relatives.

The Influence of AIDS

AIDS, which by the mid-1980s was associated largely with gay men as a result of transmission through sexual practices, increased the urgency of recognizing relationships not based on blood or marriage. Examples abounded of longtime partners or best friends of people with AIDS being excluded from hospital visitation and from decisions about medical treatment and burial or disposition of remains by the biological families of gay men with AIDS. Unmarried partners also were not given bereavement leave by public or private employers.

AIDS demonstrated the profound insufficiency of the law on decision making for a person unable to make decisions for himself. The power of attorney, an instrument that allows another person to carry on financial matters, typically could last only for as long as the person writing it remained competent, but a person with AIDS wanted to designate someone to make decisions when he was no longer able to do so. Such a designation would keep the legal next of kin—usually a spouse for a married person or a parent for an unmarried one—from obtaining that power. The saga of Sharon Kowalski also demonstrated the consequences of basing decision-making authority on the formal, traditional definition of family.

Raising Children

The gay rights movement enabled many young adults to embrace their sexual orientation. As a result men and women who in an earlier period would have married out of convention, fear, or denial, no longer did so. Some wanted to be parents. Births of nonmarital children no longer carried the stigma they did in earlier decades; medical technology increased the possibilities for conception without sexual intercourse. Lesbians began conceiving children through alternative insemination. Lesbians and gay men sought to adopt.

These developments posed new legal challenges. Laws did not easily recognize that a child might have two mothers or two fathers. Lawyers who in other contexts were redefining *family* needed new arguments for redefining *parenthood*. In addition, the increased visibility of children with lesbian and gay parents risked a backlash of restrictive laws.

Sustained national attention to the suitability of lesbians and gay men raising children emerged in 1985 in the context of foster parenting. Many states, chronically short of foster homes, licensed lesbian and gay foster parents in the decade from 1975 to 1985, a practice supported by both the American Psychological Association and the National Association of Social Workers. But in May 1985, neighbors of a gay couple who served as foster parents went to the *Boston Globe* to express their disapproval. The ensuing publicity sparked widespread debate about gay men and lesbians raising children. Massachusetts changed its policy, issuing regulations that gave preference to married couples and made it almost impossible for lesbians and gay men to become foster parents.[10]

In the wake of that controversy, in 1986 New Hampshire became the second state with an adoption ban and the first with a legislatively mandated ban on gay foster parenting.[11] In 1987 President Ronald Reagan's Interagency Task Force on Adoption recommended that "homosexual adoption should not be supported."

In other, more receptive, states, advocates for gay and lesbian parents were using court cases to develop law enabling both members of a couple to be legally recognized as a child's parent. Lawyers coined the term "second-parent adoption" to describe the equivalent of a stepparent adoption, in which a biological parent's partner adopts her child. The term "joint adoption" was used to designate adoption of a child by both members of a couple, a practice unheard of earlier unless the couple was legally married. The first second-parent adoption was granted in Alaska in 1985, and within months there were others in Oregon, Washington, and California. All were granted by trial court judges without written opinions, giving them limited value in setting precedent for other courts. The adoption decrees were circulated among a small group of advocates who used them to help develop the law in an increasing number of jurisdictions. Although law review articles first discussed these cases in 1986, there was no reported opinion granting a second-parent adoption until 1991.

The practice of second-parent adoption was not limited to same-sex couples. The principle at stake was the right of any two unmarried people to become legal parents of a child. In one Maryland case, two sisters were named the mothers of a child they were raising. When the highest court in New York approved the practice in 1995, it did so in two cases, one involving a lesbian couple and the other involving an unmarried heterosexual couple. One legal scholar urged approval of joint adoption by two coparents, not romantically involved, as a natural extension of shared parenting models within the black community.[12]

Divergence among states in attitudes toward lesbian and gay parenting continued to play out in the numerous postdivorce disputes between a lesbian or gay parent and a heterosexual ex-spouse. Successful rulings were possible because judges were required to determine the best interests of a particular child. In this less politicized, and usually less publicized, environment, some continued to be willing to accept gay men and lesbians as good parents. Researchers had begun studying the well-being of children raised by lesbian mothers, and they debunked recurring myths in court decisions—that lesbians were mentally ill or emotionally unstable; that a lesbian mother would sexually molest her child or demonstrate sexual behavior in front of her child; and that children raised by lesbian mothers would become gay or lesbian, would be confused about their gender identity, or would be socially stigmatized.

In 1980 the Massachusetts Supreme Court permitted a lesbian mother to regain custody from a guardian who had cared for her children while the mother was suffering from mental and physical illness. The court said that the mother could not lose her children because her household failed to meet "ideals approved by the community" or because she had a lifestyle "at odds with the average."[13] The Alaska Supreme Court ruled in 1985 that it was "impermissible to rely on any real or imagined social stigma attaching to mother's status as a lesbian."[14]

On the other hand, the backlash that began in the mid-1970s meant that many courts continued to rule against gay and lesbian parents. In 1985 the Virginia Supreme Court held that a gay parent living with a partner was always an unfit parent.[15] In 1986 the Nevada Supreme Court terminated a father's parental rights solely because he underwent a sex-change operation.[16] The Missouri appeals courts ruled against lesbian and gay parents nine times in the 1980s, making it the worst state in the country in which to litigate for custody or visitation.

The U.S. Supreme Court's 1986 decision in *Bowers v. Hardwick* upheld a Georgia statute prohibiting sodomy between two consenting adults.[17] The decision left standing criminal sodomy laws in twenty-four states and the District of Columbia. In some states, these statutes had been used explicitly to justify denials of or restrictions on custody or visitation. A positive decision in *Bowers* would have given advocates in those states a powerful weapon for asserting the rights of gay and lesbian parents. Instead, the Court's decision tacitly approved reasoning such as that applied by an Arizona appeals court just a few months later. That court affirmed a trial court's unwillingness to certify a bisexual man as an appropriate adoptive parent, reasoning that Arizona had a criminal sodomy statute, that such a statute was constitutional under *Bowers*, and that "it would be anomalous for the state on the one hand to declare homosexual conduct unlawful and on the other create a parent after that proscribed model, in effect approving that standard, inimical to the natural family, as head of a state-created family."[18] The ruling in *Bowers* was one precipitating event leading to the second March on Washington for Lesbian and Gay Rights in 1987. Five hundred thousand lesbian, gay, bisexual, and transgender people and their allies participated; over seven hundred were arrested on the steps of the Supreme Court in a direct protest of the *Bowers* decision.

Growing Advocacy for Family Diversity

By the late 1980s, the legal arm of the gay rights movement had a more developed infrastructure. The ACLU added a Lesbian and Gay Rights Project in 1986. The National Lesbian and Gay Law Association (NLGLA) was formed at a meeting held in conjunction with the 1987 March on Washington. In 1988 NLGLA held its first "Lavender Law" conference, which included panels on both traditional custody and visitation disputes and the issues facing planned gay and lesbian families, including access to alternative insemination, surrogacy, and adoption and second-parent adoptions. It took Lambda Legal ten years, from 1973 to 1983, to hire its first full-time attorney, but by 1989 it had four.

By the end of the 1980s, gay and lesbian advocates often played critical roles in coalition advocacy on behalf of diverse family structures. Both the state of California and the city of Los Angeles issued task force reports on family diversity. The Los Angeles report urged government to define families to reflect the way people actually live. It recommended flexible definitions of family, a ban on marital-status discrimination, and domestic partnership status for two people who lived together and shared the "common necessities of life."[19]

When the highest court in New York ruled in favor of Miguel Braschi in 1989, it was a victory won as a result of coalition efforts on behalf of diverse family forms. Certainly it was a victory for lesbian and gay couples, but the legal issue in the case was the definition of the word "family" in rent-control laws. The landlord wanted a narrow definition, limited to married couples and biological and adoptive parents and children. The strategy of the gay rights lawyers representing Mr. Braschi included the submission of numerous friend-of-the-court briefs explaining how many different types of families would be harmed by such a definition.

The ACLU's Lesbian and Gay Rights Project represented Mr. Braschi. The friend-of-the-court brief filed by Lambda Legal noted that the court's decision would affect thousands of nontraditional family units, including gay and lesbian families, heterosexual unmarried couples, and the poor. It argued that traditional families were not more worthy of government protection than alternative families. Gay Men's Health Crisis and several AIDS service agencies filed a brief detailing the circumstances of those like Mr. Braschi, who had cared for his partner who was dying of AIDS.

Briefs from other organizations acknowledged the vast diversity of families in New York and argued passionately for protection for all families. Community Action for Legal Services, a nonprofit organization for low-income New Yorkers that ran seventeen offices in the five boroughs, argued that a narrow definition of family would be devastating for its clients. It advocated a functional definition of family and pointed to court decisions describing a family as "a continuing relationship of love and care, and an assumption of responsibility for some other person." Family Service America (now the Alliance for Children and Families), then a network of 290 local agencies providing services to more than 3 million people, argued for recognizing family pluralism. The Association of the Bar of the City of New York also filed a friend-of-the-court brief. The group argued for an inquiry into whether the household was the "functional and factual equivalent of a natural family."

The *Braschi* decision identified the purpose of the state's rent-control laws as protection from the sudden loss of one's home. The court quoted *Webster's Dictionary*'s first definition of "family" as "a group of people united by certain convictions or common affiliation," and concluded that protection from eviction should extend to "those who reside in households having all the normal familial characteristics." After listing many characteristics that a trial court should consider in applying this test, the court held that the controlling factor should be the "totality of the relationship as evidenced by the dedication, caring and self-sacrifice of the parties." Miguel Braschi and Leslie Blanchard met that test.

New York's Division of Housing and Community Renewal then issued new regulations governing both rent-controlled and rent-stabilized apartments. The agency included in the list of those entitled to succession rights those "who can prove emotional and financial commitment and interdependence with the tenant," making it clear that a sexual relationship was not required. A New York State senator's proposal that the state constitution be amended to define family as spouses, parents, children, and in-laws went nowhere.

Contrasting Visions: Value Family Diversity versus Remedy the Exclusion of Same-Sex Couples from Marriage

Braschi was the most decisive legal victory to that point for both same-sex couples and other nontraditional family forms. Gay rights advocates were ecstatic. But within weeks, commentator Andrew Sullivan published an essay in the *New Republic* titled "The Conservative Case for Gay Marriage." Sullivan was less than enthusiastic about *Braschi*. Rather than allowing courts to define family, he wrote, the government should allow gay couples to marry. The generation that did not live through Stonewall (Sullivan was born in 1963) wanted to fit in, he said. "A need to rebel has quietly ceded to a desire to belong." He extolled the values of "old-style," "traditional" marriage, asking only that same-sex couples have that option as well.[20]

While Sullivan's conservative defense of marriage found little support, more activists and leaders were considering whether the time was right to challenge the exclusion of same-sex couples from marriage. Lambda Legal executive director Tom Stoddard believed that the case of Sharon Kowalski and Karen Thompson proved the imperative of achieving marriage for same-sex couples. The organization's legal director, Paula Ettelbrick, had a different analysis.

The two lawyers published side-by-side essays;[21] their frequently reprinted exchange crystallized the differences between seeking gay and lesbian inclusion in marriage and seeking diverse family recognition.

The Stoddard-Ettelbrick Debate

After acknowledging the long history of oppression of women within marriage, Stoddard advocated overturning bans on same-sex marriage as the top issue of every gay organization. First he pointed out the economic advantages of marriage, including inheritance, government benefits, preferential tax rates, conferral of citizenship on foreign spouses, and access to health insurance. Recognizing that a couple could claim some protection for their relationship using wills and other documents, he noted that this required lawyers, which required money, disadvantaging those at the bottom of the economic ladder.

Stoddard also identified marriage as "the core of the traditional notion of 'family'" and invoked a Supreme Court case that called marriage "noble" and "sacred." Exclusion from marriage marked same-sex relationships as less significant and less valuable. He argued that marriage was the political issue that would most test the commitment of nongay people to full equality for gay people and that it was also the issue most likely to end discrimination against lesbians and gay men. Stoddard identified the issue not as the desirability of marriage but as the desirability of the *right* to marry. He also argued that enlarging marriage to include same-sex couples could be the principal means of ridding marriage of its sexist and patriarchal past.

In opposing Stoddard's vision, Paula Ettelbrick emphasized the conflict between pushing for marriage and seeking validation of many forms of relationships. Conceding that from a civil rights standpoint lesbians and gay men should have a "right" to marry, she developed a distinction between rights and justice. "The fight for justice," she wrote, "has as its goal the realignment of power imbalances among individuals and classes of people in society." She argued for combining both rights and justice in setting priorities for the advancement of gay men and lesbians, and stated that making marriage a priority would set an agenda of gaining rights for a few without seeking justice for those, gay or straight, who are not married. She decried the fact that getting constitutional equal protection would require arguing that gay and straight relationships are the same, an argument she felt would undermine the transformative potential of queerness and perpetuate the notion that married couples have the highest form of relationship. She argued for the values of difference and diversity.

Addressing the undeniable economic benefits of marriage, especially the access to healthcare through a spouse's benefits, she noted that such access depended on at least one partner having a job with health benefits, something beyond the reach of those in low-paying jobs with no benefits, and she argued for healthcare for all. She also lamented the disadvantages that unmarried gay men and lesbians would continue to experience, such as exclusion from hospital visitation with respect to a sick or injured partner. She advocated *first* ending the two-tiered system of providing benefits and privileges to those who are married while ignoring the needs of those who are not. After that, she said, marriage would be a choice.

The Family Bill of Rights

The two sides of this debate sought common ground, and Lambda Legal sought to develop a document that would encompass the values of both Ettelbrick and Stoddard. Evan Wolfson, then a new Lambda Legal staff attorney, drafted a blueprint for a just policy encompassing the needs of all families, titled the "Family Bill of Rights." Wolfson advocated advancing the cause of same-sex marriage in the courts, and would go on a decade later to become one of the most widely recognized national advocates of same-sex marriage. Wolfson's draft Family Bill of Rights was an attempt to articulate a comprehensive position on the legal treatment of families that supported marriage for same-sex couples and, at the same time, urged laws reflecting the equal worth of all families. It read as follows:

> WHEREAS, the diversity of the cultures within American society and the choices individuals make result in many kinds of living arrangements sharing the values properly associated with family; and

WHEREAS, these defining family values include mutual emotional and financial commitment and interdependence, lives shared together in relationships of dedication, caring, and self-sacrifice; and

WHEREAS, the reality of American life today is that families are formed in many ways, through blood, marriage, and adoption, as well as by choice, commitment, and association, and that, therefore, family can be best defined not by reliance on fictitious legal distinctions, but rather with respect to such attributes as the level of emotional and financial commitment, the manner in which the family members have conducted their everyday lives and held themselves out to society and friends, the reliance placed upon one another for daily family services, the longevity of the family relationship, and any other pattern of conduct, agreement, or action which evidences their intention of creating long-term, emotionally committed relationships; and

WHEREAS, the American tradition of respect for individual freedom in shaping one's own destiny and making important personal choices free of government intrusion, and of encouraging diversity and pluralism warrants that all family relationships that, in the totality of circumstances, possess such attributes be accorded equal respect, recognition, and rights; and

WHEREAS, government actions should encourage, not undermine all families possessing such attributes,

NOW, THEREFORE, we representatives of all of America's diverse families, united in commitment and concern for our family members, our communities, our nation, and each other, do urge the adoption of this FAMILY BILL OF RIGHTS, to protect our equal needs and entitlements in the following areas:

I. RECOGNITION

All families have a right to secure formal recognition of their relationships. Where benefits are conditioned upon such recognition, it should not depend on marital relation, genetic history, or other arbitrary distinctions, but rather should reflect the defining family values set forth in the preamble.[22]

The Family Bill of Rights went on to address specific areas, including government and employee benefits, childrearing, and protections in civil and criminal law. Although it included a provision that same-sex couples should be allowed to marry, it made clear that marriage should not be a prerequisite for family recognition.

The unmistakable gist of the efforts in *Braschi* and the Family Bill of Rights was that no family should be penalized because it was not based on marriage. In 1991 the American Federation of Labor–Congress of Industrial Organizations (AFL-CIO) brought this expansive vision to employee benefits for families with a resolution on "Benefits for Changing Families." The union pledged to "work as appropriate to insure that fringe benefits are extended to all persons living in a household as a family."[23]

The Lotus Alternative

But another development in 1991 took domestic partnership benefits in a very different direction. That year, two large employers, Montefiore Medical Center in New York and software manufacturer Lotus Development Corporation in Massachusetts, implemented the nation's first domestic partner employee-benefits programs for same-sex couples only. They based their decisions on the exclusion of same-sex couples from marriage, calling it an equity issue for gay employees. Lotus became the largest corporation in the country to introduce domestic partnership benefits. Its decision gained widespread media attention. It also turned domestic partnership recognition into an exclusively *gay* issue, rather than an issue of recognizing an alternative to marriage.

The next year Levi Strauss, with twenty-three thousand employees, became the first Fortune 500 company to provide domestic partner benefits, and it chose to cover both same-sex and different-sex partners. "We realize that family structures are changing," said a senior vice-president, "and want to respect this diversity."[24]

In 1992 more employers implemented the "Lotus alternative." When Fortune 500 company Oracle instituted domestic partner benefits for same-sex couples the next year, it went one step further; it required the couple to sign an affidavit stating that, "We would legally marry each other if we could, and we intend to do so if marriage becomes available to us in our state of residence."[25]

Under this reasoning, the exclusion of same-sex couples from marriage emerged as an issue distinct from any criticism of marriage or any effort to value family diversity. Divergent descriptions of the problem guided law reform efforts to divergent solutions.

CHAPTER FOUR

The Right and the Marriage Movement

The Christian Right gained in influence throughout the 1980s. Its leaders used the AIDS epidemic to raise funds and incite antigay sentiment. They interpreted AIDS as God's retribution for homosexuality and did everything they could to ensure that the public linked AIDS and homosexuality.[1]

Christian religious broadcaster Pat Robertson entered the Republican presidential primary for the 1988 election. He built a precinct structure in thirty-two states and garnered 2 million votes before pulling out. The next year, starting with the mailing list from his campaign, he founded the Christian Coalition and selected Ralph Reed as executive director. The organization built support at the state and local levels, mobilizing evangelical churches and electing conservative Christians to low-profile offices.

"Family values," including the issues of family structure and gay and lesbian rights, played a significant role in the 1992 presidential campaign. As the election approached, conservative forces in the Republican Party sought to capitalize on their years of state and local organizing. Their choice for president was Pat Buchanan.

Dan Quayle Was Wrong

On May 19, 1992, Vice President Dan Quayle gave a speech about the Los Angeles riots. Four police officers had beaten African American motorist Rodney King; the beating was videotaped. On April 29, 1992, a mostly white jury acquitted the four police officers, and six days of riots followed. Quayle blamed the riots on a breakdown of family structure and traditional values, asserted that single motherhood was responsible for the rise of gangs and other social problems, and called for the welfare system to be dismantled. He took the media to task for its role in furthering such breakdown, and, in the line that gave the speech its notoriety, he said, "It doesn't help matters when prime-time TV has Murphy Brown, a character who supposedly epitomizes today's intelligent, highly paid, professional woman, mocking the importance of fathers by bearing a child alone, and calling it just another lifestyle choice."[2] The remark referred to a popular situation comedy in which Candace Bergen played a television broadcaster; in the episode watched by 38 million Americans the night before Quayle's speech, the character, who had an unplanned pregnancy, gave birth to a baby boy.

The "Murphy Brown" speech provoked immediate widespread reaction, almost all of it negative. Even President George H. W. Bush, whose daughter was a divorced mother with two children, refused to second Quayle's indictment of Murphy Brown. His assistant secretary of state, Janet Mullins, a single mother, called the comments insensitive. Single mothers across the country, including Republicans, were offended. Editorial writers and those interviewed on the news said Quayle should look to the real sources of problems, such as lack of employment and opportunity.

In mainstream newspapers, Quayle was told to update his values, develop policies to address urban education and disinvestment in cities, and to recognize that family structure was changing. Some commentators mentioned gay and lesbian parents among those family forms the vice president was overlooking. Newspapers around the country ran positive profiles of single mothers raising children. Although the Family Research Council's Gary Bauer appeared on television praising the vice president's contribution to the debate about family values, Quayle generally was cast as out of step with the issues of the time.

The same week, Democratic presidential candidate Bill Clinton spoke before an audience of lesbians and gay men and assured them that they would have a place in his administration. A Bush administration official linked these events with the comment that Clinton was wooing gay groups while Quayle was talking about family values. In a speech before the Southern Baptist Convention in June, Quayle said that people were wrong if they believed that "the family is an arbitrary arrangement of people who decide to live under the same roof, that fathers are dispensable and that parents need not be married or even of opposite sexes."[3]

When Clinton accepted his party's nomination for president that summer, he, too, spoke of family values. What he said, to great applause, was: "I want an America where family values live in our actions, not just in our speeches. An America that includes every family."[4]

The Republican National Convention proved a dramatic contrast. The local success of the Christian Coalition and its allies gave the Religious Right 42 percent of convention delegates. The party platform opposed "the efforts of the Democrat Party to redefine the traditional American family."[5] Buchanan had enough support in the primaries to earn a spot on the prime-time, opening night podium at the convention in August. He was blunt and belligerent. He said the election was a referendum on the religious and cultural war going on in the country. He attacked Hillary Clinton's criticisms of marriage as "radical feminism" and decried Bill Clinton's support of gay and lesbian rights. He inveighed that "Clinton and Clinton" would bring changes that could not be tolerated "in a nation we still call God's country."[6]

Buchanan was not the only convention speaker decrying feminism and gay rights. Robertson warned that the Clintons had a "radical plan to destroy the traditional family and transfer its functions to the federal government."[7] Marilyn Quayle, wife of the vice president, said liberals were angry because "most women do not wish to be liberated from their essential nature as women."[8] Former secretary of education William Bennett said that "family values represent a great dividing line between the parties." Speaking of "the tumultuous issue of alternative lifestyles," he said, "some ways of living are better than others."[9]

Shortly after the convention, while opposing an Iowa ballot initiative to add an equal rights amendment to the state's constitution, Robertson said, "The feminist agenda is not about equal rights for women. It is about a socialist, anti-family political movement that encourages women to leave their husbands, kill their children, practice witchcraft, destroy capitalism and become lesbians."[10]

The rhetoric that dominated the Republican convention alienated moderate Republicans. The attacks on Hillary Clinton, feminism, and lesbians and gay men failed to energize an electorate focused more on the economic downturn. Bill Clinton did energize feminists, who had lost ground during the Reagan-Bush years, and lesbian and gay activists who supported his rhetoric of inclusion and his promise to end the ban on gay men and lesbians in military service. If Buchanan was right and the election was a referendum on the culture war, Clinton's victory meant that the forces espousing antifeminist, antigay values had lost.

But there was a cloud over the election: Colorado voters approved an amendment to the state's constitution ("Amendment 2") banning state or local legislation protecting lesbians, gay men, and bisexuals from discrimination. James Dobson's Focus on the Family had moved its headquarters to Colorado Springs and played a key role, along with other Religious Right organizations, in the campaign.[11] Despite the national-level rejection, in local elections the Religious Right enjoyed some success. The Iowa equal rights amendment, which Robertson had targeted, failed by a vote of 52 percent to 48 percent.

What a Difference a Year Makes

Candidate Bill Clinton promised to end the ban on gay men and lesbians serving in the military. President Bill Clinton faced such substantial and immediate opposition to this course of action that he abandoned it, to the delight of conservative groups, who were then emboldened to attack gay rights at the state and local levels. A gleeful Pat Buchanan opined that Clinton had "opened up the center to conservatives again."[12] That same month, the National Center for Health Statistics reported that the number of births to unmarried American mothers hit a record high in 1990, rising 7 percent in one year and 75 percent over the decade.[13] Statistics such as these fueled the fire of conservative activists who were eager to capitalize on Clinton's rough start with fresh attacks on gay rights and single motherhood.

"Dan Quayle Was Right." So read the cover of the April 1993 issue of the *Atlantic Monthly.*[14] Half the issue was devoted to this topic, with a lengthy article by social historian Barbara Dafoe Whitehead. It began: "After decades of public dispute about so-called family diversity, the evidence from social science research is coming in: The dissolution of two-parent families, though it may benefit the adults involved, is harmful to many children, and dramatically undermines our society." Whitehead marshaled the work of social scientists to conclude that nonmarital births, divorce, and father absence had shattering consequences for children and that an intact two-parent family was necessary for better outcomes for children. She also presented support for the proposition that family disruption was the "central cause" of poverty, crime, and poor school performance. She criticized feminism and the diminished importance of marriage in a world where women had substantial employment opportunities.

Many voices echoed Whitehead's view. William Galston, a domestic policy adviser to President Clinton, wrote that a "stable, intact family" was the nation's best antipoverty program. He said that problems with drugs, education, teen pregnancy, and juvenile crime were traceable to one source—"broken families."[15] Sociologist Charles Murray wrote in the *Wall Street Journal* that "illegitimacy is the single most important problem of our time—more important than crime, drugs, poverty, illiteracy, welfare, or homelessness because it drives everything else." To solve the problem, he advocated withdrawing all economic support for single mothers, returning social stigma to nonmarital births, making adoption easier for married couples, and reviving orphanages.[16]

Murray's analysis featured in the debates on revamping the welfare system. President Clinton called it "essentially right." Asked in December 1993 about Dan Quayle's "Murphy Brown" speech, Clinton remarked that "there were a lot of very good things in that speech.... It is certainly true that this country would be better off if our babies were born into two-parent families," to which Dan Quayle responded, "What a difference a year makes."[17] In 1994 the Republicans won control of both houses of Congress on a platform that included slashing funding for mothers on welfare.

The rhetorical shift was a dramatic turning point in the invocation of "family values" in public policy debates. The language of social science largely superseded the language of religion. In addition to Whitehead, Galston, and Murray, David Blankenhorn of the Institute for American Values, Jean Elshtain, now chair of the organization's board of directors, and David Popenoe, now codirector with Whitehead of the National Marriage Project, traced all social problems to the decline of marriage and invoked as the solution restoring lifelong marriage to its proper place.

Sociologist Judith Stacey was the first to observe that "right-wing Republicans and fundamentalist Christians" were being supplanted in the rhetoric on the family by a "revisionist campaign" grounding its claims in "secular social science instead of religious authority."[18] In a 1994 article, she noted that

> while the right-wing family-values campaign appeals to religious and traditional patriarchal authority for its family vision, centrists are engaged in an active, indeed an entrepreneurial, process of transmuting into a newly established, social scientific "truth" one of the most widely held prejudices about family life in North America—belief in the superiority of families composed of heterosexual, married couples and their biological children.

She critiqued the "reciprocal citation practices" of these authors. Stacey demonstrated that by categorical assertions, repetition, and citation of one another, the authors had convinced President Clinton, the media, and much of the public that a "fault-free bedrock of social science research" validated their conclusions.

The social science, Stacey demonstrated, was far more in dispute than the "revisionists" claimed. Some of the studies they cited for the impact of divorce on children used no comparison groups. They ignored research showing that high-conflict marriages harm children more than low-conflict divorces do. They confused correlation and causality, and—to exaggerate the advantages of two-parent over one-parent families—they treated small differences as though they were large, and relative differences as though they were absolute. "In fact," Stacey wrote,

> most children from both kinds of families turn out reasonably all right, and when other parental resources—like income, education, self-esteem, and a supportive social environment—are roughly similar, signs of two-parent privilege largely disappear. Most research indicates that a stable, intimate relationship with one responsible, nurturing adult is a child's surest track lane to becoming one too. In short, the research scale tips handily towards those who stress the quality of family relationship over their form.[19]

The Fatherhood Movement

In the mid-1990s, two books, Blankenhorn's *Fatherless America* and Popenoe's *Life without Father*, furthered the view that father absence had catastrophic consequences, and argued for reinvigorating distinctly gendered marriage.[20] Blankenhorn dismissed as an "excess of feminism" the view that fathers should do "half the diaper changes and bottle feedings." Instead, he postulated that "the old father, with some updating" would be an adequate model of a "new father."[21] Men should be primary breadwinners and the head of their households; any other expectation would drive men from their families. Popenoe proposed a gender-linked "modified traditional nuclear family model" with women doing what they do best: taking care of children.[22]

Several organizations developed as a "fatherhood movement" building on these principles. Had this movement sought models of engaged and dedicated fathers dispelling the notion that childrearing was for mothers alone, they could have looked no further than the gay men who became parents during the 1990s. A 1993 article in *Time* magazine described two gay men, one a stay-at-home parent, raising the two children that one of them conceived with a surrogate mother.[23] The 1995 case of a gay male couple established the right of unmarried same-sex and different-sex partners to jointly adopt children in the District of Columbia.[24] The fatherhood movement did not embrace these fathers as role models, demonstrating that gendered marriage, rather than devoted fathers, was its vision.

The fatherhood movement had immediate public policy impact. The legislation ending poor children's entitlement to a social and economic safety net, otherwise known as "welfare reform," began with a recitation of four purposes, three of which directly affected marriage and fatherhood: ending dependence on the government by promoting "job preparation, work, and marriage"; preventing and reducing "out-of-wedlock" pregnancy; and encouraging the formation and maintenance of two-parent families.[25] The new law began, "Marriage is the foundation of a successful society" and "Marriage is an essential institution of a successful society which promotes the interests of children." It referred to out-of-wedlock pregnancies as a "crisis." The legislation ended Aid to Families with Dependent

Children, which, while in need of structural reform, provided a guarantee of government assistance for poor children. The new program, Temporary Assistance to Needy Families (TANF), has no such guarantee.

The Marriage Movement and Welfare Reform

By 2000, there was a new movement that named itself the "marriage movement." It overlapped with the fatherhood movement. The marriage movement emphasizes not only the importance of fathers but the urgency of tying fathers to children through marriage. Linda Waite and Maggie Gallagher published *The Case for Marriage: Why Married People Are Happier, Healthier, and Better Off Financially.* They asserted scientific support for the conclusion that marriage makes people live happier, longer, healthier lives filled with more sex and more money. They reiterated the arguments about the importance of marriage for children's well-being.[26]

With welfare reform expiring in 2002 and therefore needing congressional reauthorization, the administration of President George W. Bush, combining secular and religious arguments, escalated the emphasis on marriage and fatherhood as antipoverty strategies. Bush created a White House Office of Faith-Based and Community Initiatives and named born-again and conservative activist Don Eberly as its deputy director. As founder of the National Fatherhood Initiative, Eberly touted "diligent" social scientists for "pinpoint[ing]" the relationship between father absence and social pathologies.[27] Bush named Wade Horn, president of the National Fatherhood Initiative, as assistant secretary for children and families at the Department of Health and Human Services. Horn had written a report for the conservative Hudson Institute recommending that married couples have preference over other family forms in receiving welfare and public housing.

Bush recommended revising the goal of welfare reform to be "to encourage the formation and maintenance of two parent *married* families." He proposed $1.5 billion in welfare spending on "marriage promotion" activities; the legislation that passed devotes $750 million to such efforts. Critics argue, among other things, that these efforts fail to encourage sex equality as a norm in marriage, ignore the good reasons women have for choosing not to marry, divert money from efforts that would serve the needs of poor families, and include religious references to God's design for marriage.[28]

The National Gay and Lesbian Task Force recognized the dangers of Bush's welfare reform proposals for LGBT families, youth, and elders. In its 2001 report, *Leaving Our Children Behind: Welfare Reform and the Gay, Lesbian, Bisexual, and Transgender Community,* authors Sean Cahill and Kenneth T. Jones documented just how bad Bush's proposals would be for LGBT people. They highlighted the marriage-promotion and fatherhood initiatives, the explicitly antigay content of "abstinence-only" sex education, and the federal funding that would flow to faith-based organizations preaching antigay messages and practicing discrimination against LGBT people in access to employment and services.

They called for opposition to Bush's proposals as a matter of social justice. Urging coalition efforts with feminists and antipoverty activists, they wrote:

> The privileging of families headed by married heterosexual couples over lesbian and gay families, single parent families, and unmarried heterosexual families means that millions of children—including a disproportionate percentage of children in African American and Latino families—would be denied access to basic benefits and services that they need for a happy and healthy childhood. This we must not tolerate.[29]

Sociologist Melanie Heath studied marriage-promotion activities in Oklahoma through the Oklahoma Marriage Initiative (OMI). Oklahoma was one of the first states to implement such efforts. Heath attended thirty marriage-promotion workshops that were open to the public and interviewed many staff. She found that although OMI's stated focus was low-income people, the workshops overwhelmingly served white, middle-class couples. One employee estimated that not more than 5 percent of its efforts were going to public assistance recipients. A goal of the program was closing the marriage gap between the poor and those better off; several of those interviewed expressed concerns about the diversion of money earmarked for the needs of poor families.

Heath concluded that OMI was more interested in positioning

marriage as a morally superior family form than in meeting antipoverty concerns. The head of the public relations firm managing OMI told Heath that the program's goal was to strengthen marriages, not to support all relationships. In addition, three of the six members of the initiative's original steering committee represented conservative Christian organizations, including an Oklahoma group connected to Focus on the Family. A Christian version of the curriculum included Bible verses and an emphasis on God's design for "oneness" in marriage.[30]

Both the secular and religious versions of the OMI curriculum taught that differences between men and women were a central component of married life, with men presented as rational and strong and women as emotional and weak. Heath concluded that marriage-promotion activities were reinforcing gender inequality in marriage and funneling resources from poor women and their children.

The marriage movement consistently describes marriage as a transhistorical, transcultural core institution that must be protected against incursions from advocates of family diversity.[31] A publication on marriage and the law from the Institute for American Values and the Institute for Marriage and Public Policy begins with this quotation from an *1888* U.S. Supreme Court opinion: "[Marriage] . . . is an institution, in the maintenance of which in its purity the public is deeply interested, for it is the foundation of the family and of society, without which there would be neither civilization nor progress."[32]

At the time of this decision, marriage was the foundation of a society in which wives lost their legal identity, the assumed "separate spheres" of women and men justified denying women the vote and access to all but a handful of occupations, children born outside marriage had permanent legal disabilities, and interracial marriage was grounds for prison time or lynching. Protecting *that* institution would properly find little support today.

Faults in the Marriage Movement's Arguments

The work of family historians, including Nancy Cott, Hendrick Hartog, Marilyn Yalom, and Stephanie Coontz traces the history of marriage, demonstrating it to be far less fixed and stable than the marriage movement posits.[33] Reviewing demographic changes over time, sociologist Frank Furstenberg noted that what is universal is family diversity.[34]

More than a decade after Whitehead's "Dan Quayle Was Right" essay, the marriage movement continues to allege a "broad consensus" that married parents raising their biological children is the optimal family form and that other forms produce worse outcomes for children and disastrous consequences for society. Furstenberg counters that the majority of social scientists differ with those who sound the alarm about changing marriage patterns.[35] Preeminent researchers, some of whom have found their work enlisted to push the agendas of the marriage and fatherhood movements, have consistently and unequivocally opposed such misuse of their efforts. In 1997 Furstenberg and fellow sociologists Andrew Cherlin, Sara McLanahan, Gary Sandefur, and Lawrence Wu filed a friend-of-the-court brief opposing use of their research to block same-sex marriage. They wrote:

> The social science research does not—and cannot—support the State's assertion at trial that the presence of two biological or opposite-sex parents comprises an "optimal" childrearing environment. There is broad consensus among social scientists that child outcomes are affected by a large number of factors other than the number and types of parents present in a child's household. These factors include, inter alia, the overall quality of parenting as reflected in parental love, warmth, involvement and consistency; pre- and postnatal care; adequate nutrition and health care; whether the child was planned or wanted; the mother's age at conception; parental socioeconomic resources; quality of neighborhood and schools; influences of peers and siblings; and the child's own abilities, temperament, attitudes and psychological resources. Moreover, research reflects wide variation in child outcomes even for siblings residing in the same family. As no one study can adequately control for all factors relevant to child outcomes, and because child outcomes vary so greatly, the State's assertion at trial that the presence or absence of the single variable of residing with two biological or opposite-sex parents provides a so-called "optimal" environment for children is simply not scientifically valid.[36]

Psychologists Louise Silverstein and Carl Auerbach attacked Blankenhorn and Popenoe for misusing data to support the conclusion that mothering and fathering were distinct roles that could not be interchanged, that fathers were essential to positive child adjustment, and that marriage was the preferred family form.[37] Michael Lamb, senior research psychologist at the National Institute of Child Health and Human Development, has studied fathers' roles in child development and concluded that "very little about the gender of the parent seems to be distinctly important."[38] He testified in litigation challenging Arkansas's ban on foster parenting by lesbians and gay men that "both men and women have the capacity to be good parents and . . . there is nothing about gender, per se, that affects one's ability to be a good parent."[39]

Michael Wald of Stanford Law School, who once ran San Francisco's child welfare agency and also served as deputy general counsel of the Department of Health and Human Services, evaluated the research and arguments on care of children by gay men and lesbians. He wrote in the *Family Law Quarterly* that

> there is no consensus among researchers about either the effects of family structure or the causes for the effects that many studies find. . . . The conclusion [that the effects of divorce on children's development are modest rather than strong], which is consistent with the great majority of the research, belies the often hysterical claims of some commentators that divorce and single parenthood are destroying the lives of large numbers of children and the cause of major social problems.[40]

He noted that most researchers attribute the greater well-being of children in two-parent homes to the *presence of two parents,* because such homes generally have higher incomes, greater monitoring and supervision of children, and greater consistency in parenting because parents are less overburdened. "None of these advantages," he concluded, "turn on the sex of the two adults." Illustrating that many factors affect how well children develop, Wald cited findings that children from low-income families with two parents do less well than children from wealthier families—including wealthier families with only one parent—on grade point averages, graduation rates, and college entrance exam scores.[41]

Responding to the claim that fathers have a critical, unique role to play in child development, Wald found that "while males and females may provide children with role-modeling with respect to some aspects of gender roles, no research shows that being exposed to this role differentiation is critical to any aspects of children's development."[42] Recognizing that this might be "surprising in light of all of the political attention that is paid to the importance of both family structure and the role of fathers," he asserted that "there is no evidence that children in general do better with a father and mother than with two mothers or two fathers."[43]

The marriage movement unjustifiably argues that cohabitation *causes* poor outcomes for children.[44] Researchers Wendy Manning and Susan Brown compared families in which there were two married parents with families in which the children were biologically related to both parents but the parents were not married. They found that race, ethnicity, and education accounted for the correlation between family structure and material well-being and that "the effects of family structure are reduced to nonsignificance with just the inclusion of parent[s'] education."[45]

Numerous researchers describe "selection effect"; married couples may be better educated and wealthier because better-educated and wealthier people are more likely to marry. The characteristics that make some people more likely to marry are the same characteristics that make families relatively more successful. Correlation is different from causation. Many experts argue that the rate of marriage will increase *after* more resources are devoted to improving employment, education, and mental health and to decreasing substance abuse, domestic violence, and rates of incarceration.[46]

Social psychologist Bella DePaulo critiqued the assertions in Waite and Gallagher's *The Case for Marriage*. Her book, *Singled Out: How Singles are Stereotyped, Stigmatized, and Ignored and Still Live Happily Ever After,* presents omitted data from the studies Waite and Gallagher relied on and data from other research. She calls their claim that getting married and staying married is the means to health, happiness, and long life "ethically reckless."[47]

The Red Herring of Marriage

Government programs to promote "healthy marriage" have a benign or salutary sound to them. An overwhelming majority of Americans do marry. Researchers of low-income families have found that the women they study value marriage and would marry if they believed the union would be stable, on solid financial footing, and egalitarian. Government-funded marriage-promotion efforts now require consultation with those who provide services to victims of intimate-partner violence. And, recognizing the damage that high-conflict marriages inflict on children, the phrasing of the goal of marriage programs is now promotion of "healthy" marriages.[48]

Even with these improvements, there is reason for alarm. The sheer volume of funding and research on the subject of the significance of marriage betrays a fundamental premise that ties marriage *rather than other factors* to children's well-being. This assertion justifies spending public *antipoverty* funds on marriage promotion instead of on healthcare, preschool childcare, and improving parents' education levels.

Yet the Economic Policy Institute recently concluded that the role of family structure in determining poverty has consistently diminished over the last three decades. "An educational upgrading strategy," it wrote, "would have more of a poverty-reducing impact than one focused on changing family structure." It decried the "short shrift" that has been given the "consistent and relatively large poverty-reducing role" that improving education has played over time.[49]

One year of postsecondary education cuts in half the poverty rate of households headed by women of color, and of single mothers with college degrees and full-time jobs, only 1 percent live in poverty.[50] Public assistance rules implemented as part of welfare reform, however, require recipients to work and discourage higher education.[51]

Free market capitalism in the United States has produced increasing income inequality unknown anywhere else in the Western world.[52] Since Reagan was elected president, household income of the top 1 percent of Americans has grown 111 percent, compared to 1 percent for those in the bottom 20 percent.[53] Between 2004 and 2005,

Americans' total reported income rose by 9 percent, but average income for the bottom 90 percent of the population dropped slightly, while those in the top 1 percent saw their income rise 14 percent.[54] The George W. Bush administration cut taxes 2.9 percent for the top 1 percent, almost five times the size of the tax cut for the bottom 20 percent, equaling, in dollar terms, \$63 for the lowest fifth up to \$44,000 for the top 1 percent.[55] A child born into a two-parent black family where the family head is at least a high school graduate is twice as likely as a child born into a white family with the same characteristics to experience a long spell of poverty (33.3 percent vs. 16.7 percent).[56]

If lawmakers can be convinced that divorce and childrearing outside marriage cause "crime, drug abuse, education failure, chronic illness, child abuse, domestic violence and poverty," as the marriage movement claims,[57] they can trumpet marriage as the most effective solution and blame the unmarried, rather than their own laws and policies, for systematic social and economic problems. Law professor Vivian Hamilton calls this "the red herring of marriage," used to justify decreasing public responsibility for the economic well-being of families.[58]

Sociologist Scott Coltrane has documented the millions of dollars that conservative foundations such as the Sarah Scaife and the Lynde and Harry Bradley foundations have given to the public relations campaigns of the Institute for American Values and the National Fatherhood Initiative.[59] These funders also spend hundreds of millions of dollars opposing government intervention in the free market through such organizations as the Heritage Foundation, which offers marriage as the solution to problems that otherwise would require government funding and regulation to promote equality and social well-being. The Heritage Foundation promotes Popenoe, Whitehead, Blankenhorn, Elshtain, and Gallagher as experts on the family; news stories quoting these experts rarely associate them with this well-known conservative think tank.[60]

Comprehensive proposals to end poverty do not start with marriage. Joel Handler and Yeheskel Hasenfeld, in *Blame Welfare, Ignore Poverty and Inequality,* criticize those who demonize single mothers and ignore the institutionalized economic and social structures that are the cause of poverty and inequality. They argue that while some family-promotion programs may be worthwhile, they are not a substitute for addressing the underlying causes of poverty.[61]

Handler and Hasenfeld propose replacing public assistance with a universal children's allowance; increasing pay and benefits for low-wage work; guaranteeing employment to all who are willing to work; raising the income level at which parents lose the Earned Income Tax Credit (EITC); granting allowances for childcare; providing universal preschool; and establishing community-based social services and job training for those who face employment barriers such as low education levels, mental health problems, or physical disabilities.[62]

In April 2007 the Center for American Progress Task Force on Poverty released *From Poverty to Prosperity: A National Strategy to Cut Poverty in Half*. The report made twelve basic recommendations: raise and index the minimum wage; expand the EITC and child tax credit; promote unionization by passing the Employee Free Choice Act; guarantee childcare and promote early education; create "opportunity" housing vouchers; restore federal grants to connect young people with school and work; increase grants for higher education; help reintegrate former prisoners into jobs and communities; reform the unemployment insurance system; improve benefits for working families and services for people with disabilities; provide mortgage assistance and curb unscrupulous lending practices; and institute "saver's credits." Marriage is *not* on its list of poverty-reduction strategies.[63]

The task force believes its plan will cut poverty in half over the next ten years. It will cost $90 billion a year to implement the major recommendations. The task force proposes paying for it by eliminating some of the Bush administration tax cuts. Those cuts cost about $400 billion a year; households with annual incomes above $200,000 alone will reap $100 billion from those cuts in 2008.

The researchers who rejected the use of their research as evidence opposing same-sex marriage wrote that

> [our] research has led to a number of policy recommendations, implemented on both state and federal levels, designed to further th[e] interest [in the well-being of children] directly. These policies include access to quality health care and universal health insurance,

> supplementation and stabilization of parental income, and provision of day care for working parents. Such policies provide examples of direct means by which any state . . . could promote optimal child outcomes in all families.[64]

Professor Sheila Kamerman, codirector of the Institute for Child and Family Policy at Columbia University, also argues that direct support for all children is a critical component of social policy. Writing about the United States, Canada, Austria, Denmark, Finland, France, Germany, Italy, the Netherlands, Norway, Sweden, and the United Kingdom, Kamerman found that all the countries except the United States had universal cash benefits and a national health service or health insurance; eight guaranteed a minimum level of financial support to children of divorced parents; and most of the non-Anglo-American countries provided universal low-cost or free preschool to all or almost all children starting at age two or three. She concluded that "except in the United States, an important social infrastructure is in place for single as well as married couples and their children."[65]

Government intervention, through tax policy and transfer programs, reduces child poverty rates. Economists can measure the impact of these policies. Looking at figures for the year 2000, in other Western countries they reduced child poverty, on average, from 21.1 percent to 10.7 percent. In France, redistributive policies reduced child poverty from 27.7 percent to 7.5 percent; in Sweden, from 18 percent to 4.2 percent; in Canada, from 22.8 percent to 14.9 percent. The United States began with a child poverty rate of 26.6 percent; its redistributive policies reduced that rate to 21.9 percent. This left the United States with the highest child poverty rate by far of any country studied.[66]

Right-wing organizations and the foundations that support them oppose the government policies that are effective at reducing poverty. If they can convince the public to blame child poverty on a decline in marriage, births to unmarried women, and a high rate of divorce, they can make what is a public disgrace look like a matter of personal moral failing.

The Legal Agenda of the Marriage Movement

The marriage movement wants to make divorces harder to obtain. It also supports distinguishing the legal consequences of marriage from those associated with any other relationship.[67] In other words, it favors "special rights" for married couples unavailable to other families or relationships. It justifies this special status in order to create a "marriage culture" that will result in more children being born to married parents, thereby, it claims, reducing a host of social problems.

The religious component of the marriage movement fiercely opposes marriage by same-sex couples. When Christian Right organizations combined into the Arlington Group in 2002 for the purpose of defeating secularism, one of its principal aims was a constitutional amendment limiting marriage to a man and a woman. Adherents cite Scripture in support of their views. They believe homosexuality is a sinful, chosen "lifestyle," and they oppose all measures that further gay rights.[68]

Some secular marriage-movement publications are silent on the issue of marriage for same-sex couples; in that way, the authors obtain supporting signatures from researchers, academics, and commentators who would be unwilling to associate their names with efforts to block marriage equality. The organizations and individuals most publicly associated with the marriage movement, however, including Blankenhorn and Gallagher, vehemently oppose access to marriage for same-sex couples. They argue that marriage of same-sex couples, who can never be a child's biological mother and father, changes the meaning of marriage, and thus places American society at greater risk of "poverty, crime, juvenile delinquency, welfare dependency, child abuse, unwed teen motherhood, infant mortality, mental illness, high school dropouts and other education failures."[69]

These causal assertions of the marriage movement lack merit. In Australia, New Zealand, and Canada, the law treats unmarried couples living together almost identically to married couples; many European countries recognize same-sex marriage or registered partnership. The United States maintains a strict legal divide between the married and the unmarried and accords no federal recognition to same-sex couples, and state-level recognition in only a handful of states. Yet compared with the United States, a child in one of these other countries is less likely to die as an infant, less likely to live in poverty, equally or more likely to have educational achievement, much less likely to end up in prison, and likely to live longer.[70]

Given their emphasis on how good marriage is for children, secular marriage-movement proponents have had to articulate why it should be unavailable to the gay and lesbian couples who raise children. Their response has been insistence on the specialized roles of husbands and wives. Brigham Young University law professor Lynn Wardle, who opposes both childrearing and marriage by same-sex couples, asserted that "the union of two persons of different genders creates something of unique potential strengths and inimitable potential value to society. It is the *integration* of the universe of gender differences (profound and subtle, biological and cultural, psychological and genetic) associated with sexual identity that constitutes the core and essence of marriage."[71]

In literature and court briefs, marriage-movement proponents argue that, unlike mothers, good fathers are "made, not born," and heterosexual marriage is what makes them.[72] Whitehead and Popenoe call marriage the "glue" that binds fathers to children.[73] Proponents also claim that only marriage tames men's innately promiscuous and antisocial nature. As Glenn Stanton of Focus on the Family put it, "marriage is . . . the way societies socialize men and protect women from predatory males."[74]

As with the fatherhood movement, the marriage movement must ignore the gay men who raise children. The existence of such fathers destroys its generalization about the inherent nature of men. A core principle of the 1970s U.S. Supreme Court opinions eliminating sex-based classifications was that lawmaking based on broad generalizations about the differences between men and women is unconstitutional, yet these are precisely the justifications offered for excluding same-sex couples from marriage.

Religious organizations also assert the centrality of gender roles. In 2000 the Southern Baptist Convention released a statement of faith affirming that "[a husband] has the God-given responsibility to provide for, to protect, and to lead his family. A wife is to submit herself graciously to the servant leadership of her husband."[75] The Christ-centered organization Promise Keepers urges men to take back family leadership from their wives.[76]

Professor Carlos Ball has argued that opposition to same-sex marriage is not about the well-being of children but is rather about perpetuating patriarchy; such perpetuation is undermined by the presence of gay and lesbian couples raising children.[77] Professor Nan Hunter predicted that marriage by gay and lesbian couples has the potential to "dismantle the legal structure of gender in every marriage."[78] Such a dismantling is exactly what many in the marriage movement fear.

The marriage movement reiterates the importance of marriage—and marriage alone. Although some individuals in the secular arm of this movement support same-sex marriage, gender equality, and social supports for all families, the literature and court briefs produced by marriage-movement organizations attack these goals. Their arguments further a larger agenda of reinforcing gender norms and relieving the government and the market from any responsibility for poverty and urgent social problems.

CHAPTER FIVE

LGBT Families and the Marriage-Equality Movement

Two developments in 1993, the year "Dan Quayle Was Right," contributed to the shifting framework of legal arguments concerning LGBT families. Gay conservative thought emerged in Bruce Bawer's *A Place at the Table,* which repudiated what Bawer saw as the broader context in which claims on behalf of gay people were made.[1] Bawer argued against "alliance politics," denying any connection between the interests of homosexuals and those of women, racial minorities, and the economically disadvantaged. The gay rights movement, he said, should be about gay rights. He endorsed what he called a conservative case for gay marriage.

The other development occurred in the Hawaii Supreme Court. For the first time, a state high court ruled that a ban on marriage for same-sex couples might violate the state's constitution.[2] Once the door opened on the plausibility of legal arguments for same-sex marriage, the framework of family diversity was no longer the only basis for seeking protections for gay and lesbian relationships and families. In 1995 Andrew Sullivan, in *Virtually Normal,* called gay marriage "the only reform that truly matters."[3]

A decade later, gay conservative commentator Jonathan Rauch took Andrew Sullivan's position one step further. Rauch asserted that same-sex couples should be allowed—and expected—to marry, to protect marriage against the threats posed by alternatives such as civil unions, domestic partner benefits, and socially approved cohabitation.[4] With this, an argument in the name of gay rights converged with the marriage-movement position that the legal consequences of marriage should not be extended to unmarried couples, because this "unwisely weakens the special option of marriage."[5]

This is not the position that LGBT legal organizations take, even those most strongly advocating for access to same-sex marriage. But the marriage movement has made it harder for anyone to speak up for family diversity. As the marriage movement gained influence and cast aspersions on family diversity, it affected the arguments gay rights organizations made. It is difficult to argue how much marriage matters in one context and how little it matters in another.

Advocating marriage for same-sex couples is a sensible way to champion equal civil rights for gay men and lesbians. Unfortunately, it is not a sensible approach toward achieving just outcomes for the wide range of family structures in which LGBT people, as well as many others, live. Those outcomes depend on eliminating the "special rights" that only married couples receive and meeting the needs of a range of family forms.

Increasing Recognition of LGBT Families

Lawyers for gay and lesbian families continued to work within the framework of making marriage matter less. They were successful in many states in protecting the increasing number of children with two gay or lesbian parents. They developed documents that couples could use to protect their relationships. They benefited from successful legal arguments made on behalf of different-sex unmarried couples and were hindered when those claims failed. The workplace proved more receptive to the needs of employees with unmarried partners; the dozens of employers with domestic partner policies in the early 1990s mushroomed to many thousands by 2007, including more than half the Fortune 500 companies.[6]

When state law failed to recognize relationships outside marriage, advocates could no longer look to the Supreme Court, which in previous decades had remade marriage's legal significance. In 1986 William Rehnquist, who had once been a minority conservative voice on the Court, became its chief justice. The Rehnquist Court retreated from rulings that had advanced democracy and social justice for women, racial minorities, the poor, and other disadvantaged people. Given that *Bowers v. Hardwick* had in 1986 approved state laws that made criminals out of lesbians and gay men in sexual relationships, it was logical to conclude that the Court would not interpret the Constitution as requiring equal treatment of those relationships.

The *Bowers* decision lasted until 2003, when, in a challenge brought by Lambda Legal, the Court in *Lawrence v. Texas* overruled it, taking the unusual step of asserting that it had been wrong when it was decided.[7] In another great success, in 1996, the Court ruled in *Romer v. Evans* that a constitutional amendment passed by Colorado voters, denying state and local governments the ability to protect gay men and lesbians from discrimination, violated the federal constitution's guarantee of equal protection.[8] The Court based its decision on the 1973 case that had rebuked Congress for denying food stamps to "communal 'families' of unrelated individuals." The common thread in the two cases was the legislature's motivation to "harm a politically unpopular group"—hippie communes and LGBT people. This was not, the Court held, a legitimate exercise of governmental power. The finding opened a door to future equality claims.

Protecting the Children of Same-Sex Couples

Laura and Victoria met in 1979, had a commitment ceremony in 1983, and that year joined a support group for lesbians considering having children. In 1985 Laura gave birth to a child, Tessa Kate, conceived by unknown-donor insemination. They decided to adopt a second child, and in 1989 Victoria traveled to Nicaragua, where she had family, and adopted Maya Jo. The next year, Laura and Victoria became the first same-sex couple to petition the District of Columbia court to grant an adoption decree extending to each of them parental rights with respect to both children. The court granted the adoptions in 1991. Two years later, Victoria died when a tree branch smashed through the windshield of her car during a summer thunderstorm. Both children were in the car. Victoria's adoption of Tessa Kate assured that Tessa Kate would receive the same compensation and Social Security benefits as her sister. Laura's adoption of Maya Jo assured that Maya Jo would not be left a legal orphan.[9]

The marriage movement takes aim at childrearing outside heterosexual marriage. Yet advocates for gay and lesbian families have had success in the courts with regard to protecting the increasing number of children adopted by two gay or lesbian parents or born to them via alternative reproductive techniques.

In 1989 the mainstream media "discovered" these planned lesbian and gay families, with articles in the country's leading newspapers and shows on prime-time television. The next year, at the annual conference of Gay and Lesbian Parents Coalition International, children of lesbian and gay parents held their own meetings, out of which emerged a national organization called Children of Lesbians and Gays Everywhere (COLAGE). The first generation of children raised by lesbian mothers and gay fathers who came out in the early and mid-1970s had reached adulthood.

In 1996 Grammy Award–winning singer Melissa Etheridge appeared on the cover of *Newsweek* with her pregnant partner, Julie Cypher. Ten years later, the media covered the pregnancy of Mary Cheney, the openly lesbian daughter of the vice president of the United States, who had a child with her partner of fifteen years. During the 1990s, every major professional association concerned with children's mental health issued position statements, papers, and analyses supporting parenting by gay men and lesbians and urging legal reforms to protect their children.[10]

The principal law reform to achieve this goal was second-parent adoption, which spread across the country. Appellate courts approved it in California, the District of Columbia, Illinois, Indiana, Maine, Massachusetts, New Jersey, New York, Pennsylvania, and Vermont.[11] Connecticut and Colorado approved it by statute. Trial courts in counties in more than a dozen other states also issue second-parent adoption orders. About 46 percent of all same-sex couples now live where the law affords their children the same rights that children of unmarried heterosexual couples have—the right to a legal relationship with both parents. Getting such recognition can require a lawyer and be expensive; advocates in some of these states are working to streamline the process.

In a few courts, the partner of a biological lesbian mother, either during her pregnancy or when the child is born, can get a parentage order using the laws that permit such orders for an unmarried male partner of a woman who gives birth. Some states have read their Uniform Parentage Act—the law that emerged in the 1970s to assure a child a legal relationship with two parents—as permitting a parentage designation for a second mother.[12]

Even without a second-parent adoption or parentage order, some courts became willing to recognize the parental status of the partner of a lesbian or gay man who was the biological parent of a child that the couple planned together. The redefinition of "parent" necessary to accomplish this tracked arguments used in other contexts, such as the *Braschi* case, to expand the definition of "family." Although many courts continued to define parenthood by biology, adoption, or marriage to a woman bearing a child, some modified that definition to encompass the reality of the lives of children raised by lesbian and gay couples. These efforts also benefited children raised by unmarried heterosexual couples where only one parent was biologically related to the child.

In 2000 the American Law Institute (ALI) suggested rules for resolving family disputes that included the concept of a "parent by estoppel." Its principles state that someone who accepts full and permanent parental responsibilities for a child, with the agreement of the child's legal parent, has the same legal status as a biological or adoptive parent.[13] The examples accompanying the definition make clear that it is designed to protect a child's relationship with both parents in cases in which a gay or lesbian couple plans for and raises a child together. Not surprisingly, the marriage movement has attacked this recommendation and seeks instead to preserve a narrow definition of "parent" to go with its narrow definition of "family."[14]

A 2007 District of Columbia law defines "de facto parent" similarly to the ALI's parent by estoppel. A person who "lived with the child in the same household at the time of the child's birth or adoption by the child's parent, has taken on full and permanent responsibilities as the child's parent, and has held himself or herself out as the child's parent with the agreement of the child's parent or, if there are two parents, both parents" is entitled to custody and obligated to pay child support on the same terms as a parent.[15]

New Hampshire repealed its ban on gay adoption and foster parenting in 1999, and a court in Arkansas, in a case brought by the ACLU LGBT Project, struck down the state's ban on gay foster parenting in 2006. But lesbian and gay parents still face opposition in several states. Florida's adoption ban, dating to Anita Bryant's crusade, stands; lawsuits challenging its constitutionality have failed. Utah passed a law banning individuals living with a partner to whom they were not married—gay or straight—from adopting a child, even as a single parent. Nebraska, Ohio, and Wisconsin courts have ruled against second-parent adoptions, although all have recognized a child's relationship with his or her nonbiological parent for some purposes.

As in the early days of the gay rights movement, lesbians and gay men are still coming out after they marry and facing custody and visitation disputes with their ex-spouses when their marriages end. Despite the unanimous opinion of mainstream child welfare and mental health organizations that children raised by gay and lesbian parents suffer no harm or disadvantage, courts in some states, especially in the South, continue to rule against them.

There is a long way to go until the law stops penalizing gay and lesbian parents and their children. The marriage movement's argument that the optimal unit for raising children is two married biological parents has traction in many quarters. But lawyers and other advocates have achieved considerable legal recognition of lesbian and gay parenting using arguments crafted out of an appreciation of the diverse family forms in which children are raised.

Protecting the Interests of Couples

The tree that fell on Victoria's car had been the subject of repeated complaints to the District of Columbia's public works department. Many large branches had fallen from it; neighbors had reported that it was just a matter of time before someone was hurt. City workers did nothing—until *after* Victoria's accident, when they cut down the entire tree. Laura and the two children filed a wrongful death action against the city. The city filed a motion to dismiss Laura from the case because she was not Victoria's spouse. The trial court denied the motion. The judge ruled that in their "nonstandard family unit," Laura relied upon Victoria for support and maintenance and that their "close relationship, coupled with the fact that they were both legally recognized parents of the same two children" meant that Laura was Victoria's next of kin.[16]

Legal arguments advancing rights for unmarried couples require courts to read beyond the terms "spouse," "husband," and "wife." Laura's success was unusual. Over a strong dissent, a New York court in 1998 ruled that Donald Raum could not recover for the wrongful death of his partner of twenty years, who died of salmonella poisoning after eating a restaurant meal contaminated with the bacteria.

Seven years later, a New York court also denied the survivor of a couple who had entered into a civil union in Vermont the right to sue for damages arising from his partner's death; Lambda Legal tried, unsuccessfully, to get the court to overturn the decision in *Raum*.[17]

A few states allowed the survivor of an unmarried heterosexual relationship to sue for the loss of the relationship or for the emotional harm of witnessing a partner's death.[18] The New Mexico Supreme Court refused to limit such a claim to spouses because doing so would "exclude many persons whose loss of a significant relational interest may be just as devastating as the loss of a legal spouse." One state ruled that a woman who left her job to relocate with her unmarried different-sex partner of thirteen years could receive unemployment benefits even though she was neither his wife nor his fiancée.[19] These precedents became available to same-sex couples.

Courts considered claims by one partner against the other after a relationship ended, but only using the limited theories of property and contract law. These made recovery impossible unless a partner could prove a financial contribution to property or produce evidence of an agreement. The ALI recommended a different approach: that states treat separating domestic partners the way they treat divorcing spouses. Gay rights lawyers urged their clients to draft relationship agreements, write wills, and sign documents giving each other the ability to make healthcare and other decisions should one become disabled.

Only Washington has, in part, the rule the ALI supports. There the property either partner in an unmarried couple acquired is equitably divided between them when the relationship ends. The law applies equally to same-sex and different-sex couples.[20] In Washington, the survivor of a same-sex couple can also claim against the decedent's estate, as the state's highest court ruled in 2003 in a case a gay man brought after his partner of twenty-eight years died without a will.[21]

Arguments on behalf of unmarried couples ran directly into the claims of the marriage movement. Milagros Irizarry, a Chicago public school employee, challenged the constitutionality of a domestic partner policy that covered same-sex, but not unmarried different-sex, partners of employees.[22] She had lived with her male partner for more than twenty years and raised two children with him. In 2001 the federal appeals court ruled against her, citing many marriage-movement publications as proof that it was rational for the city to promote marriage among its heterosexual employees.

Lambda Legal filed a friend-of-the-court brief on the employee's behalf. The court found this surprising, since same-sex couples did receive the benefits. The court said Lambda was challenging the policy because it wanted to "knock marriage off its perch."

"Knocking marriage off its perch" was consistent with the claims gay rights groups had brought on behalf of children with same-sex parents. Their arguments supported all unmarried couples. In the case that established second-parent adoption in the highest court in New York, Lambda Legal successfully represented both a same-sex and an unmarried different-sex couple.[23]

But the court's marriage-movement reasoning in *Irizarry* and the impact of same-sex couples asserting the right to marry—even when such demands were decisively rebuffed—were part of what moved gay rights lawyers to challenge rules excluding unmarried couples on the gay-specific theory that their clients *could not* marry. Using this theory, the National Center for Lesbian Rights prevailed in a case that found that a surviving lesbian partner should be permitted to file a wrongful death suit after a neighbor's dog mauled her partner to death. This theory was also successful in obtaining domestic partner benefits limited to same-sex couples in states where public employers provided benefits only to married couples.

Hawaii and Its Aftermath

The national gay legal organizations did not take the lead on same-sex marriage. They had scarce resources and wanted to pick winning issues, and the underlying political disagreements about the issue, as exemplified by the 1989 Stoddard-Ettelbrick debate, remained. It took the first win, in a case the national legal groups did not bring, to get a full-fledged effort to achieve marriage for same-sex couples under way. It soon became the gay rights movement's most visible issue.

On May 5, 1993, in *Baehr v. Lewin,* the Hawaii Supreme Court ruled that the state ban on marriage by same-sex couples might violate the state constitution.[24] The court determined that permitting a woman to marry only a man and not another woman, and permitting a man to marry only a woman and not another man, was sex discrimination. The court ordered a trial at which the state would have to give compelling reasons for prohibiting same-sex marriage. Because this opinion made success in eliminating the ban on gay marriage possible, the national organizations stepped in to assist the local lawyers. Lambda Legal lawyer Evan Wolfson began working on the case, and the organization officially launched a Marriage Project.

The Right seized the opportunity the Hawaii Supreme Court opinion provided to further its own agenda. It used the possibility that other states might treat as married any couple who traveled to Hawaii and married there to push legislation saying that states would not recognize same-sex marriages performed in other jurisdictions. Focus on the Family and other right-wing groups lobbied for these measures. But well-established legal principles already allowed a state to disregard marriages from elsewhere that conflicted with its public policy.

In 1996, within three months of the presidential election, the Republican Congress handed President Clinton two pieces of legislation that he could not veto, because doing so would have jeopardized his reelection campaign: the misleadingly named Personal Responsibility and Work Opportunity Reconciliation Act, ending guaranteed financial assistance to poor families, and the equally misnamed Defense of Marriage Act (DOMA). DOMA contained two provisions. The first codified that states could decide for themselves whether to recognize same-sex marriages; even if a same-sex couple was married elsewhere, a state could disregard that marriage. The second said that for all purposes under federal law, only a man and a woman would be considered spouses. Thus a married same-sex couple would not be considered married for purposes of Social Security, Medicare, federal income tax, immigration, or any other federal law.

As it turned out, Hawaii did not approve same-sex marriage. The state defended its ban by attempting to prove that it furthered the state interest in promoting optimal child development. The trial judge ruled against the state, but before the Hawaii Supreme Court could hear the matter again, an election was held in which the voters approved a constitutional amendment giving the legislature the authority to restrict marriage to a man and a woman. The campaign to amend the constitution was led by a group heavily supported by the Catholic and Mormon churches and by groups affiliated with Focus on the Family and the Christian Coalition.

The Hawaii legislature did create a status with a new name—reciprocal beneficiaries—open to two people unable to marry—same-sex couples and relatives, such as a grandmother and grandson.[25] Reciprocal beneficiaries have some of the rights and responsibilities afforded married couples, including health-related provisions, property rights, inheritance rights, and taxation. When it was adopted in 1997, it was the most comprehensive state recognition available to same-sex couples.

When a trial court in Alaska in 1998 found that the ban on same-sex marriage violated its constitution, the state amended the constitution to define marriage as between one man and one woman.[26] Coupled with the Hawaii experience, this led lawyers to begin including in their litigation strategies the groundwork that would be required to safeguard any judicial victory from being voided in the political process.

On December 20, 1999, the Vermont Supreme Court ruled that the exclusion of same-sex couples from the benefits of marriage violated its state constitution.[27] It left to the legislature the decision whether to open marriage to same-sex couples or to create some other mechanism for providing such couples the rights and responsibilities of marriage. After an impassioned political process, in 2000 the Vermont legislature created a status called "civil unions."[28] Same-sex couples who enter civil unions are treated identically to married couples under state law. Federal law does not recognize civil unions. Outside Vermont, civil unions are legally recognized only to the extent that another state is willing to do so. Vermont also created a status of reciprocal beneficiaries for relatives. Reciprocal beneficiaries have decision-making rights in certain matters relating to healthcare and burial or disposition of remains.

Marriage Equality—Victory and Its Aftermath

In 2001 Wolfson formed Freedom to Marry, a civil rights organization dedicated solely to winning nationwide access to marriage for same-sex couples. Freedom to Marry advocates at the national, state, and local levels; works to get endorsements from a wide range of organizations; and builds the capacity of state organizations to deal with the issue of marriage equality in the state legislative and electoral processes. Wolfson does not refer to the goal as "gay marriage" or "same-sex marriage." What gay and lesbian couples want, he says, is marriage. The same marriage heterosexuals have. He named the movement to achieve that goal the "marriage equality" movement.

That year, Gay & Lesbian Advocates & Defenders (GLAD), the Boston-based legal group responsible for the Vermont case, filed a court challenge in Massachusetts on behalf of seven same-sex couples excluded from marrying. That case, *Goodridge v. Department of Public Health,* decided on November 18, 2003, established same-sex couples' right to marry in Massachusetts.[29] President Bush announced his support for an amendment to the federal constitution that would ban same-sex marriage throughout the country.

In February 2004, before the first same-sex couples married in Massachusetts, San Francisco mayor Gavin Newsom increased the visibility of the issue by ordering the city clerk to begin issuing marriage licenses to same-sex couples. Newsom acknowledged that California law did not permit such marriages, but he announced that he believed the restriction to be unconstitutional discrimination against lesbians and gay men. The first marriage, on February 12, was between Phyllis Lyon and Del Martin, the couple who, almost fifty years earlier, had founded the homophile group Daughters of Bilitis.

Over the next twenty-nine days, couples streamed to San Francisco from around the country, filling the streets in front of city hall. National news coverage bombarded the public with images of these couples. City workers volunteered to work on weekends and Presidents' Day to accommodate the crowds. The marriages continued until March 11, when a ruling from the state's supreme court halted them. Altogether, 4,161 same-sex couples wed. The California Supreme Court later ruled that the marriages were invalid. Newsom's actions prompted copycat decisions in a handful of other counties and towns.

On May 17, 2004, the first gay and lesbian couples married in Massachusetts. Congress debated but did not pass a federal marriage amendment. Efforts in Massachusetts to place on a statewide ballot a constitutional amendment that would supersede the court's ruling have so far been unsuccessful. The law enabling same-sex couples to marry in Massachusetts has been limited almost entirely to couples who live there, because a statute prohibits couples who live elsewhere from marrying if they are trying to evade marriage bans in their own states.

As of September 2007, the landscape looked like this: The highest courts of Arizona, Indiana, Maryland, New York, and Washington ruled against the couples seeking marriage. In 2006, New Jersey declared unconstitutional the exclusion of same-sex couples from the rights and obligations of marriage and left to the legislature the means to remedy this exclusion, a ruling similar to that of Vermont in 1999. As in Vermont, this led to creation of the analogous legal status of civil unions.

Four states—Connecticut, California, New Hampshire, and Oregon (the latter two effective January 1, 2008)—created an analogous status legislatively without court mandates; Connecticut and New Hampshire use the term "civil union," while California and Oregon use "domestic partnership." California's domestic partnership law is also available to different-sex couples if at least one partner is at least sixty-two. (Retirement-age different-sex couples sometimes live together without marrying to preserve certain economic benefits that might terminate or be reduced if they did marry; permitting such couples to enter domestic partnerships gives them a legal status that does not jeopardize those benefits.)

Litigation arguing the unconstitutionality of creating a "separate but equal" parallel institution continues in California and Connecticut. A case seeking marriage equality is pending in the Iowa appeals court, after a trial judge ruled in August 2007 that the exclusion of same-sex couples violated the state's constitution.

Hawaii continues to allow same-sex couples to be reciprocal beneficiaries. Maine, Washington, and the District of Columbia have a status called domestic partnership that provides limited legal consequences. In Maine and D.C. the status of domestic partnership is available to same-sex and different-sex couples. Washington is open to same-sex couples and different-sex couples where one partner is sixty-two or over. The D.C. status is also open to any two people who live together in a "committed, familial relationship"; it thus includes relatives who can register as reciprocal beneficiaries in Vermont and

Hawaii. These statutes apply to more areas of law than the domestic partner ordinances of the 1980s and 1990s but considerably less than the schemes in other states that are the legal equivalent of marriage.[30]

Widespread Hostility toward Same-Sex Marriage

These advances in a small number of states have produced a backlash. Twenty-six states have amended their constitutions to ban same-sex marriage and recognition of out-of-state same-sex marriages, most by overwhelming margins. An additional nineteen states ban recognition of same-sex marriages by statute; fifteen enacted these laws after the 1993 Hawaii Supreme Court ruling. Only Massachusetts, New Jersey, New Mexico, New York, Rhode Island, and the District of Columbia have neither a statutory nor a constitutional ban on same-sex marriage.[31] The federal Defense of Marriage Act has been upheld against court challenges in three states.

Most state constitutional amendments enacted to prevent recognition of same-sex marriages contain language that goes beyond that, to affect *unmarried* relationships of same-sex and different-sex couples. For example, the Ohio Defense of Marriage Amendment reads: "Only a union between one man and one woman may be a marriage valid in or recognized by this state and its political subdivisions. This state and its political subdivisions shall not create or recognize a legal status for relationships of unmarried individuals that intends to approximate the design, qualities, significance or effect of marriage."

In light of this amendment, some Ohio judges have found unconstitutional a law criminalizing physical abuse of a "family or household member" as defined to include "a person living as a spouse." An appeals court held that this was just the type of "quasi-marital relationship" that the Defense of Marriage Amendment was concerned about. Although the Ohio Supreme Court overturned that ruling, its opinion made clear that the state could not create a status such as civil unions for same-sex couples and hinted that public employee domestic partner benefits might also be unconstitutional.[32]

A similar Michigan constitutional amendment was interpreted to ban provision of employee benefits to domestic partners of state, county, and city employees, including staff and faculty of the University of Michigan and other public universities. The amendment reads: "To secure and preserve the benefits of marriage for our society and for future generations of children, the union of one man and one woman in marriage shall be the only agreement recognized as a marriage or similar union for any purpose."

The Michigan appeals court reviewed domestic partner benefits plans. Most required the domestic partners to sign an agreement that they were "jointly responsible for basic living and household expenses." The court ruled that granting domestic partner benefits on such a basis amounted to publicly recognizing a union similar to marriage, in violation of the constitutional amendment.[33]

Citizens for Community Values, an Ohio affiliate of Focus on the Family, contributed $1.18 million to the effort to enact Ohio's Defense of Marriage Amendment.[34] It also filed a friend-of-the-court brief arguing that the law protecting unmarried cohabiting partners from domestic violence was unconstitutional. Gary Glenn, a coauthor of Michigan's amendment and president of the American Family Association of Michigan, described the court ruling striking down domestic partner benefits as "exactly what we expected."[35]

Observers believe that public skepticism about this broad language was responsible for Arizona's defeat of Proposition 107, the "protect marriage" amendment, in 2006. Arizona already had a law limiting marriage to a man and a woman, and the state supreme court had upheld its constitutionality. The proposed amendment included language banning recognition of a "legal status for unmarried persons . . . similar to that of marriage." The amendment's opponents ran a public relations campaign emphasizing that heterosexual couples, including senior citizens, would lose their domestic partner benefits if the amendment passed.[36] Arizona is the only state where voters have rejected a constitutional amendment banning same-sex marriage; its statute having the same effect remains on the books.

Marriage equality has mobilized thousands of lesbians and gay men to become political activists, more than any issue since the government's failure to respond to AIDS in the 1980s. Judging by the results of referenda on state constitutional amendments, they have been fighting losing battles. For every state-level gay rights organization that has leveraged the issue of marriage equality into increased protections short of marriage for gay and lesbian couples, there are many where activists' incalculable time, money, and energy have been unable to stop antigay legislation and constitutional amendments. If heterosexuals in Ohio or Michigan or some other state are outraged by courts interpreting these amendments to ban domestic partnership or other rights for unmarried gay and straight couples, there might be support for a political campaign to repeal the amendments. The law affecting gay and lesbian families in those states would be where it was before marriage equality became a priority. Gay and lesbian people will be more visible, but the law will not have progressed.

Leaders in the fight for marriage equality do not judge the value of their efforts by the outcome of state referenda. They cite the six states that now have a status equivalent to marriage for same-sex couples, plus Massachusetts (which has marriage), as extraordinary progress in a short time.

Commentators are divided on the relative cost and value of fighting for marriage equality in the face of a political backlash. Historian John D'Emilio calls the campaign for same-sex marriage an "unmitigated disaster."[37] He argues that the forces of history were making marriage a less central institution, and that national gay leaders must shift course, stop arguing that full dignity will come only when gay couples can marry, and stop throwing good money after bad. Law professor Carlos Ball, on the other hand, argues that lesbians and gay men are better off in spite of the backlash.[38] He cites increased public support for some legal recognition for same-sex couples, the positive effects over time of the number of couples who will marry in Massachusetts, and the greater visibility of the fully human lives of lesbians and gay men. Even he, however, cautions against continuing to litigate for marriage equality, arguing that such efforts have reached the point of diminishing returns.

Whether or not individual states move toward or retreat from marriage equality, the current terms of the fight are problematic for the families and relationships of lesbian, gay, bisexual, and transgender people.

Flaws in the Arguments for Marriage

The arguments driving both the litigation and the political campaigns for same-sex marriage mark an abrupt shift from decades of critiques about marriage law. The shift is so pervasive that the generation of gay and straight young adults who have grown up during the culture war over same-sex marriage has no idea that the gay rights movement was once part of coalition efforts to make marriage matter less. The theme of the first three decades of advocacy for gay and lesbian families—increased recognition of family diversity in common cause with all families not conforming to one-size-fits-all marriage—has lost its prominence.

There are two causes for concern. Some rhetoric deployed in the effort to gain the right to marry shows the disturbing influence of the conservative marriage movement, which opposes family diversity. Thus it positions the gay rights movement on the wrong side of the culture war over acceptable family structures. More alarming, the logic of the arguments made to win converts to marriage equality risks reversing, rather than advancing, progress for diverse family forms, including those in which many LGBT people live. The civil rights victory of marriage for those gay and lesbian couples who seek it may come at the expense of law reforms benefiting a wider range of families.

In June 2002, Lambda Legal circulated a fund-raising letter focusing on marriage. The heading at the top of the first page read, "*These two are not two, Love has made them one* (from Benjamin Britten's 'A Wedding Anthem')." The letter continued: "One day soon, this may be a real invitation to a real wedding of a lesbian or gay couple, and the law may also make them one."

For hundreds of years the law did make a married couple one, and it took feminist agitation and litigation of more than 125 years to end the oppression embodied in such laws. The Christian Right today still preaches "oneness" in marriage. The use of such rhetorical flourish to raise money for same-sex marriage litigation panders, if unwittingly, to a social and political climate that targets family diversity as a threat to social cohesion and marriage as its only salvation.

The marriage movement and the federal government's marriage-promotion activities stress the benefits of marriage for participants and society. The rhetoric accompanying these efforts asserts that marriage is better than other family forms. These messages, understandably, affect lesbians and gay men, and advocates for same-sex marriage have picked up on them, asserting that if marriage is good for heterosexuals then it will be good for lesbians and gay men, with the ensuing benefits to society presumably flowing from their marriages as well.

To make this argument, same-sex marriage supporters borrow from flawed marriage-movement arguments that further a political agenda historically out of line with the gay rights movement. For example, psychology professor Gregory Herek argues for marriage rather than civil unions by referencing that "heterosexual cohabiting couples do not derive the same advantages as married couples from their relationships."[39] But critics of the marriage movement point out that such claims are based on bad science, reflecting "selection effect" and assuming a causal connection that cannot be proven. Similarly, cultural anthropologist Gilbert Herdt and psychiatrist Robert Kertzner assert that because "marriage supports mental and physical health," the ban on same-sex marriage "compromises the well-being [of lesbians and gay men], that of their children, and the well-being of future generations."[40]

Ellen Lewin, an anthropologist who has studied lesbian mothers and committed same-sex couples, criticizes the staking of same-sex marriage rights on the same claims the marriage movement uses to defend legal and economic advantages for married heterosexuals, deny assistance to poor single parents, and threaten to reinstitute illegitimacy. In addition, she argues that attributing mental health problems faced by gay and lesbian people to their inability to marry suggests wrongly that there is a linear relationship between this particular lack of entitlement and psychological disturbances.[41]

Gay & Lesbian Advocates & Defenders has expressed the belief that the marriage of lesbian and gay couples will strengthen the institution of marriage, not weaken it,[42] as though strengthening the institution of marriage, on the terms that rhetoric is usually deployed, is an unqualified accomplishment. When the marriage movement speaks of strengthening the institution of marriage it is always in a context that asserts the *superiority* of marriage. Marriage must be strengthened, its advocates declare, to protect society from the damage that a proliferation of diverse family structures causes. If GLAD does not want to be associated with this ideology, it shouldn't borrow from it to garner support for same-sex marriage.

Legal scholar William Eskridge and coauthor Darren Spedale also write of strengthening marriage as a by-product of extending it to same-sex couples.[43] Their work refutes marriage-movement assertions that same-sex partnership registration in Scandinavian countries has weakened marriage. But the marriage movement wins by setting the terms of the debate in this fashion.

The "Good for Children" Claim

The marriage movement uses one refrain to push its agenda: that marriage is good for children and that raising children outside marriage damages both them and society.

It's especially troubling when marriage-equality advocates make similar assertions. The constitutional mandate and law reform efforts of the late 1960s and 1970s reflected the understanding that children are not supposed to suffer harm as a result of having unmarried parents. The lifelong disabilities of "illegitimacy" have been erased. If a law discriminates between a child born to married parents and a child born to unmarried parents, it is subject to heightened scrutiny under the equal protection clause of the U.S. Constitution.

Thus, a second-parent adoption or a parentage order protects the child of a lesbian couple by ensuring her legal relationship with the mother who gave birth to her and the mother's partner. A joint adoption ensures that a couple adopting a child together are both legally recognized parents of that child. Some who urge marriage as the solution to children's needs fail to distinguish between consequences of marriage and consequences of parenthood. For example, a National Gay and Lesbian Task Force publication refers to the lack of educational assistance for the children of deceased public safety officers "who lack legal recognition of the parent-child relationship *due to the lack of marriage rights of their parents.*"[44] But a child does not need his parents to be married to get these rights; the child needs his parent to be legally recognized as his parent. The same is true for children of heterosexual parents.

A Human Rights Campaign Foundation report, *The Cost of Marriage Inequality to Children and Their Same-Sex Parents*, also confuses this issue, providing examples of how the law harms gay and lesbian couples raising children.[45] It highlights Social Security survivors' benefits, the lack of access to health insurance and family and medical leave, and some federal income tax rules. Although the report does note the availability of second-parent adoption in some parts of the country, it does not explain which of the problems it names would be cured by legally recognizing a child's parents and which require marriage of the partners to remedy those disadvantages.

One section of the report, "Protections Available to Same-Sex Couples with Children," explains that only one state permits same-sex marriage, that such marriages are not recognized for purposes of federal laws, and that states do not uniformly permit second-parent adoption. The next paragraph states: "As a result, these children cannot rely on: both their parents to be permitted to authorize medical treatment in an emergency; support from both parents in the event of their separation; or Social Security survivor benefits in the event of the death of the parent who was unable to establish a legal relationship with the child." Yet each of these three problems is solved by legally recognizing the parent-child relationship through adoption or parentage decrees. None requires marriage, either for different-sex or same-sex couples.

The report concludes that "lack of universal access" to marriage deprives children of the protections available to their peers being raised by heterosexual parents. It continues: "Until all states grant equal marriage to same-sex couples, the children in these families will continue to be deprived of the security of being recognized as a 'legal' family." This conclusion is misleading. For those advantages linked to parenthood, marriage is not necessary for the children of either same-sex or different-sex couples. For those requiring marriage of a child's parents, all children with unmarried parents suffer. All the costs to children of what the Human Rights Campaign Foundation calls "marriage inequality" would be eliminated by building on the changes started in the 1970s to eliminate the disadvantages that children of unmarried parents experience.

In fact, the Family and Medical Leave Act (FMLA), which the report mentions, already protects children raised in a variety of family structures. Any covered employee with day-to-day responsibilities for the care and support of a child is entitled to FMLA leave. The regulations say that neither a biological nor a legal relationship to the child is required. In other words, this law allows either parent in a same-sex couple to take leave to care for their child. Neither marriage *nor* adoption is necessary. The report does not convey this fact, nor does it offer it as an example of how other laws might change to protect children of same-sex couples.

Until same-sex couples can marry in every state and until DOMA is repealed, marriage provides insufficient protection for a child born to a married lesbian couple. The nonbiological mother *still* must adopt the child. This is the only guarantee that other states, and the federal government, will honor their parent-child relationship. The forty-plus state laws "defending" marriage and the federal DOMA declare that they will *not* recognize same-sex marriage or any rights flowing from it, including the rights of parenthood. For that reason, the gay legal organizations tell couples in Massachusetts and in the states with civil unions or domestic partnerships that they should still get second-parent adoptions.[46] *In other words, the option created to make marriage matter less provides greater protection for parent-child relationships.*

Marriage-equality supporters also invoke the specter of illegitimacy and quote marriage-movement rhetoric about child well-being. The American Psychological Association, in its briefs in same-sex marriage cases, has argued that children of gay and lesbian couples will benefit from their parents' marriage because nonmarital birth is widely viewed as undesirable. Referring to the historical stigma of "illegitimacy" and "bastardy," it argues that "this stigma . . . will not be visited upon the children of same-sex couples when those couples can legally marry."[47]

The National Association of Social Workers has used the language of marriage-promotion campaigns to assert in its friend-of-the-court briefs that "marriage between a child's parents uniformly is good for children. . . . It advances child welfare to permit—and indeed promote—marriage where there are children."[48] Herdt and Kertzner assert that "marriage denial has had particular effects on the well-being of children reared by lesbians and gay men by undermining family stability and perpetuating false claims about parental fitness."[49] But the research on children of gay parents uniformly finds no damage to them. The claims for marriage equality made for the sake of the children unfortunately echo claims the marriage movement makes when it blames poor child outcomes on parents' failure to marry.

Evan Wolfson, of Freedom to Marry, wrote that "all children deserve to know that their family is worthy of respect in the eyes of the law.... That respect come[s] with the freedom to marry."[50] I agree with Wolfson's premise but not his conclusion; the respect comes from the law equally valuing all family forms—the point of view Wolfson expressed in his 1989 Family Bill of Rights.

Wrongly Defining the Problem

The marriage-equality movement diminishes efforts to win legal recognition of diverse family forms in the way that it structures its arguments. First it presents problems that same-sex couples who lack legal recognition face; it presents these as stand-alone problems for gay and lesbian couples rather than as problems many types of families face. Then it posits *marriage*—rather than a broader set of legal reforms—as the solution to those problems. Consider the following example from Lambda Legal:

> Ronnie in New York City developed a grave illness and needed her partner of over twenty years, Elaine, to assist her in getting to medical appointments. Ronnie would suffer black-outs walking in the street. Elaine requested family medical leave from her employer to cover the periodic appointments, but the employer said no because Ronnie was not a "spouse."[51]

But Ronnie doesn't need a spouse; she needs care. A spouse or her nonmarital equivalent could provide that care—if she has such a partner—but so could Ronnie's niece, her sister, her closest friend, or a group of her closest friends. And such people *must* provide the care if Ronnie doesn't have a partner. The AIDS crisis, attention to which remains a part of Lambda Legal's mission, illuminates the fallacy of expecting any one person to care for someone with extensive medical needs.

What's more, Ronnie's problem with the federal Family and Medical Leave Act is not a problem only of gay and lesbian couples. For example, the law does not permit leave for parents-in-law. Nor can a grandparent or godparent take leave to care for a child. Nor can a group of close friends take leave to rotate caregiving responsibilities for a gay man with AIDS or a lesbian with cancer. The federal law's narrow nuclear family model leaves out many families and relationships.[52] In fact, because the FMLA applies only to workplaces with fifty or more employees, 40 percent of the workforce is not entitled to this benefit at all.

On the other hand, if Elaine worked for the federal government, she would be able to take Ronnie to her appointments. That's because she could use her own sick leave to care for "any individual related by blood or affinity whose close association with the employee is the equivalent of a family relationship."[53] There might be many people in Ronnie's chosen family of friends who qualify under such a definition.[54] That is also the definition in the proposed federal "Healthy Families Act," legislation that mandates seven days of paid sick leave for all employees.

Lambda Legal titled the paper referred to here "Denying Access to Marriage Harms Families." From a different angle, Ronnie's problem would be described as "Denying Access to Sick Leave Harms Families" or "Denying Access to Caretaking Leave Harms Families." The District of Columbia Family and Medical Leave Act covers extended family members and unmarried same- and different-sex partners.[55] This is not an ideal law, but it is better than the federal law and, if extended nationwide, it would meet the needs of more LGBT people than the federal law, even if same-sex couples were allowed to marry. The definition in the "Healthy Families Act" is much better. By defining the problem as lack of access to marriage, gay rights advocates overlook the possibilities for meeting the needs of more LGBT families and relationships through a different solution.

When Lambda Legal challenged the same-sex marriage ban in New Jersey, its legal director said that the "tragedies of September 11th were a painful reminder of what discrimination in marriage means as we watched gay and lesbian survivors being excluded from financial safety nets and other support because they weren't married to their lost partners." That is a *gay civil rights* lens through which to see the same-sex partners of those killed. A lens that valued all families, including all LGBT families, would use the opportunity to promote just rules for all those who depended on the deceased employees, using as models existing laws that do just that. Had the September 11 attacks occurred in California, for example, surviving same-sex partners *would* have had a financial safety net, because in that state marriage is not a prerequisite for receiving workers' compensation death benefits.

Lambda Legal chose to characterize another case as about lack of access to marriage when the relevant law itself banned discrimination on the basis of marital status. In 2007 the group filed a lawsuit on behalf of a lesbian couple whose mortgage company threatened to foreclose on their home.[56] The company explained in writing to the partner who originally owned the home how she could go about adding another person's name to the mortgage; this included changing the deed to reflect joint ownership. Yet after they sent the new deed to the mortgage company, the company claimed that the transfer violated the terms of the mortgage and demanded payment of the full mortgage—$80,000—within thirty days. The company would not have taken this position had the transfer been between spouses.

The Lambda lawsuit claims violation of the federal Equal Credit Opportunity Act, which prohibits discrimination on the basis of marital status. Lambda's legal argument—and the correct policy position—is that the company should not be permitted to discriminate against an unmarried couple. Yet the press release accompanying the filing of the complaint offered only one quote from the Lambda attorney handling the case. He said, "Everyone from kids to creditors knows what it means when two people say they are married. . . . If these two women had been able to marry in New York, this never would have happened."

The Lambda Web site claims that "a victory in this case would help remind home loan lenders throughout the nation that they must treat unmarried same-sex couples as they do married different-sex couples." But the federal law bans discrimination on the basis of marital status; *all* unmarried couples should have the right to protection from discrimination. This case was the perfect vehicle for fighting credit discrimination against all couples, but Lambda instead chose to use it to further its marriage agenda.

Plaintiffs in the cases seeking access to marriage are presented as couples who are harmed because they cannot marry. The lead plaintiffs in the Massachusetts case stated that "we still can't transfer assets to our spouse, benefit from each other's social security should one of us die, and we worry about emergencies when we travel, even with all the proper documentation." Two couples expressed the need for tax and other protections as they contemplate retirement and estate planning; three expressed concern about their ability to secure appropriate medical care in an emergency. One couple was stretched financially by the need to purchase health insurance for the partner who was a full-time student because the employed partner's insurance did not cover an unmarried couple.[57]

In the case challenging the same-sex-marriage ban in Maryland, one woman had been denied access to her partner and information about her partner's condition during the partner's emergency gall bladder surgery, and other couples expressed fears about such circumstances; one couple was separated because of restrictions on immigration that married couples can bypass, and another had spent time apart because of such restrictions; one plaintiff lost his home when his partner of thirteen years died, because the will his partner had written was not signed by the required number of witnesses; a senior citizen couple worried that they would be separated in a nursing home; two couples were unable to share employment-related health insurance; one woman, a city bus driver, worried that her partner would not receive her death benefits if she died on the job.[58]

But marriage actually hurts some couples. The Earned Income Tax Credit (EITC) is one of the most successful antipoverty programs in the country, distributing funds mostly to low- and moderate-income working families with children. Eligibility for the EITC as well as the amount of any credit is based on the combined earnings of spouses. Because of this, many low-income same-sex married parents in Massachusetts are actually better off being treated as unmarried under federal tax law, as their joint incomes would be too high to allow them to receive the credit. Similarly, if one partner needs nursing home care, the other can keep all her assets if they are unmarried. If they are married, the spouse who doesn't need the care can only keep a designated "allowance." Elder-law attorneys often advise older clients considering getting married not to do so; married couples are better off under some Medicaid-related laws and worse off under others, depending on their circumstances.

Marriage Is Not the Answer

Marriage as the solution to the problems that plaintiff couples describe bypasses better solutions that make marriage—whether it would help or hurt any particular couple for any particular purpose—matter less. When advocates for gay and lesbian couples exclude from the definition of *the problem* others who are affected by marriage's special treatment, they leave behind allies and a huge proportion of gay men and lesbians in pursuit of the *solution* of marriage for same-sex couples.

Miguel Braschi deserved protection from eviction. Had marriage been an option in New York at the time, he would have deserved this protection *even if he and Leslie Blanchard were not married.* Olivia Shelltrack and Fondray Loving, who had been together thirteen years and were raising three children, were denied an occupancy permit in 2006 in Black Jack, Missouri, because they fell outside the town's definition of family. The mayor was on record as saying that an unmarried couple with children did not meet the standard for residing there. It took a lawsuit by the local ACLU before the town granted the family the permit. The problem was not lack of access to marriage; the couple was legally allowed to marry. The problem was marriage as the standard for families welcome in the town.

In Massachusetts, some employers ended domestic partner employee benefits after same-sex couples won the right to marry. When GLAD explained its opposition to ending such benefits, it had to walk a fine line. It presented several reasons a gay couple in Massachusetts might choose not to marry. These included having a partner in the military who would face discharge, having a noncitizen partner who might face deportation, and working for an employer who might transfer the employee to a state without protections against employment discrimination based on sexual orientation. GLAD also noted that uncertainty about the legal status of marriage in the only state allowing it might "justly" make an employee pause before marrying. It said that domestic partnership policies were still important and still served the purpose of "equal pay for equal work." But once an organization successfully argues that same-sex couples must be allowed to marry because of the benefits married couples receive, it's harder to assert that a couple shouldn't have to marry to obtain that benefit.

In an August 2006 statement, Lambda Legal affirmed, "We remain committed to litigating and supporting legislative reform... for those who seek protections and respect through means other than marriage."[59] This is an important policy statement that will require care to implement. When a group alleges harm resulting from lack of marriage for same-sex couples, achieving marriage or its functional equivalent may become an end point. After urging marriage as the solution, a group may find that it has lost the ability to advocate for the diverse forms of gay, lesbian, bisexual, and transgender families and relationships. Fair treatment for those families and relationships may not seem like "gay rights" issues and may therefore appear to be someone else's problem.

In addition, in the legislative arena, where there is greater flexibility in seeking reform than there is in litigation, the marriage-discrimination mindset has caused state and national groups to advocate solutions for couples in numerous areas—for example, hospital visitation, family leave, and property tax relief—that shouldn't be limited to couples. Starting with just policies for all families, relationships, and households produces results that are more inclusive than starting with what married couples get and advocating identical treatment for some same-sex couples.

Judith Stacey, the sociologist who first sounded the alarm about the insidious secular arguments promoting fatherhood and marriage in the "Dan Quayle Was Right" era, became a strong champion of parenting by lesbians and gay men and a supporter of marriage for same-sex couples. But she is ambivalent about that support. She wrote:

> Allowing same-sex couples to join the conjugal congregation is likely to intensify social discrimination against everyone else who, whether by choice or fate, were to remain outside its privileged grounds.... This is not an outcome I consider desirable or demo-

> cratic. To love or live without marrying should not be a social scandal . . . but discriminating against those who do so should be. . . . Unless legal recognition of same-sex marriage is accompanied with social recognition and material support for the broad array of contemporary family forms which children and adults of all genders and sexual orientations now inhabit, their gain might prove to be a loss for vast numbers of other children and families.[60]

Some of the legal problems that that "broad array" of contemporary families face could be solved now by focusing on solutions other than marriage. Those solutions will improve the lives of same-sex couples as well as LGBT people not in coupled relationships, and their children. Then, when marriage equality ultimately prevails, it will be a triumph in the name of the dignity of the love between same-sex partners that does not diminish those whose lives, "by choice or fate," take a different course.

CHAPTER SIX

Countries Where Marriage Matters Less

Same-sex couples enjoy greater legal recognition in many countries outside the United States. They can marry in Belgium, Canada, the Netherlands, Spain, and South Africa. They can register as partners in at least fourteen other countries, achieving many, most, or all of the benefits and obligations accorded married couples.

While this reveals a greater acceptance of lesbians and gay men than exists in the United States, a deeper look is needed to determine whether same-sex or different-sex couples in these countries *must* marry or register to be subject to these specific legal consequences. Such an analysis reveals that, among Western countries, the United States stands largely alone in maintaining an inflexible line between married couples and everyone else.

The changes in family composition in the United States in the 1960s—brought about by increased heterosexual cohabitation and nonmarital births—occurred as well in other countries. Legal changes followed. No "Religious Right" or "marriage movement" in these countries opposed the expanding rights of unmarried couples. No theological or secular arguments for the supremacy of heterosexual marriage gained traction in their courts and legislatures.

Countries that began to recognize unmarried heterosexual couples in the 1970s have continued to do so without a backlash such as that which occurred in the United States. Incorporating same-sex couples into a legal regime available to different-sex couples was a natural progression. Those countries that later permitted partner registration or marriage for same-sex couples did not dislodge recognition available to those who did not marry or register.

Same-sex couples in the United States repeatedly identify the ban on marriage as the source of their exclusion from laws governing important matters such as retirement and death benefits, healthcare access and decision making, family leave, immigration, taxation, and dissolution of relationships. Other countries have found ways to provide legal rights involving such matters to unmarried couples. Seen from this angle, the problem in America is not that we deny marriage to gay men and lesbians but that we value married couples exclusively in providing access to laws that all families need.

Three countries, each with somewhat different laws governing gay and lesbian couples, are good examples of the ways in which this approach can be carried out. Canada allows same-sex couples to marry. It also extends to cohabiting, unmarried same- and different-sex couples virtually all the legal consequences of marriage. New Zealand allows same- and different-sex couples to enter civil unions but allows only different-sex couples to marry. Like Canada, it treats all unmarried couples virtually identically under the law. Australia bans marriage for same-sex couples, but extends to de facto heterosexual couples all of the legal consequences of marriage. Its federal government is hostile to gay and lesbian rights but comfortable giving full legal recognition to different-sex couples who do not marry. All nine Australian states recognize same-sex couples on terms virtually identical to those of unmarried different-sex couples.

In addition, many European countries permit partner registration, but unmarried/unregistered couples in those countries have many rights that in the United States come only with marriage. Although the differences between marriage/registration and cohabitation are greater in Europe than in Canada, Australia, and New Zealand, unmarried/unregistered couples in those countries still take for granted some matters—like healthcare decision making and family medical leave—that figure prominently in American arguments for same-sex marriage. Brazil and Israel also exemplify ways that law can value families beyond those created by marriage.

Canada

> Discrimination on the basis of marital status touches the essential dignity and worth of the individual. . . . [It violates] fundamental human rights norms. Specifically, it touches the individual's freedom to live life with the mate of one's choice in the fashion of one's

> choice. This is a matter of defining importance to individuals.... Discrimination on the basis of marital status may be seen as akin to discrimination on the ground of religion, to the extent that it finds its roots and expression in moral disapproval of all sexual unions except those sanctioned by the church and state.[1]

This eloquent quotation, from a 1995 opinion of the Supreme Court of Canada, explains why discrimination against unmarried couples violates the Canadian Charter of Rights and Freedoms (the counterpart to the U.S. Constitution). Marriage for same-sex couples in Canada came only *after* they, along with unmarried heterosexual couples, had received almost total legal parity with married couples. Today same-sex couples in Canada can marry if they wish to express something about their relationship by doing so; they do not *have to* marry to get legal benefits, because those benefits are already available to them. Marriage equality in Canada was a civil rights victory for lesbian and gay couples. As a matter of family law, their families were already fully recognized.

Recognition began for unmarried different-sex couples in 1972, with a British Columbia law extending spousal-support rights to cohabitants of at least two years. Laws regarding the obligations of separating partners followed. Canadian law also began recognizing unmarried couples with respect to various government programs. In the early 1970s it extended veterans' and old-age/pension benefits to different-sex couples who had lived together for at least one year or three years, depending on the circumstances.[2] Throughout the next two decades, many laws and regulations recognized unmarried couples in matters pertaining to inheritance, taxes, prison-inmate visitation, medical decision making, medical services, bereavement leave, and employee family benefits.[3]

In 1995, the Supreme Court of Canada, in *Miron v. Trudel,* found unconstitutional the exclusion of an unmarried partner from the definition of "spouse" in an automobile insurance policy, resulting in the affirmation of the equal respect due unmarried couples in the quotation that begins this section. In 1999 it ruled that the Canadian Charter required extending that respect to a lesbian requesting support payments from a former partner after their relationship had ended.[4] As a result, in 2000 the Canadian Parliament, reflecting values of "tolerance, respect, and equality," amended sixty-eight federal laws to recognize as "common law partners" both same-sex and different-sex couples who live together for at least a year. This designation carries equal rights and responsibilities to that accorded spouses.[5]

Only one major difference remains for unmarried couples. Provinces are not required to distribute property at the end of unmarried-couple relationships under the same standards used for marriages, nor must they allow inheritance if there is no will. Three provinces —Northwest Territories (1997), Saskatchewan (2001), and Manitoba (2002)—do provide identical treatment. The others follow the somewhat more onerous process of using the standards for property division at separation that the Supreme Court of Canada established in the early 1980s; these are still much easier to meet than those that address separating unmarried couples in the United States. Nova Scotia, Manitoba, and Quebec also allow both same-sex and different-sex couples to register as domestic partners, which triggers rights and obligations at death or dissolution identical to those for married couples.[6]

In 2003, after lawsuits in Ontario, British Columbia, and Quebec, those provinces extended marriage to same-sex couples. Quebec also enabled a lesbian couple having a child through assisted reproduction to place the names of both mothers on the child's birth certificate. Legislation in the Parliament followed, and marriage became available to same-sex couples throughout the country on July 20, 2005.

Same- and different-sex couples in Canada have choices. Marriage and, where available, registration as domestic partners trigger immediate legal consequences for all purposes. Couples who do not marry or register, however, will be treated almost identically to married couples after one or three years of cohabitation, depending on the relevant law, or sooner if they have children in common. Cohabitation is not rigidly defined; a 2003 Ontario case awarded temporary spousal support at the end of an eighteen-year relationship between two men, even though for some of the time the couple worked in different cities and had separate homes.[7]

For couples who have already lived together for three years at the time they consider marriage, the decision carries few legal consequences; they are already treated as spouses under all federal laws. In some provinces they will need wills to guarantee each other's ability to inherit. Otherwise the law recognizes them fully as a family.

Canada has considered, and in one province implemented, legal recognition for relationships not based on sexual affiliation. In 2001 the Law Commission of Canada, an independent federal law reform agency, released a report titled *Beyond Conjugality: Recognizing and Supporting Close Personal Adult Relationships.* The commission acknowledged that the law already treated married and unmarried couples equally. It called those relationships "conjugal." It recommended further reform to recognize the value of caring and interdependent nonconjugal relationships.[8] The recommendations have not yet been implemented on a federal level.

The province of Alberta, however, created a legal status that encompasses nonconjugal relationships, designated "adult interdependent relationships." The motive for recognizing such relationships was quite different from that expressed in *Beyond Conjugality.* Alberta is Canada's most conservative province, and its legislators were dismayed with the Canadian Supreme Court decisions invalidating distinctions between married and unmarried couples, including same-sex couples.[9] Because the province did not want to single out unmarried straight and gay couples for recognition, it created a broader status that recognizes more than conjugal couples. Alberta wanted to keep marriage for different-sex couples only, but of course has been unable to do so since the 2005 mandate allowing such marriages throughout the country.[10]

Under the 2002 Adult Interdependent Relationships Act, two people in such a relationship are treated identically to a married couple for many of the legal consequences applicable to marriage. The relationship is created for legal purposes via a written agreement or in the case of couples living in an interdependent relationship for three years. If there is a child by birth or adoption, the three-year requirement is dropped, but the relationship must be "of some permanence." Any two unmarried people, not already in another interdependent relationship, may become adult interdependent partners (AIPs). The two people must live together, share each other's lives, be emotionally committed to each other, and function as an economic and domestic unit; a sexual relationship between the partners is not required.

AIPs are now included in many laws previously applicable to spouses and/or family members. Extended healthcare benefits that Alberta residents receive if they or their spouses are sixty-five or older now apply to AIPs if one of the partners is sixty-five or older. AIPs may not be compelled to testify in court against each other. An AIP may make decisions about organ and tissue donation for a dying partner.

AIPs inherit under the same circumstances as does a spouse if one partner dies without a will; if the decedent has both a surviving spouse and a surviving AIP, the one who was living with the decedent at the time of death inherits. An AIP, like a spouse, also cannot be disinherited by his or her partner but rather is entitled to some portion of the estate even if there is a will to the contrary. When the relationship dissolves, an AIP may bring an action for ongoing support if the facts merit it. Alberta's Workers' Compensation Act provides a pension benefit to the spouse or AIP of a deceased worker. If the worker has both a spouse and an AIP, the law says that the spouse receives the pension if the spouse is dependent, but if the spouse is not dependent and the AIP is, then the AIP gets the pension.

Canada thus provides a dramatic contrast to the United States with respect to nonmarital relationships. Canadian law sought to accommodate the sexual revolution that brought into society different-sex cohabitation without marriage. It first eschewed marital-status discrimination and then applied the mandate of equality in its Charter of Rights and Freedoms to recognize same-sex couples. From there it opened marriage to same-sex couples. Canada will achieve even greater justice for all families if the law embraces the principles of the *Beyond Conjugality* report and considers the Alberta Adult Interdependent Relationships Act a model from which to build other protections for nonconjugal relationships.

Australia

Australia has an approach different from that of both the United States and Canada.[11] Unlike that of the United States, Australian law recognizes unmarried heterosexual couples who live together as almost identical to married couples. Indeed, such recognition is even more sweeping than in Canada; few laws require the couple to have lived together for a certain amount of time.

The areas addressed under Australian federal law, and thus equally available to married and unmarried different-sex couples, include immigration, veterans' benefits, income tax, social security and family-assistance benefits, superannuation retirement benefits (called pensions in the United States), death benefits, caretaking and bereavement leave, and bankruptcy. The terms used in the federal laws include "de facto spouse," "member of a couple," "partner," and "marital" or "marriage-like" relationship. The most common language in the definitions of these terms describes living with someone of a different sex "on a genuine domestic basis."

Unlike in Canada, Australian federal law does not extend this recognition to same-sex couples. A small number of federal laws extend coverage to those in an "interdependent" partnership or relationship, including same-sex partners. The most significant of these is the ability to sponsor for immigration someone with whom the Australian citizen shares an "interdependent relationship." The Australian military also recognizes same-sex couples as interdependent partners for purposes of housing, relocation expenses, travel, and other benefits. A survivor of an interdependent relationship is also entitled to the favorable tax treatment of certain death benefits.

Eligibility to marry in Australia is set by federal law and requires that the couple be a man and a woman. Other matters of family law, however, are left to the eight states. There, with the exception of parenting laws in some states, unmarried same-sex and different-sex couples are treated identically.

States began recognizing different-sex de facto relationships in the 1980s. Gay and lesbian community groups studied issues of relationship recognition and produced a report, *The Bride Wore Pink*, in 1994, urging recognition of a range of relationships. It explicitly disdained marriage as the benchmark, and acknowledged "chosen family" beyond conjugal relationships.[12]

In 1999, New South Wales, where Sydney is located, became the first state to include same-sex partners in the term "de facto relationships." The term encompasses two unmarried adults who "live together as a couple." While no one factor is required to determine that such a relationship exists, the criteria to be considered include how long they have been together; their reputation; their financial interdependence; their arrangements for financial support, ownership or use of property, and living together; care of the home and children; and their mutual commitment to a shared life.

Although some Australian states use "domestic" partnership or relationship rather than "de facto," all use the factors New South Wales first listed. A couple is not required to live together a certain amount of time to be covered by these laws, except for the right to inherit and to divide property upon dissolution; these require two years of cohabitation, unless the couple has a child. A judge has the discretion to waive the two-year rule.

Victoria, where Melbourne is, also extends numerous laws to couples who do not live together "where one or each of them provides personal and financial support of a domestic nature for the material benefit of the other."[13] In 2003, Tasmania went even further. It introduced both the concept of "significant relationship" with a definition similar to that of other states and a registration system that by itself establishes proof of the existence of a "significant relationship." *Neither* scheme requires that the couple live together.

Tasmania also created the status of "caring relationship" for noncouples. This is defined as "a relationship other than a marriage or significant relationship between two adult persons whether or not related by family, one or each of whom provides the other with domestic support and personal care."[14] A registration system for caring relationships triggers fewer rights and obligations than those accorded significant relationships, but it includes, among other things, access to workers' compensation, what happens when someone dies without a will, property and support obligations, and state retirement benefits.

Australia provides an interesting contrast to the United States. The federal government extends to heterosexual couples who do not marry the same family recognition it provides married couples. In doing so it violates a basic premise of the American marriage movement, reflected in U.S. federal laws and policies, that the law must maintain a bright-line distinction between married and unmarried couples. On the other hand, it is hostile to same-sex couples. Federal law bans both same-sex marriage and recognition of same-sex marriages validly entered into in other countries, although the recognition of interdependent relationships does provide more rights to same-sex couples in Australia than in the United States.

New Zealand

New Zealand bans discrimination on the basis of both sexual orientation and marital status. "Marital status" includes a ban on discrimination against cohabiting unmarried couples, called de facto couples.[15] For most purposes, since a 2002 law revision, they are treated identically to married couples. For example, partners are each other's next of kin; their income is considered a single economic unit; they have decision-making authority in health matters and with respect to disposition of remains. To inherit from each other without a will and to divide property at separation, however, the couple must have lived together for three years, unless they have a child. To avoid "serious injustice" a court may waive the three-year rule.

Since April 2005, same- and different-sex couples in New Zealand have been able to enter civil unions. Only different-sex couples may marry. The consequences of marriage and civil union are almost identical. New Zealand allows a different-sex couple to enter a civil union because it does not want to discriminate on the basis of sexual orientation. The female partner of a woman who bears a child through assisted reproduction is presumed a parent of that child.

Other Countries

Formalization of same-sex relationships began in Europe with Denmark, which in 1989 passed its "registered partnership" law for same-sex couples only; Norway (1991), Sweden (1994), Iceland (1996), and Finland (2001) followed. The United Kingdom followed in 2005 with a status for same-sex couples called "civil partnership." In 1998, the Netherlands set up a registration scheme for both different-sex and same-sex couples. Registration under all these laws grants rights and obligations identical to those of married couples, except in some areas of parenting, which separate laws address. Although U.S. commentators sometimes use the term "gay marriage" to describe the legal status available in Denmark and other Scandinavian countries, this is inaccurate because those countries reserve the word "marriage" for heterosexual couples. Andorra, the Czech Republic, France, Germany, Luxembourg, Slovenia, and Switzerland all allow partner registration, although the accompanying rights and obligations are less than those for married couples.[16]

In 2001, the Netherlands became the first country in the world to allow same-sex marriage. It kept its registered partnership option for both same-sex and different-sex couples. Currently, Belgium, Spain, and South Africa (in addition to Canada) also allow same-sex couples to marry.[17]

Even with these formalization regimes in place, no European country draws a bright line for all purposes between married/registered relationships and the relationships of unmarried couples. Rather, they continue changes that began in the 1970s with respect to recognizing unmarried couples. Listed here are some of the legal consequences that attach to unmarried and unregistered couples who live together.

- If they are raising a child, the surviving partner receives social security–type benefits (Norway, Sweden, the Netherlands, and Iceland).
- The survivor can sue for compensation based on wrongful death (Finland, France, the Netherlands, Sweden, Denmark, Norway, Iceland, and Belgium).
- Cohabiting partners are considered next of kin for purposes of medical decision making (Belgium, Finland, the Netherlands, Norway, Sweden, France, and Germany).
- The survivor can remain in the couple's rental home, even if the only name on the lease was that of the deceased partner (Germany, Denmark, France, Iceland, the Netherlands, Sweden, Finland, and Norway).

Outside Europe, Brazil has no partnership registration but has a long tradition of recognizing the status of nonmarital different-sex cohabitants, which has recently been extended to same-sex couples. The right of a woman to recover for the wrongful death of her nonmarital partner was established in 1912. The concept of de facto partnerships allows a partner who contributed domestic services to a relationship to obtain financial compensation when the relationship dissolves or one partner dies. The first case to extend this doctrine to same-sex couples was decided in 1989.[18]

Brazil also recognizes a "stable union" between a man and a woman. The relationship must be public and lasting, but the couple is not required to live together. A stable union is a family, and treated the same as a married couple with respect to inheritance, taxation, insurance, and healthcare. Brazil extended social security benefits to dependents, including different-sex unmarried partners of government employees, in the early 1960s, and to same-sex partners through court decisions in the late 1990s. In 2001 a state supreme court recognized a same-sex relationship as a stable union. Others have followed. In 2006, Brazil's Supreme Federal Court ruled that same-sex couples should be considered family entities.[19]

In Israel, religious institutions control marriage law. Many different-sex couples are unable to marry because both partners are not Jewish. Court cases and legislation have extended to them a variety of rights. These include pension rights, intestate succession (the right to inherit when there is no will), and financial support if the relationship dissolves. Some of these have been extended to same-sex partners.[20]

The American marriage movement demands that the law rigidly distinguish between heterosexual married couples and all other relationships. It claims that this distinction is needed to promote a "marriage culture" and that a marriage culture is required for the well-being of children and society. Many countries do not make this rigid distinction in their laws. If the marriage movement's premise were accurate, one would expect dire consequences to society resulting from family law in these countries, yet no such consequences emerge. Comparing one important measure, for example, the data show that the percentage of children living in poverty in the United States is 22 percent, compared with 16 percent in the United Kingdom, 7 percent in France, 2 percent in Denmark, and 4 percent in Norway and Sweden.[21]

Immigration: A Case Study

Immigration laws have been a focus of lesbian and gay rights advocacy for many years and are an excellent example of the different approaches to family definition in the United States and elsewhere. Human Rights Watch and Immigration Equality compiled the laws in a 2006 report, *Family, Unvalued: Discrimination, Denial, and the Fate of Binational Same-Sex Couples under U.S. Law.*[22]

U.S. law allows someone to sponsor his or her spouse for immigration to the United States; even engaged persons are permitted entry. When one person in a same-sex couple is a U.S. citizen (or permanent resident) and the other is not, they have no such ability. Advocates for gay and lesbian couples have been seeking to amend the law. They propose including "permanent partners" defined as those in an "intimate relationship . . . in which both parties intend a lifelong commitment," are financially interdependent, and are unable to marry the U.S.-national partner in a marriage recognized by current law.

At least twenty countries extend indefinite residency and permission to work to the same-sex partners of their citizens. The overwhelming majority of these countries extend this ability to unmarried heterosexual partners as well. Some countries require the couple to have lived together for a minimum period of time; others require proof of the stability of the relationship. Even in countries that allow a same-sex couple to marry or register their relationship, such formalization is rarely required for immigration.

- Of the five countries that allow same-sex marriage (Belgium, Canada, the Netherlands, South Africa, and Spain), all except Spain allowed unmarried same- or different-sex partners to immigrate before it allowed same-sex marriage, and they continue to allow unmarried-partner immigration.
- Of the countries that allow partner registration, only Germany and Switzerland require registration before a foreign-national partner can immigrate.
- Australia, Brazil, Israel, and Portugal do not have national partner registration but do allow immigration of both the same- and different-sex partners of citizens or residents.

This array of countries demonstrates not only support for gay and lesbian couples but overwhelming recognition that unmarried and unregistered couples form families that should be able to live together. The United States is concerned with immigration fraud, but this is one area in which the government recognizes that *marriage* can take place for fraudulent purposes; procedures are in place to weed out such fraud. In fact, if the United States adopted a minimum period of cohabitation for unmarried couples it would likely find *less* fraud in administering that requirement than it finds with marriages; current law allows an American to sponsor a spouse for immigration as long as the couple has met in person *once*.

The current effort to help binational same-sex couples, through the Uniting American Families Act, often invokes the number of other countries that permit immigration of same-sex partners, but it overlooks the fact that almost all of those nations extend identical rights to unmarried different-sex couples. Those countries have assimilated same-sex couples into a system of family recognition that does not hold *marriage* as the benchmark.

Internationally, gay and lesbian law reform efforts support the ability to marry without elevating marriage above other family forms. At the International Conference on LGBT Human Rights held in Montreal in 2006, the assembly adopted the "Declaration of Montreal."[23] This declaration lists and explains necessary changes and seeks to build an agenda for global action. The section on relationships and families calls for access to marriage as a matter of equality and states that "doing justice to the changing realities of family life also entails recognizing and granting equal rights to non-marital relationships." It is the same sentiment found in the Family Bill of Rights drafted at Lambda Legal in 1989.

In the almost twenty years since the draft Family Bill of Rights, other countries have moved toward gay and lesbian civil rights *after* incorporating nonmarital relationships and households into their family law. Both results are necessary to secure justice for all families. An exclusive focus on obtaining for same-sex couples what married couples have risks leaving behind many other households, families, and relationships of LGBT—and indeed all—people.

CHAPTER SEVEN

Valuing All Families

Marriage brings with it a staggering number of legal consequences. A 2004 U.S. Government Accountability Office report identified 1,138 provisions of federal law that treat a relationship between two people who are married differently from any other relationship.[1] The same is true at the state level. For example, *Marriage Inequality in the State of Maryland*, a 2006 report by the LGBT rights group Equality Maryland, lists more than 425 state provisions that exclude same-sex couples because they depend on marriage or immediate-family status.[2]

Advocates for same-sex marriage invoke these facts as evidence of the justness of same-sex couples' demand to be permitted to marry. They present the stories of couples whose family life mirrors that of married couples. They document the undesirable—sometimes tragic—consequences of excluding these couples from a legal status uniquely available to different-sex couples who marry. In the stories they tell, the *harm* is exclusion from marriage, and so the *remedy* is allowing same-sex couples to marry.

But the injustice same-sex couples suffer is not unique. When law makes marriage the dividing line, it harms all unmarried people, including those with children. The harm is the dividing line. The remedy is drawing a different line more closely tailored to achieving the law's purpose.

Others have criticized laws that attach consequences to marriage and no other relationship; two family law scholars and one law reform commission have been especially insightful. Martha Albertson Fineman believes the relationship to which the law should grant privileges is the one between a dependent and that dependent's caretaker. Grace Ganz Blumberg argues that unmarried couples and married couples should be treated identically. The Law Commission of Canada stated that government should not advantage relationships based on sexual affiliation—conjugal relationships—over others able to fulfill critical social goals.

The Caretaker-Dependent Dyad

Fineman coined the terms "inevitable dependency" and "derivative dependency."[3] Inevitable dependents are those who cannot care for themselves, typically children, but also the ill, elderly, and disabled. Derivative dependents are those who provide the care to inevitable dependents; to provide uncompensated care they depend on others for resources. When caretaking is treated as a private, rather than a collective, responsibility, it is assigned to the family, where women perform most of it.

Unlike many feminists, Fineman does not argue that fathers should do more caretaking and thus reduce the difference in mothers' and fathers' roles. Rather, she maintains that family should be redefined with the caretaking dyad, prototypically the mother and child, at its core. Caring for inevitable dependents should be a collective responsibility, supported by policies that channel resources to such units, not to the sexual dyad of a man and a woman. Even if the sexual-dyad model included same-sex couples, she says, such units should have no preferential claim to social resources.

Everyone is dependent at some point, but only some people care for dependents. Those caregivers perform work critical to the government, the economy, and the society, so they deserve compensation and accommodation. "We all lead subsidized lives," Fineman writes, arguing that autonomy is a myth. The government subsidizes business and industry; it bails out farmers, airlines, car companies, and savings and loans. The tax code subsidizes home ownership and other endeavors. Uncompensated work caring for others subsidizes those who receive it and the society that needs this work done.[4]

In Fineman's view, society should ask what functions it expects families to perform and then consider how it can help families carry out their responsibilities. Among the solutions she advocates are direct state subsidies—such as childcare allowances—and restructuring the workplace to make it more compatible with caretaking so that the market assumes a fair share of the burdens of dependency.

Recognizing All Couples

Since the 1970s, law professor Grace Blumberg has advocated treating unmarried couples similarly to married couples. "All conjugal families need legal rules that respond to dependence and vulnerability, the hallmarks and pitfalls of conjugal relationships," she wrote. Blumberg argued that after two years of cohabitation, or any cohabitation if the couple had a child, the couple should be treated as married when the relationship ended. She also argued that Social Security, income tax, and workers' compensation should take into account unmarried cohabitants, based either on cohabitation alone, cohabitation for a set time, or cohabitation with birth of a child.[5] More than twenty years later, after California passed a comprehensive domestic partnership law granting same-sex couples virtually all of the state-law consequences of marriage, Blumberg expressed concern that recognizing marriage or registration for same-sex couples would reduce the likelihood of moving U.S. law in the direction Canada took: recognizing unmarried couples, both same-sex and different-sex. The American Law Institute's *Principles of the Law of Family Dissolution: Analysis and Recommendations,* which Blumberg helped draft, applies the same rules to the dissolution of domestic partnerships that it does to divorces.[6]

Canada: *Beyond Conjugality*

Canada has implemented the heart of Blumberg's proposals—the functional equivalence of married and unmarried couples. As discussed in the previous chapter, the Law Commission of Canada recommended further reform to recognize caring and interdependent nonconjugal relationships in its report *Beyond Conjugality,* which affirmed that "the freedom to choose whether and with whom to form close personal relationships is a fundamental value in free and democratic societies."[7]

The commission developed a method for evaluating any law. It includes allowing people to choose which relationships should be subject to the law where appropriate. For example, an employee should be able to identify for herself the people so close to her that she would take bereavement leave if one of them died. When it is not appropriate for an individual to self-define the relevant relationships, as with laws designed to avoid a public official's financial conflict of interest, then the law should apply to both the formal and the functional relationships that are relevant to achieving the objectives of the particular law. The commission applied this method to many Canadian laws, including those governing who may be compensated when someone dies due to someone else's negligence, who can take bereavement or caregiver leave, who may be sponsored under immigration law, who should be considered a family member in various conflict-of-interest rules, and who tax and pension laws cover.

Marriage: The Wrong Dividing Line

Laws that make marriage—only marriage and always marriage—different from all other relationships must be reevaluated. Many laws apply only to marriage because of marriage's historically gendered nature; these stray far from their original purpose. Until recently "husband" and "wife" remained distinctly gendered states, backed by distinctly gendered laws. In the 1970s the Supreme Court struck down gender-based distinctions. This left two options: extend a law equally to husbands and wives or eliminate it. Courts and legislatures did both. When they extended the laws, husbands and wives were then treated the same—a legal framework that would have shocked societies and legislatures and judges of previous centuries—but unlike everyone else.

These laws no longer serve their original purpose, which was tied to legally mandated sex roles in marriage. Laws enacted before no-fault divorce, the end of illegitimacy, and the elimination of rigid norms of gender and sexual expression must be reevaluated. When children are involved, the law already ties rights and responsibilities to *parenthood,* not to *marriage*; when a law's purpose is to protect children, marriage is never an appropriate dividing line. A legal system in a pluralistic society that values all families should meld as closely as possible the purposes of a law with the relationships that that law covers. *Marriage* is not the right dividing line.

Real Support Should Count

Those who advocate marriage for same-sex couples stress that such couples are willing to assume the responsibilities of marriage. An argument that the "special rights" given marriage reflect the "special obligations" couples have to each other has rhetorical appeal but little support in contemporary law.

Laws that used to codify a wife's dependence on her husband formed the core of an elaborate system maintaining "separate spheres" for women and men, ensuring male domination and control at home, in the economy, and in public life. Such a purpose has no place in contemporary law, as the Supreme Court recognized in the 1970s and 1980s in finding sex-based classifications unconstitutional.

Courts and legislatures responded to the Supreme Court's gender-neutrality mandate by either eliminating a husband's duty to support his wife, or placing the obligation of support on both spouses, or obliging a spouse to pay for his or her spouse's "necessaries" only if the debt-incurring spouse was unable to do so. Cases involving the "necessaries doctrine" now almost exclusively concern hospitals seeking payment for medical services.

Maryland, Michigan, and Florida have abolished the necessaries doctrine; spouses there do *not* have the obligation to pay for each other's necessaries, including healthcare. If a hospital cannot collect from the patient or the patient's estate, it cannot make a claim against the patient's spouse. Virginia and Missouri have extended the doctrine to both spouses; New Jersey and New Hampshire place secondary liability on the spouse.[8] Despite this varied legal framework, married couples in all states are entitled to, for example, spousal health insurance coverage and Social Security retirement benefits. These benefits are not tied to any obligation the spouses have under their state's necessaries doctrine.

About half the states have criminal nonsupport statutes that apply to spouses, mostly triggered only when a spouse is left "destitute." No contemporary cases apply such laws; a standard text summarizing family law contains only six cases after 1950 and none after 1970.[9] A few states have "family expense" laws that make both parents responsible for family expenses and children's education. These laws are overwhelmingly applied in circumstances concerning the support of children. Only a handful of cases in the past twenty-five years involved spousal support, and, as with the necessaries doctrine, most concern medical bills.[10]

Any remaining support obligation must be analyzed in light of no-fault divorce. Whatever the obligation may be, it is no longer lifelong. Either party can end any obligation by ending the marriage, with or without the other's consent. Most states also allow two people planning to marry to write a prenuptial contract in which they agree that neither will have a financial obligation to the other if they divorce, regardless of the reason for dissolution. They still count as "married" for the special benefits the law provides.

While most states allow alimony, requirements to get it are stringent and awards are rare. When alimony is awarded, it is almost always for a specified number of years, not for life. For example, a Maryland study found alimony awards in 8 percent of cases in 1999 and 6 percent in 2003.[11] Several laws recognize that the duty to support a spouse is the wrong basis for a rule. Alimony ends if the ex-wife remarries, based on its original theory that the new husband picks up the obligation to support her. But courts now often end alimony if the recipient begins living with a partner in a "marriage-like" relationship. Some do this automatically; others assess whether the partner is contributing to the recipient's support or whether the new arrangement has decreased the recipient's need for alimony.

While looking at the recipient's economic circumstances is sensible, a decision cannot be based on the partner's legal obligation to support the woman he lives with, because no obligation exists. In fact, if that relationship ends, the woman will have no claim to support from her ex-partner. So marriage is a rigid dividing line for receiving alimony but not a rigid dividing line for losing it.[12] In a 2007 Virginia case, the court ended an ex-husband's alimony obligation because his ex-wife was living with a lesbian partner.[13] It did so even though a state constitutional amendment bars legal recognition of that lesbian relationship.

Recipients of government assistance face similar laws. Federal Temporary Assistance to Needy Families rules permit a state, if it wishes, to deem the income of a mother's cohabiting unmarried partner available to the family unit; if the mother and her partner have a child together and there are also other children who are not the partner's children, the partner's income *must* be counted. Thus, although a man has no legal obligation to support his partner or any of her children who are not also legally his, his income can render the family ineligible for public assistance.

This picture should dislodge the notion that benefits flow to married couples because they have an obligation to support each other. It is better to extend benefits to family units that *actually are* supporting each other, regardless of any legal obligation. In fact, it is nonsensical to deny a benefit, such as health insurance coverage, to a couple who *are* supporting each other on the ground that they are not *required* to do so. Giving privileges to those who make an unenforceable promise of commitment over those who have carried out that commitment is the triumph of formalism over function. It's the life together, not the promise, that the law should recognize.

Recognizing Higher Values than Speed and Efficiency

A law that includes spouses and excludes everyone else is relatively easy to apply, even though uncertainty and complexity, in some cases, reign. Ten states permit common law marriage, and every state recognizes as married a couple who had a common law marriage in a state that permits it.[14] In such situations, uncertainty often exists about whether a couple is married. Sometimes laws make exceptions that require scrutiny, such as when a woman "marries" a man who was married to someone else: Did she know that he was already married, and if so, when did she find out, and what did she do when she learned the truth? The law expects administrative agencies and courts to apply these complex rules.

Still, in most instances marriage is a clear distinction that is simple to apply. Application ease should sound like a disturbingly familiar justification. States offered it, and the Supreme Court rejected it, in many cases. Illinois argued that most fathers of children born outside marriage were unfit, so it should not be required to hold hearings after a mother died; it should simply be permitted to remove the children from their home. The Supreme Court responded with the pronouncement that "the Constitution recognizes higher values than speed and efficiency."[15]

The facts were compelling. Joan and Peter Stanley had lived together intermittently for eighteen years and had three children. It was 1972, four years after the Court first found unconstitutional a distinction based on a child's "illegitimacy." The sexual revolution was well established. The rule disregarding as a parent the father of children born outside marriage was consistent with centuries of law that such children were not legally his, but it was clearly not good for these children. After Joan Stanley died, if the state had removed the children from their home it would have been depriving the children of their sole remaining parent. The Court dispensed with centuries of law to avoid an unwise result.

The outcome of *Stanley v. Illinois* may seem obvious today—how could it possibly be in children's best interests to lose their father after they have lost their mother? But it was extraordinary in 1972. The Supreme Court found that Peter Stanley's right to raise his children had been violated, and the decision required *every* state to revise its laws.

In *Reed v. Reed* in 1971, the state also justified its law preferring men over women as estate administrators based on application ease. In that case, both the mother and the father of a deceased child sought to administer the child's estate. Idaho did not want to hold hearings on the merits of competing relatives, and the Supreme Court was sympathetic to the state's desire to reduce the probate court's workload. Yet it ruled that mandatory preference based on sex, "merely to accomplish the elimination of hearings on the merits," violated the equal protection clause of the Constitution.[16]

The Court was affected by the fact that women's lives had changed, and their demands for equality, paraded in the streets as well as in courtrooms, had grown louder and stronger. As the decade progressed, the Court repeatedly rejected government arguments that it was cheaper and easier to make decisions based on sex-role stereotypes than to hold hearings.

These sentiments should animate contemporary family law. Once the law made assumptions about nonmarital children and sex roles, that produced certain and streamlined rules. It is more efficient to give a husband the sole and absolute right to select a child's surname and where the family lives. It is more certain to consider a man's children only those born to his wife. The law has accommodated a less certain and less efficient system that is more consistent with modern values. When the law today makes assumptions about marriage as compared with other family forms, it achieves certainty or efficiency based on outdated generalizations at the expense of the well-being of much of the population.

Even so, law reform designed to value all families should be as easy to apply as possible. Under the valuing-all-families approach, states would keep marriage, but give it a new name—civil partnership—and extend it to same-sex couples. While all marriages/partnerships would not have the same legal consequences, most would trigger specific rules, facilitating straightforward treatment. In addition, states would keep records under a "designated family relationship" registration system. People who register would be publicly declaring that their relationship should count as family under laws that now list family members defined only by marriage, biology, or adoption.

Beyond that, deciding what relationships would be covered depends on discerning each law's purpose. Some laws' purpose is to give people maximum autonomy by allowing them to make decisions for themselves, such as with respect to disposition of their remains after death. Recognizing that people sometimes don't or can't make such decisions for themselves, the law allows them to select someone to make decisions for them. When no one has been designated, the law should determine who should make decisions on that person's behalf based on whom the person would most want in this role. When it is inappropriate for people to make their own decisions—for example, society values supporting all minor children, thus the law will not allow parents to withhold support from those born outside marriage—the law's purpose is the driving principle.

The current system sometimes draws lines based on a law's objective rather than on marriage alone. The valuing-all-families approach extends this method to more laws. Where appropriate, the law would minimize uncertainty through presumptions tied to the law's purpose. For example, a law designed to account for economic and emotional interdependence would automatically include those who had lived together interdependently for a certain period.

Family Law That Values All Families

Marriage/Civil Partnership

The valuing-all-families legal system keeps marriage and extends it to same-sex couples, although with a new official name—civil partnership. Over the past four decades, family laws have shed words laden with outmoded and undesirable meanings. The change in nomenclature symbolizes a break with the past.

For example, "custody" and "visitation," when referring to the post-divorce care of children, have been replaced with, among others, "parenting time," "decision-making responsibility," and "parental rights and responsibilities." The old words implied that one parent "won" control of the children and the other "lost." The new words remove the implication that one parent matters more than the other.

"Support" and "maintenance" have replaced "alimony," a word that conjures a man's lifelong obligation to support a woman, the price a man pays for ending a marriage, and a form of blood money sapping beleaguered men in favor of undeserving women. "Dissolution" sometimes replaces "divorce." "Divorce" can be a nasty affair, presuming one spouse at fault and stigmatizing the participants. "Dissolution" is a less value-laden and contentious word for ending a relationship. Residents of California, Oregon, and Missouri say they are "divorced" after they have been to court to end their marriages, but they have received a "Judgment of Dissolution of Marriage."

"Marriage" has a long history of exclusion; slaves, interracial couples, and same-sex couples have been denied it. "Marriage" has a long, sex-stereotyped past that is both unconstitutional and inconsistent with modern values. For many people, "marriage" is moored to religious doctrine that belongs in churches, synagogues, and mosques. The terminology of civil partnership distances this legal status from its past and from the components of marriage that religions define. The legal terms "husband" and "wife" should also change, making way for the gender-neutral terms "spouse" and "partner."

A valuing-all-families approach will alter marriage's legal consequences, something the law has done repeatedly over the centuries. In this instance, with the relationships included in a law dependent on that law's purpose, a law might encompass some marriages and not others. If a law is designed to recognize or facilitate childrearing, for example, a marriage without children would be excluded and any household raising children would be included. While divorcing couples now have one set of rules for the economic consequences of separation and unmarried couples who split up have another, laws might instead differentiate not based on marriage but based on whether the couple has raised a child or on some other criteria.

California's domestic partnership law, for example, which confers a status equal to that accorded spouses, allows dissolution of a domestic partnership by filing of a notice with the secretary of state, without having to go to court, if the couple meets certain criteria. These include that they have been registered for less than five years, have no children, own no real property, have relatively little money or other assets, and have signed a property settlement agreement. The scheme reflects the sound principle that not all marriages should trigger the same legal consequences.

Finally, with marriage neither necessary nor sufficient to access particular laws, marriage would be a real *choice.* While the movement for marriage equality has insisted it is fighting for same-sex couples to have the choice to marry, marriage is not a choice if it is the *only* way to achieve economic well-being and peace of mind.

Designated Family Relationships

In areas of the law that give people the right to make their own decisions, a statute must determine what happens if someone does not exercise his right. The most important legal matters in this category are who makes healthcare decisions for an incapacitated patient; who determines the disposition of a person's remains; and who inherits property.

Everyone can execute documents saying who should make medical decisions if he is incapacitated and what should happen with his remains. Everyone can write a will distributing his property. Most people don't. State laws then determine how to proceed, naming people with certain relationships to the patient or deceased. In general, a spouse tops the list, followed by children, parents, siblings, and more distant blood relatives (relatives by adoption were added only recently). In other words, the law assumes that the one family member a person has chosen—his spouse—is the one who should be preferred, but that otherwise family is not a matter of choice but of biology.

Since the purpose of laws in these areas is furthering autonomy, the theory for the priority is that the person would most likely want the result that the laws provide. After all, it is not feasible to hold a court hearing in every case and ask a judge to rule on whom a dead or incapacitated person would choose to make decisions on her behalf. But the current model fails those who choose important family relationships without marrying and would want such people, not biological relatives, to have rights and decision-making authority.

A simple way to implement the valuing-all-families approach is a registration system for those who lack a spouse/partner but wish to identify someone considered a family member. With such a system, a person listed as a patient's or deceased's "designated family" would be treated as a spouse is now treated under the relevant laws. The designated family member would have the authority to make healthcare and disposition-of-remains decisions unless the patient/deceased had indicated a different preference. If someone died without a will, his designated family member would receive the same share of his estate that a spouse would have received; that percentage varies by state law and generally depends on whether parents or children survive him.

The current state laws operating most closely to this proposed designated family relationship system are the Vermont category of "reciprocal beneficiaries" and the Maine and Washington domestic partner laws. The Vermont law is limited to relatives only; the Washington one to same-sex partners and different-sex partners over sixty-two who live together; the Maine one to same- and different-sex couples who have lived together for a year. The Vermont law does not include the right to inherit without a will, but since only relatives may register as reciprocal beneficiaries there, and relatives are already on the list of who inherits without a will, this was unnecessary in Vermont.

A designated family relationship registration system would not have the limits of those in these three states; it would be open to all unmarried/unpartnered people who wanted a chosen family relationship to be legally recognized. "Designated family relationship" is a better term than "reciprocal beneficiaries" because it concisely expresses exactly what the two people mean by registering—that they are family. It is a better term than "domestic partners" because, as the Maine and Washington laws demonstrate, the common usage of that term is for couples. Because the purpose of this registry is allowing anyone to designate a "next of kin," neither a couple relationship nor living in the same home are relevant requirements.

When the Law's Purpose Is Maximizing Autonomy

Anna Nicole Smith died unexpectedly at the age of thirty-nine. Four parties—her mother, from whom she had been estranged for more than ten years; the lawyer appointed to represent the interests of her five-month-old daughter; the man she lived with; and another man with whom she had an affair (both of whom claimed to be the daughter's father)—argued in court over several days about who should have the right to decide where to bury her. The trial judge gave the right to the child's lawyer. Two state laws authorized release of remains for burial to the legal next of kin eighteen or older, so Smith's mother appealed. The appeals court ruled that a person has the right to decide for herself where she wants to be buried. Smith had put nothing in writing, but the testimony was undisputed that Smith wanted to be buried next to her son in the Bahamas. The court ordered that result.[17]

The laws gave the right to Smith's mother, who had no real relationship with her and who wanted to bury her in Texas. The court had to do some creative interpretation to reach the result Smith would have wanted; in a routine case attracting less attention it might not have done so. Many partners and friends of gay, lesbian, bisexual, and transgender people have stories of being excluded from both disposition-of-remains decisions and their loved one's funerals by parents unsupportive of their child's sexual orientation or gender identity.

To maximize autonomy for unmarried people who have not designated a family relationship, the law should do two things. First, designating one's own wishes or the name of someone else to make the decision should be easier, more routine, and not require lawyers to draw up documents. Second, when someone does not put his wishes in writing, the rules should maximize the chance of doing what he would have wanted.

This requires including an unmarried partner on the default list. A New York law, enacted with strong support from gay health services groups, gives control to a domestic partner but does not require that the relationship be formally registered. It considers someone a domestic partner based on the circumstances of the relationship.[18]

Disposition-of-remains laws should also be harmonized with the best statutes on surrogate healthcare decision-making, because so much thought has gone into getting the result a patient would want. The best laws include "close friends" in the list of those who can serve as healthcare proxies, and they authorize a person lower on the list to receive decision-making authority if she can show that she had a close relationship with the person and was most likely to know her wishes. Such a law would have made clear that Anna Nicole Smith's estranged mother did not have the right to bury her. Ordinary unmarried people also need the tools to achieve the right result.

How a Law Changes When Its Purpose Changes

Nancy no longer lived with her husband, Joseph. Over the course of two days he struck her with his fists and threatened her at her place of work. She sought a protection order, but the Maryland Domestic Violence Act applied only to spouses living together when the acts occurred.[19]

A Delaware woman went to court to seek an order protecting her from her same-sex partner's violence. The judge told her to take her "funny relationship" out of his courtroom. The woman filed a misconduct complaint about the judge in which she stated: "I am a human being. I am a taxpaying citizen. I am a proud black American. I am a proud lesbian American, and I am a mother with a duty to teach my daughter values. I am not some alien from another planet with 'funny relationships.'"[20]

Laws dealing with intimate-partner violence show how reconsidering a law's purpose can expand beyond marriage those subject to the law. Every state has laws designed to protect victims in abusive relationships. These civil laws allow a victim to get a protection order and related remedies, such as exclusive use of a jointly owned home and temporary child custody.[21] They greatly enhance a victim's options, unlike criminal prosecution, which is at the prosecutor's discretion. And traditional civil remedies are not usually helpful because they give the victim the same status as any other injured person, they may require lengthy legal actions and a lawyer, and the only result available is money damages. These options are not tailored to the circumstances of a terrified abuse victim seeking immediate safety.

Each state's law identifies categories of relationships that allow someone to apply for a protection order. These categories have changed as the laws' purpose has changed. Early laws applied only to married couples living together because their purpose was to "reach and treat the roots of family discord" and save marriages.[22] When feminist activists and lawyers named the problem of violence against women in the late 1960s and 1970s,[23] they demanded that the state respond more forcefully and, among other things, they lobbied for more effective laws.[24]

Once the goal was stopping violence, not saving marriages or treating household problems, the laws were expanded. Advocates argued that family members covered by laws should reflect "all concepts of family as they exist in the reality of our diverse family relationships" and all intimate and dating relationships. Almost every state covers unmarried partners living together, including same-sex partners.[25]

The expansion of partner-violence laws demonstrates an evolving understanding of those laws' purpose. Marriage—sometimes restricted to married couples who were still living together—used to be the line between who was excluded and who was allowed access to these laws. Hence Nancy's experience. That is no longer the case *anywhere*. Other laws should be rewritten to change the categories of included relationships based on their contemporary purpose.

Three Key Principles for Valuing All Families

Three principles should play a role in determining dividing lines other than marriage. They are: (1) place the needs of children and their caretakers above the claims of able-bodied adult spouses/partners; (2) support the needs of children in all family constellations; and (3) recognize adult interdependency.

Place the Needs of Children First

Pfc. Hannah McKinney married just before deploying to Iraq. She entrusted her two-year-old son from an earlier relationship to her parents. Hannah died in Iraq, and the military paid a $100,000 death benefit to her husband, not to her parents, who will raise her son.[26] When a service member has a spouse and dies on duty, the government pays $100,000 to the spouse. When the service member has a child from a previous relationship, and that child is not being raised by the widow or widower, the child gets none of this benefit.

This rule may be based on the assumption that a service member's children will be *with* his or her surviving spouse, so that by paying the spouse, the military is providing for the children. This assumption might have been valid in 1908, when Congress created the benefit and it went to surviving wives. Divorce was rare. If a man had a child outside of marriage, he had no obligation to support her.

Today, many married service members have children who are not the child of their current spouse. That child may be in the custody of a former spouse or unmarried partner, a grandparent, or another relative. Determining who should get the money depends on the benefit's purpose. If it's to support dependents, the money should go *first* to the ones who have no choice but to be dependent: minor children. If such children exist, it's possible that none of the funds should go to a widow or widower who is not caring for the service member's children.

In a *Washington Post* story on this topic, a military spokesman justified the rule as easy to apply.[27] In the "vast majority" of instances, he said, the spouse has the greatest need when the service member's paychecks stop. The rule allows the military to distribute the benefit quickly, protecting the spouse from immediate financial distress. In other words, this rule places speed and efficiency above other values.

Soon after the article was published, legislation was introduced in Congress to "fix" the problem. Unfortunately, it does not address the purpose of this death benefit and identify beneficiaries based on that purpose. It proposes that if there is a spouse, the benefit goes to the spouse, even if there were no children of that marriage. Even if the marriage lasted only weeks. Even if the surviving spouse is self-supporting.

Only if there is no spouse does the benefit go to the service member's parent or sibling who is caring for the service member's child. If someone else is caring for the child, that person cannot get the benefit at all; it will be held until the child reaches adulthood and then given to the child, ignoring the fact that money is needed to raise the child. The solution that addresses the needs of children would give the benefit to anyone raising the child.

The law places spouses above children in other areas as well. Laws about wills exist to protect someone's freedom to distribute his estate as he wishes, with one exception: a married person cannot completely disinherit his spouse. But a parent can, in almost every state, disinherit minor children; if someone dies and leaves a minor child, the law doesn't require any assets to go to the child. The law does require that some assets go to the surviving spouse, so if the spouse is caring for the child, presumably those resources will help support the child. But if the child is in someone else's care (for example, with the parent's former spouse or former unmarried partner), the child may end up with none of the parent's assets. The law restricts the rights of the person who died to the benefit of the spouse but ignores the child's needs.

These schemes reflect family life in the past. When there was no divorce and no obligation to children born outside marriage, legislators could assume that minor children would be with the surviving spouse. Children did not need support for as long as they do now; they started working at a young age and became economic assets to the family. The legal disabilities of wives, on the other hand, justified economic protection for them.

This system has a certain logic, but it's wrong for today's families. It's time to revisit laws such as these. Laws that confer financial benefits on spouses by virtue of marriage alone and disregard children and their caretakers must be reexamined.

Support Children in All Family Forms

Some laws directly address the needs of children, but only if they live in certain family structures. The proposal to amend the military death benefit is one; it would direct funds to the custodian of the deceased service member's child, but only if that custodian was the service member's parent or sibling.

The tax code's definition of a dependent child is similarly flawed. Consider its application to the Earned Income Tax Credit (EITC), which is the mechanism through which the tax code supports children in low-income families. The program is widely heralded; antipoverty proposals routinely advocate increasing the ceiling on the income a worker can earn without losing its benefits. A worker who has no children must have an income close to the poverty level to get any benefit. The bulk of the money distributed through this program goes to low-income workers with children. A taxpayer living with and providing financial support to another adult—spouse, unmarried partner, friend, parent—cannot claim that person to receive the credit. This is appropriate for a program whose primary purpose is addressing the needs of poor children.

Despite this program's importance in reducing child poverty, a taxpayer can only claim the credit for a "qualifying" child. To qualify, the child must have a specific relationship to the taxpayer. The definition includes children, stepchildren, and children placed through foster care or court order; whole, half, and stepsiblings; and the descendants of any of these (grandchildren, nieces, nephews, etc.). A taxpayer living with an unmarried partner—same-sex or different-sex—and supporting that partner's children cannot claim the children to receive the credit. If two single parents live together and pool financial and childcare resources (for example, one parent earns the income and the other cares for the children), the income-earning parent cannot claim the EITC for all the children. A taxpayer also cannot claim a godchild or more distant kin.

The distinction in the law is not based on a taxpayer's legal obligation, as she has no legal obligation to grandchildren, siblings, nieces, or, generally, stepchildren. It draws a line beyond marriage but short of supporting the needs of children whatever their family structure. This should change.

For purposes of the Family and Medical Leave Act, the federal law that requires employers to extend twelve weeks of unpaid leave to employees for the care of seriously ill family members, coverage is extended to the "child of a person standing *in loco parentis.*" The regulations define such a person as one who has "day-to-day responsibilities to care for and financially support a child. . . . A biological or legal relationship is not necessary."[28] That definition should apply to the EITC and other laws designed to provide for dependent children.

Acknowledge Adult Relationships and Interdependency

Adults build relationships for purposes other than childrearing. Whether married or unmarried, sexual or platonic, connected through biology, adoption, extended family, or choice, adults create relationships that contribute to their health, happiness, well-being, identity, and security. A society that cares about the welfare of its people will make laws that value and support those relationships. Laws must also justly address the consequences of these relationships when they end through death or dissolution.

Bella and Fran had lived together for more than eleven years when they lost their apartment and became homeless. Bella was on dialysis and Fran had recently had brain surgery. At the homeless shelter in the Bronx they were treated as two single women. When they went to the Adult Family Intake Center in Manhattan, the shelter for couples, they were told they needed to register as domestic partners with the city to be housed together. They also needed to bring proof of jointly paid bills and other documentation of how long they had lived together. They sat in the waiting area for two days, and when they hadn't produced the documentation they were sent back to the Bronx shelter.[29]

Bella and Fran have a life together. Their relationship is as valuable as that of a married couple. They lost their home. They should be able to hang on to each other. If the city can accommodate married couples together, it should meet the needs of other adult interdependent relationships.

Queers for Economic Justice, a New York progressive organization focused on the needs of poor LGBT people, organized for two years to reduce the likelihood that couples like Bella and Fran would be separated while homeless. Their advocacy focused on maximizing the possibility that anyone entering the homeless shelter system would be housed with the person they live with or rely on. Couples with domestic partner certificates no longer need additional proof of the length of their relationship. Couples referred from the street by an outreach worker don't need domestic partnership certificates at all. Any two adults will be housed together if one is medically dependent on the other. Homeless adult relatives who lived together for six of the last twelve months will also be housed together. In addition, the manager of the Adult Family Intake Center has the discretion under extraordinary circumstances to house together any two people who have lived together for six months.[30]

Maria also faced a battle with New York City when she wanted her elderly father added to her Section 8 subsidized household. Had she married, living with her husband in a one-bedroom apartment would have been acceptable; living with her father was deemed "overcrowding." Maria successfully challenged the termination of her Section 8 subsidy, but only by appearing at hearings on four different dates spread over a year.[31]

Government regulations and benefit programs that single out spouses for special treatment need to be reassessed according to their contemporary purposes and in light of current demographics. Law professor Frank Alexander has documented the shifting definitions of "overcrowding" that have been used to regulate who can live together, especially in immigrant communities.[32] He says that housing laws should not be used "to define the relationships that count."

Financial benefits that spouses but no other adult relationships receive also need to be reassessed according to their contemporary purpose. For example, a woman may receive Social Security retirement benefits based entirely on her husband's earnings regardless of whether she raised a child with him *and if she was married to him for only a year before he retired.* The provision is essentially unchanged since the program began in 1939, although the composition of families and of the workforce has changed dramatically since then.

Considering this program's purpose today requires deciding why we pay a benefit to spouses of retired workers. If it flows from an appreciation of *derivative dependency*—the assumption that the spouse has earned less because she cared for *inevitable dependents,* namely children—then it should not go to spouses who have not raised children. And it should go to a family unit that has raised children—an unmarried couple, same-sex or different-sex, or a nonconjugal pair such as a mother and her mother. If instead it is recognition of the economic interdependency of two adults, then it should go to those whose lives are economically interdependent. Marriage, again, is not the right dividing line.

A Valuing-All-Families Victory Is an LGBT Victory

The valuing-all-families approach is not specific to lesbian and gay families. But any move toward valuing all families will benefit the full range of LGBT families and relationships.

After the September 11, 2001, attacks, Congress passed a law benefiting same-sex partners, but not in the name of gay rights.[33] The Mychal Judge Act, named after the openly gay New York City fire department chaplain who died inside the World Trade Center, ensures that the federal government will recognize every public safety officer killed in the line of duty by conferring a $250,000 death benefit.

The previous law gave this benefit to a surviving spouse, minor or otherwise dependent child, or parent. Had the law's purpose been compensation for a deceased officer's dependents, then bypassing officers without dependents would have been appropriate. But Judge and nine other public safety officers died that day without qualified survivors, and Congress wanted to honor them. Judge was singled out because he was the first confirmed death, because the media filmed his body's removal from the wreckage, because he was much loved in the fire department, and because of the poignancy of his death while administering last rites to others.

The new law splits payment between a surviving spouse and minor/dependent child if there are both, and awards it to a spouse or children if there are not. If there are neither minor children nor a spouse, the payment goes to whomever the officer designated. Judge had designated his two sisters to receive his life insurance proceeds, and they received the benefit.

So the Mychal Judge Act was good for lesbian and gay families and other families. It was not a public affirmation of same-sex relationships. The only "face" on the proposed legislation was that of a celibate priest whose sexual orientation was then unacknowledged in all but the gay media. If the rhetoric accompanying the measure is the standard, it was not a gay rights victory.

But if advocates want LGBT people to have their families' financial well-being protected, then it was a great victory. Judge named his *two* sisters as beneficiaries. A gay or lesbian police officer or firefighter could name his partner as his sole beneficiary. A heterosexual officer could name his partner as well; unlike many gay-specific laws, this one does not require that a heterosexual couple marry to get the benefits. Someone who defines family more broadly, through communal living not based on sexual affiliation, through a polyamorous relationship, or through a network of interdependent friends who do not live together, can divide the benefit as he wishes. The law does not prefer marriage-like, same-sex couples over other family arrangements. It also allows an officer to name the grandmother who raised him, the uncle who paid for his education, the close friend with whom he pooled resources to buy a home they shared, or the "godchild" he helped support (whether that is the child of his sister or his best friend from college, or the son of the lesbian couple who asked him to be a male role model).

Legislators and policymakers increasingly respond to pressure to recognize gay and lesbian couples with proposals that recognize a range of relationships. Thus they avoid appearing to validate LGBT relationships. This occurred in Salt Lake City's efforts to provide its employees with domestic partner benefits.

Gay rights advocates should take advantage of a political climate open to such proposals. A victory for diverse family forms, as the Mychal Judge Act shows, protects more LGBT people because it includes a wider variety of LGBT relationships. When the law includes *unmarried* heterosexual couples, as this one does, it's a total win. It's not a consolation prize for those "rightly" excluded from marriage; it's a law that bypasses marriage entirely and therefore better serves its purpose.

In places where the political climate welcomes gay rights claims, advocates should not limit themselves to reforms that benefit only marriage-like couples. Many marriage-equality advocates focus on achieving for same-sex couples what the law gives married couples.

Although understandable as a civil rights approach, this fails to address the needs of the full range of LGBT relationships and families. If all families were valued in the law, the harms same-sex couples say come from their inability to marry—and the harms many other families endure—would be alleviated.

CHAPTER EIGHT

Domestic Partner Benefits for All Families

As an employee of the state of Maryland, Jo cannot enroll her partner, Takia, or Takia's children, in the state health plan. Until recently, Takia was working part-time, and so she and the children were forced to go without insurance. During that time the couple struggled to afford medical care for their son's asthma. Now that Takia is a full-time employee, she and her children are covered, but the insurance is inferior to the coverage Jo receives from the state.[1]

In 1999, Vega left her job to move with Mala to Olympia, Washington. She was uninsured during the five months that she was unemployed, and she could not be insured through Mala because they were not married.[2]

Marriage is not the solution to the problem these couples describe. The solution is universal access to healthcare. All of the 45 million uninsured people in the United States[3]—lesbian, gay, bisexual, transgender, and heterosexual—should have healthcare. The number of uninsured and the cost of healthcare and health insurance premiums have skyrocketed in the past fifteen years. Medical expenses trigger more than half of all personal bankruptcies. A job lucrative enough to provide health insurance, or partnership/marriage to someone with such a job, should not be a prerequisite to obtaining health care.

In the absence of a national healthcare program in the United States, however, access for all but the very poor, who are covered by Medicaid, and those over sixty-five, who are covered by Medicare, depends primarily on benefits provided to employees and their families. Today, 80 percent of people who are not elderly and who have health insurance receive that coverage through their job or through the job of a family member.[4] Defining what family members should be eligible requires assessing the purpose of this type of program.

The Job-Insurance Connection

Coming out of the Depression, during World War II, government imposed wage and price controls to avoid inflation. Pressure from unions to raise workers' standard of living resulted in government rulings that allowed employers to offer employee benefits instead of wage increases, along with favorable tax treatment of such benefits.[5]

After World War II, employee health and welfare benefits increased. European countries developed policies to serve the health needs of all. The United States instead fostered a system connected to employment and amended federal tax laws to subsidize the practice. This favorable tax treatment remains today; an employer can deduct the costs of benefits from its taxable earnings, and the value of the benefits, unlike wages, is not taxable to employees. (For the moment this is *not* true of benefits to unmarried partners.)

Like that of many laws and policies that distinguish between married couples and everyone else, the history of benefits as part of a compensation package includes assumptions that date back to the sex-specific roles of women and men. The "family wage" concept, developed in the nineteenth century, assumed that a man needed to earn enough money to support himself, his wife, and his children. A working woman was assumed to have either another source of income—her father or husband—or no dependents or both. This justified paying women less than men for doing the same job. Consistent with the concept of the family wage, when benefits became a part of employee compensation, employers took into account a worker's responsibility to support his wife and children. Women, presumed not to have such needs, did not receive equal benefits.[6]

The expansion of healthcare benefits after World War II coincided with new family characteristics that made the 1950s unique, including a decrease in the age at which people married and an increase in the birth rate.[7] In 1950 only 23 percent of married women were in the paid labor force.[8] The 1950 census, for the first time, counted families related by blood, marriage, and adoption, rather than households consisting of all those who lived as a single housekeeping unit. The term "nuclear family" entered common usage in 1949.[9] Employee benefits covering spouses and children reflected the demographics of families.

The 1963 Equal Pay Act required equal pay, including equal benefits, for men and women doing the same jobs. Wage stagnation has eliminated the family wage, and 71 percent of married mothers with children under fifteen are in the labor force.[10] Still, employers with generous compensation packages provide health insurance not only for employees but for their spouses and children as well. This singles out married couples for a benefit that, until recently, was unavailable to other family members who might rely on the employee for support.

Employee benefits are designed to attract and retain good employees, improve worker productivity, display a corporate image that might generate interest in a company's goods or services, and manifest an employer's values. Permitting an employee to cover family members serves these purposes as well. The definition of family members eligible for coverage when health insurance benefits were instituted after World War II reflected the composition of American families. While the census did not count the number of unmarried couples living together until 1990, there were an estimated sixty-four thousand such couples in 1960.[11] At that time, their sexual relations violated criminal laws and their children were legally bastards.

The purpose of such programs today is best fulfilled by adjusting eligibility to reflect today's families. Hiring, retention, and worker productivity depend on responding to employees' real needs. Those needs have changed as the way people organize their families has changed. There were 3.2 million cohabiting couples in 1990, 5.5 million in 2000, and 6 million in 2005.[12] The number of children in these households almost doubled between 1990 and 2000. Unmarried couples are almost as likely as married couples to have minor children in their homes. The Constitution mandates equal legal treatment of those children.

Employers adjusting benefits to today's demographics should cover these families. Marriage should not be required. A person with an unmarried partner of either sex is twice as likely as a married person to lack health insurance. For married couples, coverage as a dependent is almost as important a predictor of having health insurance as coverage through one's own full-time job. Thirty-six percent of married people are insured through a spouse's employer-based coverage; less than 5 percent of those with unmarried partners have such coverage.[13]

Employers will always consider the expense of any benefits program.[14] The principles of the valuing-all-families approach point to appropriate priorities when funds are limited. Employers should extend benefits *first* to employees' minor children, who are inevitable dependents and have no way to provide for their own needs. Government targets children first when it allocates scarce funds to healthcare, and the private sector should do the same.[15]

Employers should extend healthcare benefits to any child an employee supports in her home, regardless of legal relationship. Employees may raise stepchildren, grandchildren, siblings, or the children of their unmarried same- and different-sex partners. The fact that employees are not these children's legal parents is immaterial to the goals of establishing a program that will attract and retain workers and increase their productivity by relieving them of concerns about their family members' health needs. As with an adult partner, the condition of *actually supporting* a family justifies the benefit.

As discussed in the previous chapter, the federal Family and Medical Leave Act uses the term "in loco parentis," defining someone who stands in loco parentis to a child as a person who has "day-to-day responsibilities to care for and financially support" that child. The regulations state clearly that "a biological or legal relationship is not necessary."[16] Employers must provide FMLA leave to employees considered in loco parentis to children who are ill. They should have no difficulty using this definition to determine which children are eligible for coverage on an employee's health insurance policy. If an employer has enough funds to provide healthcare benefits to another adult, the criteria should be dependence or interdependence.

Toward Domestic Partnership Benefits

Gay rights activists in the early 1980s spearheaded efforts to extend employee health insurance benefits beyond spouses. By then, the legal significance of marriage had been transformed. More straight couples were living together, giving gay activists allies in demanding that marriage cease to be required for coverage as an employee's family member. They urged employers to recognize their employees' "domestic partners."

Three definitions of domestic partner emerged in that concept's first decade. The earliest policies covered unmarried partners, both same- and different sex; this recognized that marriage had become more optional and that an unmarried couple was a family. A handful of policies later used a wider definition of relationships beyond conjugal couples, such as the District of Columbia's term, "committed, familial relationship." In 1991, some employers began covering same-sex partners only in their domestic partner policies. This was not a rejection of marriage as a measure of who was a family member but rather an adjustment for the unavailability of marriage for same-sex couples. Same-sex-only domestic partnership policies demonstrated an employer's commitment to equal treatment of its gay and lesbian employees.

The movement for domestic partner health insurance benefits has had considerable success; the number of public and private employers with such policies has mushroomed to over 9,000. This includes 13 states, 144 cities and counties, 299 colleges and universities, and more than half of the Fortune 500 companies.

State courts and legislatures cannot require private employers to provide domestic partner benefits. Federal law governs private employer pension and benefits plans, and, because it does not mandate inclusion of domestic partners, employers are free to decide for themselves. Unions and other employee groups, through collective bargaining or other negotiations, have played a major role in securing domestic partner coverage.

Gay rights lawyers and activists have sought and achieved domestic partner public employee benefits for same-sex couples. Lawsuits against Alaska in 2005, Montana in 2004, New Hampshire in 2006, and Oregon in 1998 were successful on the theory that extending public employee benefits only to spouses was discrimination on the basis of sexual orientation because same-sex couples could not marry.[17] Advocates in San Francisco in 1996, furious at state and federal "defense of marriage" acts, lobbied for and won an "equal benefits ordinance" that requires contractors with the city to treat their employees' spouses and same-sex partners alike. This served as a model for other cities.

These are civil rights victories for gay men and lesbians, but they are not good family law. They leave such a scheme vulnerable to elimination when a state grants a legal status—marriage, civil union, or domestic partnership—to same-sex couples. Some employers in Massachusetts and Vermont did precisely that after marriage and civil unions, respectively, were enacted in those states. California adopted an "equal benefits" law for all state contractors, but the equality it requires is between spouses and registered domestic partners. Employers can still discriminate against the families of unmarried and unregistered employees.

A better approach, the one that values all families, would not make this distinction. An employer should not protect only the partners of employees whose relationships have been granted formal status by a state. The principles behind making marriage matter less that animated early domestic partnership policies still apply. Given the vast increase in couples living together without marrying, in the context of a legal system that has made getting married and staying married more optional, there is no basis for requiring marriage or its same-sex analogue for someone to count as a family member.

What's more, a public or private employer with two different pathways for its employees to get family health benefits risks excluding the families of transgender employees. For example, if a state does not allow a female-to-male transsexual to marry a woman, or the couple doesn't want to be the test case to find out if this is possible, the couple would have to request domestic partner benefits as a same-sex couple. Employee "John" would then have to explain why his partner "Anne" is a *same-sex* partner. This would require coming out as a transgender person and risking discrimination on that basis. Neither Alaska, New Hampshire, nor Montana—all sites of recent court victories for same-sex-only domestic partner benefits—bans employment discrimination on the basis of gender identity.[18]

Every same-sex-only domestic partner policy could put couples with one transgender partner in this bind. When the first same-sex-only policies appeared in 1991, gay rights groups paid much less attention to transgender people's needs. Now transgender equality is part of their mission—another reason to seek more inclusive policies.

Eligibility also should not be limited to "couples." A lesbian and gay man can decide to raise a child together in one home. Two lesbian mothers can commit to being a family unit based on caring but not romance. A gay man with no partner or children may be the one among his adult siblings best situated to move in with, support, and care for an aging parent or grandparent. A benefits program that values the families of all its employees will not exclude these families.

Some employers already recognize a wide range of employees' families. For example, Nationwide Insurance began offering "household member" benefits in 1999. Anyone who has lived with the employee for six months is eligible. A company spokesman said that the company wanted employees to determine who their own family members were.[19] Prudential allows an employee to cover either a same- or different-sex domestic partner or an extended family member for whom the employee provides more than 50 percent financial support. Both categories must have lived with the employee for six months. Although the policy includes a list of relatives, the definition of "extended family member" also includes anyone who is a member of the employee's household.

Motives and Results

In a political climate filled with "defense of marriage" acts and marriage-movement rhetoric, the controversy over eligibility for domestic partner coverage has taken on a novel anti-gay-rights dimension. Some public and private employers are offering broad eligibility criteria, not because they value all families but because they do not want to provide a benefit specifically to gay couples. Pressured by market forces to reach beyond spousal coverage, but adamant about avoiding the appearance of condoning homosexuality or even unmarried heterosexual partners, they select broad language precisely so that gay rights advocates cannot claim a civil rights victory.

Gay and lesbian organizations have responded lukewarmly to these developments. Even when a policy will cover same-sex couples —as well as any LGBT person whose primary relationship is not with a conjugal partner—advocates seeking affirmation of gay and lesbian relationships are reluctant to embrace an approach couched solely in terms of family diversity and inclusivity.

This is a mistake. Litigation to allow same-sex couples to marry highlights the harms couples experience because the law fails to protect their relationships. When evaluating a change in the legal treatment of families, a law or policy that eliminates those harms should be applauded, as long as it does not *deprive* others of the same opportunities. If an employee benefits policy eliminates the harms other unmarried family units suffer, that is a great result, one that helps an even larger group of gay men and lesbians because it extends recognition to nonconjugal relationships. If the political and legal climate accommodates lesbian and gay families' needs as part of embracing other family forms, advocates should seize that opportunity. Once a truly expansive policy is in place, gay rights groups can claim the policy as a victory regardless of the intent of those who enacted it.

Questionable Motives: The Salt Lake City Example

Motives for expanding employees' family benefits clashed in Salt Lake City in 2005. In July, the county council rejected a proposal that would have granted health insurance benefits to county employees' domestic partners.[20] Later that year, the city's mayor signed an executive order that did exactly that for *city* employees. It defined "domestic partner" as "an individual with whom an eligible employee has a long-term committed relationship of mutual caring and support." The requirements were sharing a household for six months, common financial obligations, and joint responsibility for each other's welfare. As with all definitions of domestic partner that apply only to those in a "marriage-like" relationship, it excluded those related to the employee to a degree that would prohibit marriage (for example, a brother and sister). A domestic partner's children could also be covered.[21]

Mayor Ross Anderson said that discrimination on the basis of marital status and sexual orientation harmed the city's "general welfare," that domestic partner benefits could help the city hire and keep good workers, and that such benefits are "one of the hallmarks of a progressive employer that values diversity."[22]

A few months later, the Salt Lake City Council passed an ordinance allowing employees to identify an "adult designee" who would be entitled to health insurance benefits. The requirements were: living with the employee for more than a year with an intent to continue living together; being at least eighteen years old; and being economically dependent or interdependent. Benefits extended to children of the adult designee. While an employee's same-sex or different-sex partner could qualify, this definition was broad enough to encompass any family unit.[23]

Anderson vetoed the ordinance even though it provided the same benefits to gay and lesbian employees and their partners that his executive order did. He asserted his goal was equality among employees regardless of sexual orientation or marital status, and that he aimed to provide parity between married employees and those with "spousal-like" relationships. Anderson said extending benefits to others was unjustified and designed solely to avoid "marital status equality, especially as it concerns gay and lesbian employees."[24]

The council overrode the mayor's veto. One member noted that single employees had been subsidizing the insurance pool and that the ordinance recognized nontraditional families and support systems. Another noted that everyone pays when people lack health insurance. One councilmember said that the council's approach allowed single employees to provide for a primary family member and that true equality recognized the needs and living situations of all employees. While not gay-specific, these comments were not antigay, nor were gay and lesbian families excluded from the ordinance's benefits.[25]

The council's action not only protected more families, it also insulated the program from legal challenge. The antigay Alliance Defense Fund had challenged the mayor's order as a violation of the state's statutes and constitution. Like many states, Utah has a Defense of Marriage Act that prohibits laws creating rights or benefits "substantially equivalent" to those provided a married man and woman. It also has a constitutional amendment defining marriage as between a man and a woman and prohibiting any other "domestic union" from receiving "substantially the same legal effect." The lawsuit became moot once the city council's "adult designee" law superseded the mayor's "domestic partner" program.

Utah's antigay groups did bring a new lawsuit on the same grounds against the council's benefits law, which failed. The judge noted that "single employees may have relationships outside of marriage, whether motivated by family feeling, emotional attachment or practical considerations, which draw on their resources to provide the necessaries of life, including health care."[26] In other words, the judge described a valuing-all-families rationale.

While no LGBT group in Utah opposed the council's program, the city's gay and lesbian employee association said it would have preferred the domestic partner plan. Mike Thompson, director of Equality Utah, commended the council's work as progress and said that the more residents receiving healthcare the better. Still, no gay rights advocates were present at the city council votes. This contrasted with the ten gay rights advocates who had appeared with Mayor Anderson when he signed the domestic partner executive order.

In 2007, Jenny Wilson, the Salt Lake County councilwoman who failed to get domestic partner benefits for county employees two years earlier, spearheaded an effort to cover "adult designees," borrowing from the Salt Lake City program. The Republican who cast the deciding vote against the plan in 2005 said he would support it because it was about "fair health care" and didn't define a "new legally protected class of people."[27] Thompson supported the measure, saying he hoped such a "progressive decision" would shift the way people think about the state of Utah.

Questionable Motives, Less Inclusive Policies

The Salt Lake City policy should shift the way people think about employee benefits (although its one-year-minimum cohabiting requirement is too long). Other, less inclusive, policies fall short. Georgetown University, a Jesuit institution, came late to the trend among colleges to extend domestic partner benefits, no doubt because of conflicts with Church doctrine on homosexuality and sex outside marriage. In 2006 it extended coverage to an employee's "legally domiciled adult"—a person in an interdependent "close personal relationship" living with the employee. This resembles the Salt Lake City model, but it fails to cover a legally domiciled adult's children.

In 2006 Colorado considered extending benefits to "reciprocal beneficiaries." This term was created in Hawaii in 1997, after the constitutional amendment that allowed the legislature to prohibit same-sex marriage passed. To be eligible for registration as reciprocal beneficiaries, the two people must be barred from marrying. In other words, the status is for same-sex couples and those whose familial relationship precludes marriage, such as a brother and sister or a grandmother and grandson.

The Colorado bill's Republican sponsor said that the legislation would help same-sex couples without treating them as the legal or moral equivalent of married couples.[28] To the surprise of many conservative groups, Focus on the Family endorsed this legislation as about "need" rather than sexual relationships; its chairman James Dobson mentioned elderly siblings living together or a parent caring for a child.[29] Most right-wing groups opposed the bill.

This proposal did not cover a reciprocal beneficiary's children. It was also different because it excluded unmarried different-sex couples. Legislation the marriage movement supports will always exclude different-sex partners, because the movement's ideology insists that a man and a woman marry, thus preserving the "special" status of marriage. Antigay organizations will always oppose exclusive coverage for same-sex couples, but some will support a proposal such as the one in Colorado.

What's a Gay Rights Group to Do?

Although gay rights groups would be smart to embrace the Salt Lake City model, the Colorado proposal is more problematic. It neither values all families nor champions gay rights. This presents a dilemma.

Opposing inclusion of family members barred from marriage in order to achieve a "pure" gay civil rights win separates the needs of same-sex couples from the needs of extended-family relationships. Asking employers to address the health needs of fewer people than they are willing to protect disrespects the needs of others who suffer from the "special rights" given married couples. On the other hand, it is hard to be enthusiastic about the Colorado approach when its supporters make dismissive or derogatory comments about same-sex couples. A policy that covers fewer employees—only those in same-sex couples—is at least a gay rights victory.

Looking solely at the substance of the Colorado proposal, its core problem is identical to that which any policy that excludes different-sex couples poses: it preserves the "specialness" of marriage. It is bad family policy, because it coerces couples to marry, reversing the gains that have made marriage matter less. And it leaves couples with one transgender partner vulnerable.

If it seems politically difficult to argue for benefits for unmarried different-sex couples, LGBT advocates need to recognize that conservative marriage-movement rhetoric created this political climate. The movement's adherents make bogus claims that those who do not marry, especially if they have children, are responsible for every conceivable social problem, neglecting to hold government accountable for actions and inactions that are responsible for childhood poverty, education failure, and other deplorable social and economic circumstances.

Sean Cahill, former director of the NGLTF Policy Institute, has shown how marriage-movement efforts to control both heterosexuality and homosexuality are two sides of the same coin.[30] Given the drawbacks of embracing a policy that excludes unmarried different-sex couples, gay rights advocates should go this route only as a last resort. This means they should seek out allies who will argue for the healthcare needs of unmarried couples. It was the norm in the 1980s to work in coalition with such groups in the name of family diversity, and this is still the best approach. Once formed, such a coalition may realize that it should strive for coverage of relationships outside the conjugal model—the Salt Lake City approach.

Looking Ahead in Congress

As part of a tax code that singles out marriage for a special status, employee benefits to those who are not spouses are not tax deductible to the employer, and the employee must pay taxes on them (unless the recipient is a "tax dependent" of the employee, something few domestic partners would qualify for). Some states exempt partner benefits from tax, but only Congress can change the law for the purpose of federal taxation.

Congress gave these tax breaks sixty years ago to encourage employers to provide these benefits. The family has changed since then, and the tax rules should change as well. Congress should pass the pending "Domestic Partner Tax Equity for Health Plan Beneficiaries Act," which will extend the benefits that now only spouses receive to anyone covered by an employer's health benefits.[31] This would support advocacy for the most inclusive possible definition of whose health an employee can protect.

Today, access to healthcare is on the national political agenda. In the 1960s, President Lyndon Johnson and a Democratic Congress established the Medicare and Medicaid programs to ensure that older people and very poor people would have healthcare. Healthcare costs increased dramatically as did the number of Americans without health insurance coverage. The AIDS crisis in the 1980s turned the attention of gay activists to many aspects of the U.S. healthcare system. In 1993, President Bill Clinton tried to achieve widespread healthcare reform, but that effort failed.

If a plan for access to healthcare emerges in the coming years that favors employment-based coverage for workers and their families, gay rights organizations can work with others to protect the widest possible range of families. If any politicians propose an individual-based system like Medicare or the Canadian or European models, gay rights groups should urge its adoption. A plan for *everyone* is a plan for all LGBT people.

CHAPTER NINE

Coping with Illness

Medical Care and Family and Medical Leave

When Robert was transferred by helicopter from a community hospital to a shock trauma center in Baltimore with severe complications of AIDS, medical staff said that his partner, Bill, was not a family member and thus could not see Robert, learn anything about his condition, or speak to his doctors. Bill and Robert were registered domestic partners who lived in San Francisco; they were traveling through Maryland en route to visit Robert's sister. Bill had Robert's healthcare power of attorney, which had been placed in Robert's medical record at the community hospital. Bill knew Robert's end-of-life wishes, including that Robert did not want to be placed on a respirator. Bill watched, distraught, as families of other patients were permitted to visit their loved ones. The hospital excluded Bill until Robert's sister and mother arrived four hours later. The hospital gave *them* information about Robert's status and allowed all three to see Robert, but by then medical staff had inserted a breathing tube and Robert was unconscious. He died two days later.[1]

After nine years in a committed relationship, Julie and Hillary planned to have a child together. Julie had complications resulting in a difficult cesarean section, and after the birth, their daughter was placed in neonatal intensive care. Hillary was not allowed to see either Julie or their daughter; hospital staff said she was not immediate family. She was allowed in after she lied and said she was Julie's sister. Julie and Hillary had adopted the same surname, Goodridge, so that they could claim to be sisters in an emergency.[2]

Janet and Carol have been a committed couple for more than thirty years. Janet has had frequent hospitalizations. After Carol waited during an eight-hour surgery to remove Janet's life-threatening liver tumors, she was not allowed to visit Janet in intensive care because she wasn't immediate family. When she explained that she was Janet's partner, the attending nurse said she didn't know what that meant. During another hospitalization, Janet was not allowed to identify Carol as her next of kin.[3]

Karen was planning to give birth at the only hospital in her county that offered birthing services. The hospital informed her that Edward, the baby's father, would not be allowed in the delivery room because she and Edward were not married, although they lived together with Karen's child from a former marriage. Hospital policy allowed only a spouse or member of the mother's immediate family to be present during delivery. Karen and Edward sued the hospital. The trial court ruled against them. On appeal, the court found that this was discrimination in public services on the basis of marital status, in violation of the state's civil rights law.[4]

Who Makes Decisions and Who Visits?

The concern that LGBT couples suing for the right to marry voice most often is that one partner will be denied access to the other in the hospital or during a medical emergency, and denied the right to make healthcare decisions on a partner's behalf. Couples pay lawyers to draw up documents that they hope hospitals will honor, and yet they fear that such measures will not be enough. The examples above show that these concerns are well founded.

The couples state that only marriage will quell their fears. Lambda Legal opined that Bill and Robert "paid a terrible price for [marriage] discrimination."[5] The Human Rights Campaign used the issue to make a video ad for marriage equality. But the problem isn't lack of marriage; Karen and Edward could have married. And marriage is not the solution, because it will be ineffective until every state to which a couple travels recognizes their marriage. Better solutions are attainable more quickly.

The law gives every adult the autonomy to make healthcare decisions and to delegate that authority to another person through a document such as a healthcare power of attorney. The problem is that the law is not uniformly well implemented. The solution is better implementation, including a national advance-directive registry. New laws are needed that allow patients to decide who may visit them in the hospital. Laws governing healthcare decision-making must be reformed, using as models laws already in effect in some states, to meet the needs of all families and relationships, including LGBT people who do not have partners.

Lawyers serving LGBT people should hesitate before using Julie and Hillary, Robert and Bill, and the other couples mentioned here, as evidence supporting a focus on the legalization of same-sex marriage. The law should facilitate autonomy for married and unmarried people alike in matters of hospital visitation and medical decision-making. Reforms ensuring that hospitals follow patients' instructions with regard to visitation, and the implementation of a nationwide advance-directive registry to cover those who enter hospitals in emergency situations, would help all persons, married and unmarried, LGBT and straight—and such reforms could be accomplished relatively quickly.

For the foreseeable future, marriage for same-sex couples, when it is enacted, will be a civil rights triumph, but it will *not* achieve the peace of mind that all LGBT families crave. Because of federal and state laws "defending" marriage, most states will not give married/partnered same-sex couples the rights they have in their own states. Even if a couple is able to marry where they live, if they leave the state they will be no better off than they are now.

Because patient autonomy is universally understood as the proper purpose of any policy in this area, gay rights advocates would find many allies in reform efforts.

Making It Easier to Name a Surrogate Medical Decision-Maker

A patient has the right to make her own decisions about medical treatment. The federal law also requires hospitals to tell patients that they have the right to name someone to make these decisions if they become unable to do so.[6] That person is called a healthcare agent, proxy, or surrogate. The document's name varies from state to state, but common names include healthcare power of attorney, durable power of attorney, and advance directive.

A few states, including Arizona, Idaho, Maryland, North Carolina, and Vermont, have advance directive registries. A person can register both her choice of healthcare proxy if she is incapacitated and her desires about end-of-life treatment (generally called a "living will"). These registries are in an Internet database accessible to healthcare providers. State Web sites walk users through the steps to create the proper documents, eliminating the need to pay an attorney. Maryland law lets residents note on their driver's licenses or government ID cards that they have an advance directive in the registry; Idaho issues a card like a driver's license with a scannable bar code.

Every state should establish a registry, and registries should be linked through a national database all hospitals can access. Federal regulation should require that hospitals search the national database whenever a patient is not able to designate a proxy at the time of admission. With such a system, the Baltimore hospital that treated Robert would have found his California designation.

Regardless of whether a state or national registry exists, hospitals should improve procedures that secure a healthcare agent from competent patients. In a recent study of outpatients at a Chicago hospital clinic, only 18 percent of those surveyed had a durable power of attorney for healthcare, but 100 percent were able to name the person they would want to act as proxy, and 87 percent would have completed a form on the spot if a doctor had asked them to do so.[7] Hospitals should not assume that a married patient would select her spouse; the Chicago study showed that 33 percent of married patients would select someone else. A study of elderly people in Detroit showed that 50 percent of married people did not choose their spouses.[8] The law already gives everyone the right to name whomever they want; hospitals need to do a better job of making such designations happen.

If a patient is conscious and competent but not able to sign a document, verbal designations should be allowed. The Uniform Health-Care Decisions Act (UHCDA), adopted by the National Conference of Commissioners on Uniform State Laws and approved by the American Bar Association in 1994, maximizes patient autonomy by allowing someone to make known orally to his primary healthcare provider who he wants to make medical decisions on his behalf.[9] A 2002 report by the national coalition Last Acts graded states on the quality of their advance directive laws; giving patients the ability to express their wishes in their own way, rather than requiring mandatory forms or language, was one component of that grade.[10] About ten states have approved this method of designating a proxy. Hospitals need this provision to ensure that doctors who act on what they know to be the patient's wishes will not be subject to lawsuits just because the instructions were oral rather than written.

What to Do When There's No Named Healthcare Surrogate

Laws that determine what happens when patients have not designated anyone to make medical decisions on their behalf should do a better job of reflecting contemporary families and relationships. In 2000, 81 million people in the United States—40 percent of those over eighteen—were not married.[11] Most laws say that in those cases biological or adoptive kin make the decisions. This overlooks the circumstances of all people estranged from their families of origin—including gay men, lesbians, bisexuals, and transgender people rejected because of their sexual orientation or gender identity—and all unmarried couples.

Gay rights advocates do not meet the healthcare-agent needs of their constituency by winning marriage, civil unions, or domestic partnerships. Many same-sex couples will not marry/register, and they should not have to in order to make healthcare decisions for their partners; an ideal default law places an intimate partner at the top of the default list.

Two jurisdictions do this now. The District of Columbia calls this person a "domestic partner," defined as "an adult person living with, but not married to, another adult person in a committed, intimate relationship."[12] Notably, the District does have a formal domestic partner registration system for both different- and same-sex couples, but registration is *not* required under the surrogate healthcare law. New Mexico uses the following definition: "an individual in a long-term relationship of indefinite duration with the patient in which the individual has demonstrated an actual commitment to the patient similar to the commitment of a spouse and in which the individual and the patient consider themselves to be responsible for each other's well-being."[13]

A law referring to committed, intimate relationships has some ambiguity, but it serves the needs of same-sex couples. It authorizes hospitals to rely on someone who identifies himself as the partner when no one else is present, as they do now when someone identifies himself as a patient's spouse. Hospital staff would no longer be able to say, as did Janet's nurse, that she doesn't know what "partner" means. A biological relative disagreeing with a partner's decision would have to prove there was no such relationship. If this had been the standard when Karen Thompson clashed with Sharon Kowalski's parents, Thompson would have won.

Model healthcare proxy laws include a relationship that serves the needs of many LGBT people: "close friends." The UHCDA defines such a person as: "an adult who has exhibited special care and concern for the patient, who is familiar with the patient's personal values."[14] About twenty state laws include this category on the list of those eligible to be named surrogates.[15] The Last Acts coalition identified including "close friend" in the list of default surrogates as one component of the grade it assigned to states. The report noted that this category recognizes that "'family' in today's world often extends beyond the nuclear family."[16]

In every instance, the right choice as the surrogate decision maker is the person who is most likely to know what medical decisions the patient would make if she were able to. To achieve this goal, a law needs flexibility. One example of such flexibility is in place in Colorado. The law defines "interested persons" as the patient's spouse, parent, adult child, sibling, grandchild, and any close friend.[17] The law instructs this group to select a proxy decision maker who has a close relationship with the patient and is most likely to know the patient's wishes. If the group cannot reach consensus, any of them may petition the court for guardianship.

The D.C. law, which lists spouse, domestic partner, adult child, parent, sibling, and close friend in that *presumptive* order, says someone lower on the list can rebut the presumption if he knows the patient's wishes better or is "better able to demonstrate a good-faith belief as to the interests of the patient."[18] A close friend is likely to know the patient's wishes better than an estranged parent or distant sibling. Hospital staff should explain this law if a conflict arises between a close friend and a biological or adoptive relative, thus discouraging those relatives who have had little contact with the patient from challenging the friend's authority.

Gay rights groups can channel the justifiable anxieties many

LGBT people have into advocacy efforts that would quell their worst fears. They'll fall short if they use those fears to gather support for access to marriage when a solution lies elsewhere.

The Best Hospital Visitation Policies

The stories of the plaintiffs seeking access to marriage include dozens of examples of exclusion from hospital rooms. Medical staff turn to "immediate" family at such times. Different-sex couples have an advantage; they can say they are married even when they are not. Intensive-care nurses do not routinely ask a "husband" to produce a marriage license before visiting his "wife." Karen and Edward's story illustrates that when they tell the truth, different-sex unmarried couples also may not be counted as "immediate family." A lesbian may succeed by identifying herself as a patient's sister. This deception is humiliating and should be unnecessary.

Little dispute exists about what policies *should* be in this area. The purpose of all hospital care is the patient's health and well-being. A decision about who can visit the patient must be tailored to achieve that goal, which is why hospital staff must sometimes be able to prevent anyone from visiting. If visits are permitted, patient well-being is promoted by allowing the patient to choose her visitors. So it is inappropriate for a hospital to limit visits to immediate family.

A simple amendment to the federal law that regulates hospitals would require them to allow every entering patient to list those they most want to visit them. This should include designation by a pregnant woman of those who can visit her newborn child. Virginia enacted a law in 2007 requiring its hospitals to allow patients to see whomever they wish. Hospitals and the AARP supported the bill, as did conservative state legislators. As one said, "Why would anybody say no to that?"[19]

Gay rights advocates should seek this broad protection because it helps all same-sex couples and all LGBT people who are not coupled but who want contact with friends when they are hospitalized.

Hospitals need a visitation policy for emergency admissions when the patient can't make a designation. The most effective solutions to this problem are adding to any advance directive form a section declaring that the person wants hospital visiting privileges for her healthcare agent and enacting legislation stating that anyone named as a healthcare agent must be allowed to visit. Maryland law provides for this now, thanks to the efforts of the gay rights group Equality Maryland.

A law is needed to address the situation of anyone who has not written or registered hospital visitation wishes. The recent Virginia law is silent on this issue. New York has a hospital visitation law for a "domestic partner"; it includes those registered anywhere and those "dependent or mutually interdependent" on one another for support. It lists a number of factors that can be considered in determining a "mutual intent to be domestic partners"; most involve financial sharing, but others include having a child in common or the length of the relationship.[20]

Anyone in a committed partner relationship with the patient should be permitted to visit, and if the patient does not have such a person, a close friend should be allowed to visit. References to those in committed relationships and to close friends appear in many laws authorizing surrogate healthcare decision making. It is a much more weighty matter to determine who can make a decision that may mean life or death than to name who can visit. Visitation laws should take a cue from these related laws and incorporate the concepts of committed relationships and close friends.

When a same-sex partner is denied visitation, the consequence often is that no one visits. This disregard of the meaning of friendship is cruel. LGBT advocates could find allies among the elderly and other patient advocacy groups for the single patient's right to visits from friends.

In the few instances when more than one person requests to visit or be transported with the patient, and medical circumstances require that only one person be chosen, the priority should be: (1) the person named in a document the patient signed authorizing visitation and/or surrogate decision making or listed in an advance directive registry; (2) the formal spouse or partner; (3) the person named as a designated family relationship, should a state implement such a registry; (4) the person in a committed relationship with the patient, in which the two consider themselves responsible for each other's well-being; (5) any adult child, parent, or adult sibling; (6)

a close friend who has exhibited special care and concern for the patient.

The most critical provision in a law is that *anyone* on this list *must* be allowed to visit or be transported with the patient as long as it isn't medically contraindicated. That assures that a patient unable to speak for himself will not be left alone simply because medical staff wish to impose a narrow definition of family. It also attempts to prioritize based on what can reasonably be assumed to be the patient's wishes. As soon as the patient is able to communicate his desires, those would govern.

The Maryland Experience

In 2005 the Maryland legislature passed a bill—the Medical Decision Making Act—creating a status called "life partners," open to same- and different-sex couples who lived together in a mutually interdependent relationship.[21] Equality Maryland worked to ensure the law's passage. Registered life partners were authorized to make surrogate medical decisions, visit each other in a hospital, accompany each other on medical transfers, share a room in a healthcare facility, make decisions about disposition of remains, and authorize anatomical gifts. A person in an interdependent relationship with the patient but not registered as a life partner would be able to visit and accompany the patient but would not have the other rights.

Republican governor Robert Erhlich vetoed the act. In the veto message, he expressed sympathy with the "compassionate goals" of the legislation but said that codifying a relationship called life partners "could lead to the erosion of traditional marriage." He said he hoped he could work with the legislature to find a compromise that would help those in need while "respecting the uniqueness of traditional marriage under Maryland law."[22]

Erhlich kept his word. The bill he proposed established the state's advance directive registry and required the motor vehicle administration to enable those with registered advance directives to have that fact noted on their driver's licenses. The bill passed, and Maryland joined the list of states where residents, including LGBT couples, need not pay lawyers to draw up documents and then carry those documents with them in case of emergency.[23]

The governor's message was an offensive collection of right-wing incantations. But he isn't governor anymore. Maryland has an advance directive registry that will benefit everyone and move the country closer to having a nationwide database. Equality Maryland worked to achieve a law that adds to the advance directive form the right to visit a patient, to accompany a patient, and to determine disposition of remains. It became law without the governor's signature. Maryland now has a model for states whose advance directives make no reference to these other issues.

The Maryland bill creating life partners addressed LGBT couples' needs while ignoring the needs of those not in couples. It would have required partner registration to achieve most of its benefits. That approach mixes up the civil rights goal of equal rights for same-sex partners with the needs that all people have to control their healthcare circumstances. Had Ehrlich signed the law, Maryland probably wouldn't have an advance directive registry, and all Marylanders would be worse off. Now Equality Maryland can focus on implementing the registry, reforms needed to protect the interests of those who do not register, and its civil rights and progressive agenda.

Here's what Dan Furmansky, head of Equality Maryland, said about their efforts: "Lack of resources keeps us focused on equal protection for LGBT people, and we look to various means to the end. In this case, advance directives was a great route, and it's nice to work on things that will benefit a more broad contingency than just our own community."[24]

Other state-level LGBT groups could learn from this insight. Not only did Equality Maryland's work benefit those outside the LGBT community, it helped more LGBT people because its focus was broader than "couples." Because marriage equality claims loom so large on the political and legal horizon, a focus on "equal protection for LGBT people" too easily starts with a look at what different-sex *married* couples have. An emphasis instead on what all LGBT people need can produce better results.

Family and Medical Leave

After twenty-five years with the same Pennsylvania employer, David received a call while at work that his partner of twenty-three years had suffered a heart attack and been airlifted to a hospital. David, who had never come out at work, notified his boss he needed to leave for personal reasons. The next day, he returned to work, explained his situation, and requested family leave. His boss refused the request. David exhausted his personal and vacation leave caring for his partner.[25]

Mary, a Denver social worker, requested three days of family leave to care for her sick same-sex partner. Her request was denied because the list of "immediate family" members in the city's regulations did not include unmarried partners. Mary argued that this was unlawful under another city regulation banning discrimination on the basis of sexual orientation. The court ruled against her. It held that the city was treating all unmarried couples identically, and that therefore it was not discrimination on the basis of sexual orientation.[26]

Under the federal Family and Medical Leave Act, an employer with more than fifty workers must provide twelve weeks of unpaid leave to employees who have a serious health condition; or who must care for a spouse, minor child, disabled adult child, or parent with a serious health condition; or who give birth to or adopt a child. Unmarried couples are not entitled to leave to care for their partners. Because of the federal Defense of Marriage Act, couples married in Massachusetts are not entitled to this leave either.

The proposed FMLA originally did not allow even spouses to take leave to care for each other; its purpose was ensuring that women who needed time off for childbirth would not be fired. Congressional hearings in 1984 focused on the need for maternity leave only; feminist lawmakers insisted on caretaking leave for both mothers and fathers. In other words, the bill's original focus was the inevitable dependency of children.

Business groups opposed employers being required to grant any leave. Some Republicans argued that such a program should be limited to mothers, because fathers would abuse the law, taking time off but not really caring for their children. In 1986 lawmakers revised the bill to permit leave to care for a spouse or parent; this garnered the AARP's strong support. Over the next few years spousal coverage was the most controversial part of the proposal. President Ronald Reagan made clear he would veto any bill. By the time supporters were able to overcome the persistent opposition of the business community, George H. W. Bush was president, and he did veto the bill—twice. Fulfilling a campaign pledge, President Bill Clinton signed it in 1993 during his first month in office.[27]

To take the law at its word, its purpose is to "promote the stability and economic security of families, and to promote national interests in preserving family integrity." The need for the law came from changing demographics: more mothers with children and more people with aging parents were in the workforce.

Every part of the legislation reflects a compromise between employers' interests in narrowing its mandates and employees' interests in expanding it. The requirement of a "serious health condition" means leave is not mandated for routine doctor's appointments or brief illness. Because it mandates only unpaid leave, its value in promoting economic security is limited. The vast majority of countries provide paid annual leave, sick leave, and maternity leave; dozens provide paid parenting leave to both men and women.[28] The leave policies in many Western countries extend to care of unmarried partners, any member of the employee's household, or anyone who depends on the employee for care.

In 2004 California became the first state to provide partially paid family leave; employees receive 55 percent of their weekly pay, up to about $850, for six weeks, to care for a child, parent, spouse, or registered domestic partner, or to bond with a newborn or newly adopted child. The program is funded through a payroll deduction and administered by a state agency. Approximately 138,000 workers received an average $409 a week during the program's first year.[29]

A few states require employers to allow their workers to use *sick* leave to care for sick family members. The federal government and forty-eight states allow public employees to use sick leave this way but do not mandate it for private employers. Paid sick leave and family leave are critical to the well-being of all workers and their families. Workplace policies that compensate those who must leave work to care for others are one way to implement the collective responsibility for dependency. These efforts are incomplete, however, if they narrowly limit whom an employee can take leave to care for.

Who Is Covered

The FMLA started as a bill about the parenting of infants. When it was expanded to encompass care of sick children, the law included the "child of a person standing *in loco parentis.*" The regulations define such a person as one who has "day-to-day responsibilities to care for and financially support a child.... A biological or legal relationship is not necessary."[30] This enables the same-sex partner of a child's biological parent to take leave to care for her child. This definition should be a model for the definition of "child" in many laws and policies that have economic impact on a family, including federal and state tax laws, employee health benefits that cover family members, and various government benefits programs.

A law whose primary purpose is facilitating care of inevitable dependents—especially children—should allow a broader range of employees leave to provide that care. Grandparents, godparents, and other extended family members should be given leave to care for sick children who are not their day-to-day responsibility. This is especially critical for single parents unable to afford taking unpaid leave. Lack of affordable childcare already restricts the employment options of single mothers; childcare for *sick* children is almost nonexistent. Widening the list of those eligible to take leave to care for a sick child is an appropriate way to broaden collective responsibility for children.

Some state laws cover other family members. New Jersey, Oregon, Rhode Island, Vermont, and Wisconsin cover parents-in-law. Oregon covers same-sex domestic partners. Rhode Island covers same-sex and different-sex domestic partners. California, Connecticut, Hawaii, New Jersey, and Vermont extend coverage to those same-sex couples who register under their domestic partnership/civil union/reciprocal beneficiaries laws.

The District of Columbia passed its own family leave law three years before the federal government did. It covers those who live together, or have in the past year lived together, in a "committed relationship."[31] D.C. allows both same- and different-sex couples to register as domestic partners, but registering is not required for taking family leave. D.C. also provides leave to care for any child living with the employee "for whom the employee permanently assumes and discharges parental responsibility" and for people related by biology or marriage—in other words, extended family.

The FMLA has not proved as burdensome as businesses feared.[32] Some employers voluntarily extend leave to care for domestic partners. Developing an ideal group of people for whom an employee could use leave requires balancing an employer's legitimate needs against the diversity of employees' caregiving obligations. The main tool to address employer needs, however, should *not* be how family is defined. The purpose of a family and medical leave policy is facilitating care of those unable to care for themselves; the law should encompass the broadest possible range of relationships.

A Better Model

The "Healthy Families Act," introduced in 2007 in both houses of Congress, would make four dramatic improvements on current law.[33] It provides for some paid leave; it applies to smaller businesses; it eliminates the requirement of a "serious" illness; and it broadens the group of eligible care recipients.

The bill provides for seven days a year of paid sick leave. Half of all workers have no sick leave, and almost 80 percent of those who earn in the lowest one-quarter of pay do not. It also allows leave for doctor's appointments and shorter illnesses and to care for an adult family member "in need of care" beyond the listed medical reasons.

The bill uses the term "sick leave," but defines leave as available for both a worker's own medical needs and those of others. Specifically, it allows leave "for the purpose of caring for a child, a parent, a spouse, or any other individual related by blood or affinity whose close association with the employee is the equivalent of a family relationship." This definition comes from the *current* regulation governing use of sick leave by federal government employees. In other words, the federal government has already approved the ability of its workers to use their paid sick leave to care for a very broad category of family members.[34]

This definition responds directly to the problem that family leave is designed to address: the need to care for loved ones. If it passes, the result will be better than that achieved by marriage or civil union/partnership laws; they merely extend the ability to take leave to an employee's spouse or registered partner. Unmarried partners, both same-sex and different-sex, are harmed if marriage/registration is a requirement. It also broadens the definition of "child" to encompass those not in the employees' day-to-day care. A witness at the Senate committee hearing on the Healthy Families Act supported the definition of "family" in the bill because her extensive research on workers' lives demonstrated that only such a broad definition would reflect the "needs and commitments of American families."[35]

The AARP support for the FMLA was critical, and that is the reason the FMLA doesn't require that the employee live with the person she wants leave to care for; the group's constituency includes parents of an employee who do not live with their children but rely on them for care. The AARP is likely to support the broader definition in the Healthy Families Act because it both enables more of an elderly person's relatives to provide care and enables grandparents to take leave to care for grandchildren.

The act would require all employers with fifteen or more employees to provide seven days' paid leave for the stated purposes. The FMLA would still mandate that larger employers provide longer unpaid leave. Reforms at the state level also may follow two different tracks. The definition of a covered family member, however, should be the same for both paid and unpaid leave.

The act provides model language for state efforts. A gay civil rights approach concentrates on getting for same-sex couples what married couples now have, either through a formal status such as civil unions or through listing same-sex partners in the included categories, as Oregon does. The District of Columbia does better by including all unmarried couples (thereby recognizing that care needs are as strong among those who do not marry as among those who do) and all extended family. A valuing-all-families approach, epitomized in the Healthy Families Act, would garner many allies under a banner of family diversity and protect the wide range of caring LGBT families and relationships.

CHAPTER TEN

When a Relationship Ends through Dissolution or Death

Distributing Assets and Providing for Children

Helen and Lisa lived together for more than ten years. During that time they had five children. In 1990, Lisa gave birth to the first child, Scott, born using unknown-donor insemination obtained through a fertility clinic. Helen quit her job and stayed home with Scott. When they decided to have another child, a medical condition prevented Helen from becoming pregnant, so Lisa again conceived, using the same donor semen from the same fertility clinic. Pregnant with quadruplets, Lisa became incapacitated, and Helen cared for her as well as for Scott.

The quadruplets were born in 1993. Lisa went back to work at the end of her maternity leave. Helen stayed home with the five children. Lisa pursued career advancement as a civilian employee of the United States Navy, where she achieved a GS-14 professional position. She paid the bills. Helen was the stay-at-home mom. The couple split up when the quadruplets were four years old.[1]

This case entered the court system in Pennsylvania when Helen filed for custody of the children. The couple settled their dispute, with an agreement giving Helen joint legal custody and Lisa physical custody. Lisa moved to California with the children. Helen had specified weeks of visitation. Helen took a job as a light-machinery operator. Lisa petitioned for child support. Helen argued that she was more like a stepparent and should not be required to support the children. The court disagreed and ordered that Helen pay the same amount under the state's child support guideline that any noncustodial parent was obliged to pay.

On the issue of child support, the case reached the right result.

It's what was not at issue in the case that's troubling. Helen stayed home with one and then five children for seven years. During that time, Lisa's career advanced. When their relationship ended, Lisa walked away with her increased earning power and paid nothing to Helen, who was, as she said, a stay-at-home mom. Nothing in Pennsylvania law, or the law of any state, gave Helen the right to request temporary support while she got back into the labor market. Nothing gave her the right to ask for money from Lisa to offset the ten years of retirement benefits Lisa accumulated or a share of any property that wasn't titled in both of their names. Had they been married, Helen would have had the right in a divorce action to request such relief.

The Financial Consequences of Splitting Up

The plaintiffs in marriage-equality cases do not say that they want to marry so that if they split up the property division and support rules that accompany divorce will apply to them. Like all couples who plan to marry, they do not expect to divorce. But the different rules for settling money issues at the end of a marriage versus an unmarried relationship can cause indefensible hardship.

Same-sex couples who marry in Massachusetts or enter civil unions/domestic partnerships in Vermont, New Jersey, New Hampshire, the District of Columbia, Oregon, or California will have divorce laws apply if they separate. That reform is not sufficient. Formalization should not be required for achieving a fair allocation of the costs associated with the end of a couple's life together.

Applying the valuing-all-families approach requires first considering why rules apply to the end of marriages that are different from those that apply to other private disagreements about who owns what property and who owes whom what amount of money. Until the changes in divorce laws in the 1970s, the forty-two "common law" property states did not treat the end of a marriage as an event needing specific rules for determining who got what property. The person whose name appeared on the title to land or the bank account kept it. Untitled property belonged to the spouse who paid for it. Obviously, this meant the husband owned most of the property during the marriage and kept it when the marriage ended.

For example, in a 1974 case at the end of a twenty-two-year marriage, a wife who had no outside employment for the first ten years while she cared for the children, and who kept homemaking even when she had paid employment, received her personal items and her car. Her husband kept a 265-acre farm, the family home, machinery, and livestock. The court said the result was "harsh" but required by the law.[2] With no-fault divorces and many more marriages ending in divorce, courts and legislatures in common law property states came to see the outcomes as unfair because they failed to take into account noneconomic contributions to the household. They established new laws allowing judges to transfer title to property—something that would have shocked our ancestors—to achieve a result that was "equitable."

The law governing the end of unmarried relationships has not caught up with the times. Traditionally, the law would not even enforce deals in which a man *agreed* to provide for a woman with whom he "cohabited." The law considered such arrangements no different from prostitution. When the California Supreme Court ruled in 1976 that actor Lee Marvin *could* be required to support Michelle Triola Marvin if he had agreed to do so, it heralded a more modern treatment of unmarried couples.[3]

Unfortunately, *Marvin v. Marvin* proved to be an end point, rather than the beginning of a more appropriate legal treatment of all families. Law books are filled with decisions denying assets and support to "stay-at-home moms" like Helen who lived with male partners, raised children, and got nothing when those relationships ended. Some were together for decades. All they had available to them when their relationships ended was the opportunity to prove a contract with their former partner or *financial* contributions to the former partner's property. Their status as a partner who devoted years to home and family counted for nothing.

In fact, Michelle Triola received nothing. She was unable to prove a contract with Marvin, and the court refused to approve an award of temporary support based solely on the equities of their situation. Contracts are hard to prove. In a 2006 case at the end of a thirteen-year lesbian relationship, Harriet argued for compensation based on her partner Sara's pension, which was valued at close to $250,000 for the period the couple was together. The judge ruled against her, finding that Sara had not agreed to share her pension if their relationship ended.[4] Even when couples have agreements, a few states still adhere to the pre-*Marvin* rule and refuse to enforce them.[5]

In the thirty years since *Marvin*, the number of unmarried couples living together has increased exponentially. In 2003, there were about 5.5 million such couples. Among different-sex couples, 44 percent of them had children under eighteen. Thirty-eight percent of female same-sex couples and 27 percent of male same-sex couples also had children under eighteen.[6] Two people who filled the same roles in their respective homes should not be treated differently based on whether they had a marriage license. When the relationship ends, the court has all the information it needs about how the couple lived and should have the power to transfer property and order support to achieve just results.

One state goes part of the way toward a just result now. If a couple lives together in Washington, that state will treat the property they accumulate as the equivalent of community property and apportion it equitably between them. In a 1995 case, the Washington Supreme Court ruled that the property acquired during a seven-year relationship was presumed owned by both parties and that the name on the title was irrelevant. The man's net worth had almost doubled from $1.4 million to $2.7 million during that time. The court said he could overcome the presumption of joint ownership only by showing that he bought the property using money he had before their relationship began.[7] Subsequently, the court applied this doctrine to the separation of a lesbian couple.[8]

A just result can be reached through applying Martha Fineman's observations about inevitable and derivative dependency. *Someone* needed to take care of Helen and Lisa's five children. Helen did this, and cared for Lisa as well. That made her dependent on Lisa for financial support, and it hindered her ability to support herself because she was out of the workforce for seven years. The law needs to acknowledge this type of commitment.

The ALI Principles

The vast increase in the number of unmarried couples living together prompted the American Law Institute to include "domestic partners" in its *Principles of the Law of Family Dissolution*. If a couple meets the criteria for domestic partners, then the rules governing the financial consequences of their dissolution are the same as those applied to married couples, unless they make an agreement to the contrary. The authors, including law professor Grace Blumberg, base this doctrine on "the familiar principle that legal rights and obligations may arise from the conduct of the parties with respect to one another, even though they have created no formal document or agreement setting forth such an undertaking."[9]

The ALI principles define as domestic partners two individuals who are "not married to one another, who for a significant period of time share a primary residence and a life together as a couple."[10] They presume that a couple who lives together for three years meets this test. If they have a child, they meet it after two years.

The principles list thirteen factors relevant to determining whether two people "share a life together as a couple."[11] They include written and oral statements and promises made to one another about the relationship; statements to others and the couple's reputation in the community as a couple; commingling of finances; economic interdependence, or dependence of one person on the other; assumption by the parties of specialized or collaborative roles; changes in the life of either or both as a result of the relationship; naming of each other as financial beneficiaries or in documents, such as wills; participation in a commitment ceremony or partnership registration; jointly raising a child; and the parties' emotional or physical intimacy.

Stepping into the Culture War

Blumberg and the ALI were vilified by marriage-movement ideologues for including domestic partners in their recommendations, a step opponents claimed would "secularize the culture and hasten the 'deinstitutionalization' of marriage." "[The ALI] want[s] marriage to mean nothing," said Representative Marilyn Musgrave, sponsor of the constitutional amendment to ban same-sex marriage. *U.S. News and World Report* columnist John Leo blasted the "drastic notion" in the ALI principles that "marriage is just one arrangement among many." Brigham Young law professor Lynn Wardle said the principles "reflect an ideological bias against family relations based on marriage" and a continuation of "the war on the traditional family and traditional sexual morality that has been waged over three decades." Bush administration welfare policy advisor Ron Haskins was the most blunt. "Cohabitation is a plague," he said, "and we should do what we can [to] discourage it."[12]

David Blankenhorn stated: "Anyone who cares about the state of marriage, which is weak enough already, if you want it to become weaker still, knock away legal protections marriage enjoys."[13] Of course, the ALI was not knocking any protections away from marriage; it was extending them to unmarried couples who also needed them.

The lawyers and law professors who wrote the ALI principles rejected these criticisms. Blumberg remarked that it was a good thing to acknowledge reality. Katharine Bartlett, the dean of Duke Law School, who was also a principal drafter of the principles, affirmed that law needed to deal with families as it found them and do the best it could for all children. A Pennsylvania lawyer who advised the ALI maintained that the divorce code wasn't about "protecting marriage"; it was about dealing with the realities of a breakup.[14]

The marriage movement isn't looking for the most just way to resolve the family disputes of unmarried couples. It is drawing a line to keep marriage "special," even if this causes others great harm.

Deciding Not to Marry Doesn't Justify Not Dividing Property

Some commentators say it is inappropriate to require a separating couple who has chosen not to marry to divide their assets as though they had. They argue that the choice not to marry means neither party agreed to share assets with the other if the relationship ended, and they suggest it is paternalistic to impose financial obligations on couples who chose to live together without marrying. They would apply this argument with equal force to an unmarried/unregistered same-sex couple in Massachusetts, Vermont, New Hampshire, New Jersey, California, or any other state that allows same-sex couples to formalize their relationship.

The argument has a fatal flaw. Couples who marry have no idea what economic obligations accompany their marriage, either while they are together or if they divorce. They couldn't possibly. The law is so different from state to state that unless they research the laws of their specific state—and any state they move to while married—they can in no sense be seen as having *agreed* to the legal consequences of their marriage.[15]

Most states differentiate between "marital property" and "separate property." Separate property is owned before marriage or acquired through gift or inheritance. When people divorce, most states divide only marital property. Some allow a judge to divide separate property to avoid an unfair result. Still others consider all property either party owns up for grabs.

Certainly a divorcing spouse with inherited wealth might be surprised to learn that his spouse could get a share of it, especially if his brother, who lives in a different state, was able to shield his inheritance during his divorce because it was separate property. He might say he never thought marriage would give his wife a claim on his inherited wealth. The wife might also have assumed she had no claim on those assets until she consulted a lawyer. The law is set to establish a norm for all regardless of what they think or intend.

Even marital property rules differ from state to state. Some statutes *require* a fifty-fifty division. Some *presume* a fifty-fifty division but let a judge rule otherwise. Some instruct a judge simply to do what is "just" or "fair" or "equitable." Some states consider why the marriage ended; some think that's irrelevant.

Spouses don't know when they marry whether their sexual infidelity or other marital "fault" could have economic consequences when they divorce. They couldn't. The law on that also differs from state to state. An unfaithful wife will be barred from alimony in North Carolina but not in New Jersey. An unfaithful husband may have to "pay" for his transgression in North Carolina but not in Delaware. In some states a divorced spouse cannot receive alimony unless he cannot support himself.

A wife who supports her husband through medical school in New York can claim a share of his earning ability if they divorce. A wife who does the same in Indiana won't even get back the money she spent supporting her husband while he was in school.

Each state sets rules for the economic consequences of divorce based on what it thinks fair and appropriate. It is equally legitimate to set rules for the end of "a life together as a couple" that recognizes the interdependency and vulnerabilities of such a shared life.

How They Do It in Australia and New Zealand

Australia has incorporated unmarried couples into the dissolution laws that apply to divorces. Australia considers two people who "live together as a couple" to be in a de facto relationship. The ALI considered the list of factors used in Australia when it developed its criteria for domestic partnerships. The Australian factors are: the length of the relationship; the nature and extent of common residence; whether a sexual relationship exists; the degree of financial dependence or interdependence; any arrangements for financial support between the parties; the ownership, use, and acquisition of property; the degree of mutual commitment to a shared life; the care and support of children; the performance of household duties; and the couple's reputation.[16]

Australia began applying these principles to unmarried heterosexual couples in the mid-1980s. Most Australian states require two years of cohabitation in order to apply marital property rules to the end of a relationship, but the law gives judges the flexibility to waive this requirement to avoid great hardship. In 1999, New South Wales became the first state to extend these rules to the dissolution of same-sex relationships. All now do so.

New Zealand also treats separating unmarried and married couples alike, but its laws have an additional component especially significant with respect to matching the reach of a law to the law's purpose. When a married couple divorces, the applicable property-division laws depend upon whether the couple has been married for at least three years. In other words, *marriage* is not the dividing line in New Zealand for what laws apply to the end of a relationship.

When a couple has been married less than three years, each spouse leaves the marriage with what he contributed.[17] After three years, principles requiring sharing of marital property kick in. New Zealand applies the same standard to unmarried couples. The ALI principles require a minimum period of living together before marital property-division rules apply to a cohabiting couple. If the purpose is to ensure that the couple really has a shared life, it makes sense to judge marriages in the same way. A couple who marries vows to stay together until death does them part. A divorce in less than three years shows that to be an empty promise. New Zealand's law holding all couples to the same standard is a good example of deciding that marriage, by itself, should not determine "special" legal consequences.

What Happens to the Children?

Lisa and Janet lived in Virginia. They traveled to Vermont in 2000 and entered into a civil union. They decided to have a child, and Lisa gave birth to Isabella, who was conceived using unknown-donor semen, in April 2002. The couple moved to Vermont in August. They separated in September 2003. Lisa moved back to Virginia with the baby. She filed an action in Vermont to dissolve the civil union and asked for custody of Isabella with visitation rights going to Janet. The court issued a temporary custody and visitation order in June 2004. In July 2004, after Virginia passed a constitutional amendment banning recognition of same-sex unions, Lisa filed an action in Virginia asking to be determined Isabella's sole parent.[18]

Although this case garnered much press attention about interstate recognition of same-sex couples, the case turns on the completely separate question of which state had authority to issue a custody and visitation order. Under both federal and state law, Vermont had that power because Isabella lived in Vermont during the six-month period before Lisa filed for custody and visitation there. Once Vermont made a decision about Isabella, no other state had the authority to do so. These rules exist to stop parents from "forum shopping" until they find a state willing to change another state's custody order. The Virginia trial judge incorrectly granted Lisa's request and was reversed by the Virginia appeals court.

Couples seeking the right to marry often say they want it for their children. With the prominence of advocacy for marriage equality, the claims of same-sex parents raising children have been mistakenly conflated with the issue of whether to recognize the parents' relationships with each other. That accounts for the Virginia trial judge's mistake. In fact, same-sex parents have been raising children together, and courts have been grappling with the law that governs their families, for more than twenty-five years.

When a same-sex couple with a child splits up, the legal landscape that affects them depends on a number of circumstances. If they have both adopted the child, or if one partner is the biological parent and the other completed a second-parent adoption, then they have equal rights and responsibilities toward the child. They are no different from two unmarried different-sex parents. The children of same-sex parents have benefited from the constitutional and statutory reforms that ended discrimination against all children born outside of marriage. Over 45 percent of same-sex couples live in states or counties that grant second-parent adoptions, and all states are required to recognize adoptions granted in other states.

The ALI developed rules for disputes over children when there has not been a second-parent adoption. When a child is born to a same-sex couple with the agreement that the couple will each have "full parental rights and responsibilities," the second parent is a "parent by estoppel." A person can become a parent by estoppel even if she and the biological parent did not have an agreement before the child was born; this requires living with the child for two years, "holding out and accepting full and permanent responsibilities as a parent, pursuant to an agreement with the child's parent." A parent by estoppel has parental rights and obligations identical to that of the biological parent.[19]

At least fourteen states allow a parent who did not give birth to or adopt the child the right to a continued relationship with the child and the obligation to pay child support.[20] That's why Helen, with Scott and the quadruplets, had joint legal custody, visitation rights, and an obligation to pay child support.

In fact, all the states that gay rights lawyers targeted for marriage-equality litigation *already* protected the relationships between children and both their same-sex parents. Having those protections first made it easier to argue for marriage because the state could not credibly claim that same-sex couples should be denied marriage as a way of denying them the ability to parent.

As long as federal and state "defense of marriage" acts exist, a parent-child relationship based on the couple's marriage or civil union is vulnerable. An adoption decree is not. Every state and the federal government must honor it. That's why lawyers representing same-sex couples in the states that grant couples a formal legal status urge their clients to obtain adoption decrees as well.

When Death Does Them Part

Sam and Earl lived for twenty-three years on a ranch in Oklahoma that was titled in Earl's name alone. They raised Sam's three children from his former marriage. Earl worked a full-time job and Sam ran the ranch. In later years, Sam cared for Earl's elderly mother, Viola. Viola considered Sam her son-in-law and asked his children to call her "Grandma." Earl had a stroke in 1997 and Sam was his primary caregiver. None of Earl's relatives came to visit, although they lived less than thirty miles away.

Earl was diagnosed with cancer in 2000 and died within three months. Sam sought to probate the will Earl had written, leaving him the ranch and all his possessions. But the signed and witnessed will was one witness short of the number required under Oklahoma law. Five of Earl's cousins challenged the will. Although Earl's intent was completely clear, the court awarded all of Earl's property to his cousins.[21]

Randall and Ronald lived together in Colorado for twenty years. One year, at Randall's birthday party, in the presence of two friends, Ronald gave Randall a card containing a typed, signed letter stating that if anything should happen to him all he owned should go to Randall. The letter said that Randall, their pets, and an aunt were his only family and that "everyone else is dead to me." The next year Ronald died of a heart attack. When Randall sought to probate the letter as Ronald's will, Margaret, the mother of Ronald's three nephews, argued that the document was not a valid will and that Ronald's nephews should inherit all of Ronald's property.

This document complied with even fewer formalities than Earl's will. It didn't say it was a will and it had no witness signatures. Nonetheless, Randall was entitled to prove that Ronald intended it to be his will. The two people present when Ronald gave the letter to Randall could testify about what Ronald said as a way of proving his intent.[22]

Probating a Will as the Deceased Intended

Had Sam and Earl lived in neighboring Colorado, Sam would still have his ranch. The difference between the two cases is not the ability to marry. The difference is that Colorado has adopted Section 2–503 of the Uniform Probate Code.[23] That statute permits probate of a will that fails to comply with all the will formalities if it can be shown that the deceased intended the document to be his will.

The reasoning of this "harmless error" rule is that a technical defect in will formalities should not defeat the intent of the deceased. The only purpose of the formalities is to ensure that the will does represent the deceased's intended disposition of his property. The National Conference of Commissioners on Uniform State Laws determined in 1990 that proof of intent should trump the requirement of formalities. Their Uniform Probate Code described the success of such rules in Australia, Canada, and Israel. The American Law Institute reached the same conclusion, and urged that courts adopt this approach even without a statute authorizing it.[24]

Experts on wills consider it embarrassing that a relative might be "unjustly enriched" through inheriting property contrary to the clear intent of the deceased. Examples of unjust results abound, affecting many more people than just same-sex couples. In one case, the will left the decedent's property to his stepson. It was denied probate because it lacked all the formalities; the decedent had no heirs because he had no relatives listed in the intestate succession statute, so the decedent's assets were given to the state.[25]

It will be a long time before marriage or civil union for same-sex couples comes to Oklahoma. The statewide LGBT advocacy group Oklahomans for Equality points out that LGBT people there can be turned down or fired from a job, denied or evicted from rental housing, denied or refused service in a public place, and turned down for a home mortgage loan. When the U.S. Supreme Court in 2003 declared unconstitutional a Texas law criminalizing private, consensual, same-sex sodomy, Oklahoma was one of three other states with an identical law on the books. The crime was a felony punishable by up to ten years in prison. That's the legal environment Sam faced when he went to court trying to inherit under Earl's will.

It need not be long before states adopt the harmless-error rule, thereby assuring the result everyone agrees is the purpose of the law of wills—that a person should be able to decide for himself who inherits when he dies. No one should have to marry, even if they could, to achieve that result.

Inheriting without a Will

When Earl's will was denied probate, his property passed according to his state's law of intestate succession. A spouse always receives a share of the estate, and may receive all of it if the deceased had no children. The property of an unmarried person with no children passes to "next of kin"—relatives in an order specified in the statute. That's why Earl's cousins got the ranch.

Christine and Andre met in 1983. They built a home in a New Hampshire town and lived there until Andre died in 2003. They weren't married but were generally considered husband and wife. Andre had worked for the post office for more than ten years. His widow was entitled to federal employee retirement system benefits. Christine applied for them, and the government argued that she was not eligible.[26]

New Hampshire does not recognize common law marriage, so the couple wasn't married while they lived together. That's why an administrative judge ruled against Christine's claim for benefits. But New Hampshire has a unique statute that recognizes a couple as married after one of them dies, if they lived together and were considered husband and wife for three years before the death.[27] For purposes of intestate succession, therefore, Christine was Andre's spouse. Her case claiming federal benefits as his survivor is still pending.

The law of intestate succession has two main purposes: to make it easy to distribute the decedent's property, and to distribute it in a way that approximates what the decedent would have wanted. Because the order of descent consists of family members, definitions of family form a critical component of intestate succession laws. Adopted children and children born outside of marriage were once entirely excluded from inheritance. Stepchildren are still in most instances excluded, even from inheriting from a stepparent who raised them, and even though they qualify as a decedent's child with respect to other purposes.

Courts do not have the power to stray from intestate succession statutes. They have no authority to allow proof of the intent of a person who dies without a will concerning how he wanted his property distributed. Several scholars have proposed categories for inclusion in such statutes that would make inheritance more feasible for a surviving same-sex or unmarried different-sex partner, including cohabitation in a "marriage-like" relationship or living together "as a couple" according to a list of factors.[28] With the exception of the New Hampshire statute, no state takes such an approach.

Two legal scholars, Mary Louise Fellows of the University of Minnesota and Gary Spitko of Santa Clara University, propose adding to those who inherit by intestate succession someone named to benefit from a "will substitute" such as life insurance and retirement or pension assets. Those proceeds pass outside of a will to the designated person. Sam did receive Earl's life insurance and retirement fund proceeds. When Congress passed a statute awarding a death benefit on behalf of every public service officer killed in the line of duty, it selected as the recipient for someone without a spouse or child the person named as beneficiary on the officer's life insurance policy.

This proposal shows promise as a way of matching intestate succession laws with their purpose—distributing an estate as the decedent would have chosen had he made a will. A person's choice to confer financial benefits on someone not on the intestate succession list is one way he demonstrates that his wishes are not defined by bloodlines alone—or at all. This proposal has the further advantage of valuing relationships beyond the couples who would benefit from adding "committed partner" to the list of those entitled to inherit.

Registration

When Hawaii became the first state to make a formal status with limited rights available to same-sex couples, one of the rights it enumerated was intestate succession on par with that of spouses. Hawaii calls its status "reciprocal beneficiaries." In the handful of states that now afford same-sex couples the opportunity to obtain all the state-level consequences of marriage (Connecticut, Vermont, New Jersey, California, New Hampshire, and Oregon) those couples are treated as spouses for purposes of inheritance. In addition, the District of Columbia and two states, Maine and Washington, have enacted statewide domestic partnership that includes intestate succession as one of its legal consequences. If a couple moves to a state with a constitutional amendment banning recognition of same-sex couples, however, that state would likely not recognize rights deriving from these statutes.

A registration mechanism is well suited to the circumstances of intestate succession because it provides certainty. But it's a mistake to conflate registration for this purpose with marriage or civil union. Everyone should have the opportunity to, in essence, choose a family member. Current law affords that chance only to intimate partners, who exercise their choice by marrying. Those who are unmarried are "stuck" with blood relatives. They are of course free to write a will, but so many people don't that an alternate mechanism is desirable.

A registration system that allows a person to designate who is a member of his family can resolve this issue. A designated person would have surrogate medical decision making authority and control of disposition of remains in the absence of a written indication otherwise. These are also rights normally assigned to "next of kin" —the same people listed in intestacy statutes. For inheritance purposes, in the absence of a will, a "designated family member" would, like reciprocal beneficiaries in Hawaii, inherit in the same way as a spouse. In most states, if a decedent has children, the assets are split between the spouse and the children; that same split would apply here.

Marriage Is Too Special

Marriage is a bright line in inheritance law. A spouse instantly rises to the top of the list of those who inherit without a will. The length of the marriage is immaterial. What's more, for those who write wills, in every state except Georgia a spouse cannot be disinherited, unless she waives her right to inherit in a prenuptial agreement or other acceptable document. One part of rethinking the role of marriage should be rethinking why all marriages receive this special status.

In keeping with the valuing-all-families principle that the needs of dependent children come before those of able-bodied spouses, the law should not permit disinheritance of minor children. Right now every state except Louisiana and Massachusetts allows people to do this.

Furthermore, intestacy should be expanded to reach any child a decedent lives with and supports, or supported when the child was a minor. This would allow stepchildren, children of an unmarried partner, godchildren, and others to inherit if the decedent did not make a will. For decades, adopted children were disadvantaged in inheritance law because the law protected distribution of property along bloodlines. That is no longer an acceptable justification for discriminating against adopted children. Intestacy is supposed to do what the deceased would have wanted. In the modern world of diverse and blended families, the law should presume that a person who has raised a child wants that child to be considered an heir.

Earl treated Sam's children as his sons. He took the boys to company Christmas parties and carried them on his insurance. It's a sure bet that Earl would have preferred them—not his distant cousins—to inherit the ranch.

The Tax Consequences of Death

The sisters Joyce, eighty-eight, and Sybil, eighty, have lived together all their lives. They own a home on thirty acres of English farmland, which they lease out. They live off the rental income they receive. They each have wills naming the other as beneficiary. When one of the sisters dies, the 40 percent inheritance tax her estate is obligated to pay will make it necessary for the survivor to sell the land and move.[29]

When Jodie, Mary's partner of twelve years, died in 2004, the home they owned together in California was retitled in Mary's name; Mary's property taxes nearly doubled.[30]

Protecting the Homes of Everyone

Mary and Sybil and Joyce face a different set of laws that give married couples who live together an advantage that no other family form receives. Tax laws in Britain and the U.S. exempt spouses from the taxes that are otherwise due when assets pass from one person to another. Bequeathing your share of your home by will to anyone other than a spouse, as Sybil and Joyce want to do, is a "taxable event." It may produce so much tax liability that, after losing a life partner, the survivor also loses her home. Spouses do not face this loss.

In California, property taxes remain stable, no matter what the value of the property, until ownership is transferred. Then the property value is reassessed and the tax increases to meet the new value. When this law was enacted in 1978, only transfers between spouses were exempt from reassessment. In 1986, transfers between parents and children were added to the exemptions, and in 1996, transfers between grandparents and grandchildren were exempted. As of January 1, 2006, transfers between domestic partners registered with the state are also exempt from reassessments.[31] This change came too late for Mary.

Michele, fifty-eight, and Jenny, fifty-five, had been friends in Ohio for fifteen years when they decided to pool their resources, build a home together in Florida, and "enjoy the pleasures of female friendship."[32]

Brenda and Dan, close friends in their forties in the San Francisco Bay Area, bought a house jointly to raise their children together and have been doing so for many years.[33]

The California domestic partnership law won't help Brenda and Dan, and if Michele and Jenny had built their home in California it wouldn't help them either. When the first of these two co-owners dies, the property would be reassessed. If the increased taxes were prohibitively expensive, the survivor would have to sell the home and move.

Mary and other same-sex couples who experienced property tax hikes compared themselves to married couples, who were spared these increases. The executive director of Equality California invoked the specter of a widowed partner forced out of his home while grieving the loss of his loved one. If denial of access to marriage is the cause of their difficulty, then marriage equality or the second-best solution of a domestic partnership/civil union law is the way to alleviate that problem. But that still leaves families constructed in other ways—sisters, friends, coparents—vulnerable.

Allowing same-sex couples to marry is not the solution to this problem. The example of Sybil and Joyce shows why that helps too few people. Sybil and Joyce took their case to the European Court of Human Rights. They live in the United Kingdom, which allows same-sex partners to enter civil partnerships. They complained, quite rightly, that if they were a lesbian couple the survivor would not face the loss of her home. In December 2006 the court narrowly ruled against them in a 4–3 vote.[34]

The solution is reforming tax laws so that *no one* loses their primary home because a co-owner dies. California doesn't do this. Instead, California law allows children to move into wildly expensive homes they inherit upon the death of their parents or grandparents. The children could not afford to buy those homes now and could not afford to keep them if they were taxed at their present value. But the survivor of Brenda and Dan or Michelle and Jenny might lose *her own home* because of its reassessed value. So could the survivor of any unmarried, unregistered couple.

Here's the principle that should drive tax law on housing: *No one* should lose the home they live in because of the tax consequences of the death of an owner. California does not reassess property tax when one spouse dies, because it doesn't want the other spouse to lose her home. *Anyone* who lives in a home, and who inherits it upon the death of a spouse, partner, sibling, friend, or coparent, should not have to lose it upon a co-owner's death. California is protecting the wrong people—children and grandchildren who don't live in the home—and abandoning the people most entitled to protection from the loss of their home due to increased tax liability.

Tax on Inherited Pensions

Until 2006, when a person died with funds in a retirement account, the beneficiary of those funds had to pay income taxes on them immediately. The only exception was for spouses. A spouse could roll the funds over into his own retirement account, thus deferring tax liability until he used the funds during his own retirement. Congress changed the law in its pension-reform legislation in 2006. It created a way for *any* beneficiary to move funds in an inherited retirement account into his own retirement account with no tax consequences. It also extended from spouses only to any beneficiary the ability to use retirement funds early without tax penalty for medical and financial emergencies.[35]

The Human Rights Campaign lobbied for this change "without fanfare" for three years. Immediately after passage, HRC staffers hailed its impact on LGBT couples. Legal director Lara Schwartz said that HRC made the case for "more fair treatment" by sharing stories of how real people were affected by the existing tax penalties. A Republican senator said the change would help the "large group of

Americans that are left behind in traditional pension benefit models." A Democratic congressman affirmed that "all families need to be able to plan and save for their future."[36]

All tax matters raise questions of distributive justice. These should never be resolved by drawing a line between spouses and everyone else. That makes the result HRC achieved better than a result singling out marriage for special treatment—even if same-sex couples *could* marry.

CHAPTER ELEVEN

Losing an Economic Provider

Wrongful Death, Workers' Compensation, and Social Security

Diane Whipple was mauled to death in the hallway of her apartment building by her neighbors' dogs, one of which had, on a previous occasion, bitten her on the wrist. Owner Marjorie Knoller, who was with the dogs at the time, was convicted of second-degree murder in Whipple's death; co-owner Robert Noel was convicted of involuntary manslaughter. Whipple was survived by her partner of seven years, Sharon Smith.[1]

Recovering for Wrongful Death

Under common law, there was no such thing as recovering money damages from someone whose negligent or intentional actions resulted in another's death. Oddly, this made it cheaper to kill someone than to injure him. If death resulted, the criminal law could step in, but survivors could not bring lawsuits (except for husbands, who could sue for the loss of their wives' "services").[2]

In the mid-nineteenth century, England enacted a statute authorizing such suits with the goal of compensating dependents. American states followed. The statutes specify who may bring such actions. Sharon Smith faced a motion to dismiss her wrongful death suit against the dog owners and the landlord who allowed them to keep their dogs, because unmarried partners are not specified in the statute as among those who can bring such an action.

Wrongful death statutes vary from state to state, but their lists of who can bring a claim look much like the lists governing who inherits by intestate succession. A spouse tops the list, followed by children, parents, siblings, and other relatives. It's time to update these statutes to accord with modern life and the purpose of compensating for loss.

The overturning of a wrongful death statute ushered in the end of discrimination against children born outside of marriage. In cases decided on the same day in 1968, the U.S. Supreme Court ruled that a child born to an unmarried woman had a constitutional right to recover for her wrongful death and that a mother had the same right with respect to her nonmarital child; both groups were excluded under the Louisiana wrongful death statute.[3]

Justice William Douglas reasoned that the children depended on their mother, writing pointedly: "The rights asserted here involve the intimate, familial relationship between a child and his own mother. When the child's claim of damage for loss of his mother is in issue, why . . . should the [wrongdoers] go free merely because the child is illegitimate?"[4] In the companion case brought by a mother whose son was killed in a car accident, Douglas wrote that the law denying her recovery created "an open season on illegitimates in the area of automobile accidents," giving a windfall to wrongdoers.[5]

A judge refused to dismiss Smith's wrongful death action. The opinion echoed the reasoning of the Supreme Court in the "illegitimacy" cases; the judge said the purpose of the statute was compensation for loss, the plaintiff's sexual orientation was irrelevant to that loss, and "denying recovery would be a windfall for the [wrongdoer]."[6] But the judge could not just rewrite the statute. Like the child of an unmarried woman or the unmarried mother of a child in the Louisiana cases, Sharon could proceed only if the statute's exclusion of her was deemed unconstitutional. The judge ruled that it was, because Sharon and Diane had been denied the opportunity to come within the statute by marrying.

California has since amended its statute to allow registered domestic partners to bring wrongful death actions. This is an improvement that will help same-sex couples who register, but it misses the point. The purpose of the statute is compensation for loss. Even with the addition of registered domestic partners, the statute falls short of achieving that goal. Sharon should have been allowed to sue for wrongful death, regardless of whether she and Diane had a formalized relationship, because she suffered the greatest loss at Diane's death.

A Better Approach: Compensating Dependents

A handful of states come closer to meeting the purpose of a wrongful death statute. If the deceased had no spouse, child, or parent, Arizona allows suit by anyone named in the decedent's will. Michigan covers anyone named in the decedent's will, regardless of whether there are other survivors. The September 11th Victim Compensation Fund also adopted this approach; same-sex surviving partners who were named in the wills of those who died on September 11 recovered from the fund without difficulty. West Virginia does the best job by including anyone "financially dependent" on the deceased.[7] Smith accepted a settlement in her wrongful death suit, so the trial judge's decision to let her proceed was not tested in an appeals court.

The California statute does a better job with respect to children who may recover for an adult's wrongful death. It allows suits by children, dependent stepchildren, and any minor who lived with the deceased for the 180 days preceding her death and was dependent on her for at least half his support.[8] Thus, if Sharon Smith had a child who had not been adopted by Diane, the child would have been entitled to recover if Diane was responsible for at least half her expenses. The distinction between one's legal children and others in the statute, however, is inappropriate; stepchildren should not have to show dependency to the extent of 50 percent support. No child should have to meet this hurdle.

A wrongful death statute should allow all those dependent in whole or in part upon the deceased to recover from whoever was responsible for the death. Any other result creates either the kind of "open season" that lets a wrongdoer off the hook or the "unjust enrichment" of distant relatives, as in the intestacy statutes described in the previous chapter.

A few states have allowed suits for emotional loss upon a loved one's death. The New Hampshire Supreme Court ultimately allowed Catrina Graves to recover for the harm of seeing her partner of seven years killed when a car struck the motorcycle he was riding.[9] New

Mexico allowed a woman to sue for the loss of companionship of her unmarried partner, and, using similar reasoning, allowed a grandmother to sue for the loss of companionship when a pharmacy error resulted in the death of the granddaughter she was raising.[10] These more expansive understandings of who is harmed when a family member is hurt or killed should be models for other courts. California could have taken a more expansive view if it had borrowed the model in its workers' compensation statute.

Workers' Compensation Death Benefits

Joe Lopes and Bill Valentine met in San Francisco in 1980. They began living together in 1982. The next year, Joe was hired as a flight attendant for American Airlines. When he was transferred to New York in 1984, Bill moved with him. In 1994, they registered as domestic partners with the city. In 1995, they purchased an apartment together. Bill and Joe had a long-term financial plan. Bill was going to leave his job and enroll in journalism school; Joe was going to support him. On November 12, 2001, Joe died when the flight he was working, American Airlines Flight 587, crashed near Kennedy Airport. Bill applied for workers' compensation death benefits, but the claim was denied because he was not Joe's "surviving spouse."[11]

When San Francisco supervisor and gay community leader Harvey Milk was assassinated in 1978, his partner of five years, Scott Smith, received death benefits approved by the state's Workman's Compensation Appeals Board.[12]

The difference in outcomes in these two cases did not hinge on marriage. Scott Smith and Harvey Milk were not married; they were not even registered domestic partners, a status that was not created until many years after Milk's death. The difference hinged on the fact that California awards workers' comp death benefits based on dependency.

Workers' compensation began early in the twentieth century. It addressed the growing problem of industrial accidents causing injury and death. Before workers' comp, an injured employee, or the survivors of a deceased employee, could recover money only by proving that the employer's *fault* caused the injury or death. Those unable to meet this burden of proof could be left with no income; if a worker died his dependents lost their source of support.

Workers' comp is a type of no-fault insurance system. All employers pay into a state fund. Benefits are paid from that fund. In exchange for paying into the fund, the employer is immune from suit by an injured employee. The employee's only compensation comes through the administrative agency in charge of the state's workers' compensation system. Similarly, if an employee dies as a result of an injury on the job, survivors cannot sue the employer; they receive death benefits from the state-administered fund. Each statute establishes its own criteria for every aspect of the program, including who counts as a survivor, how much money they receive, for how long, and under what circumstances the payments cease.

Until 1972, a state could deny workers' compensation benefits to a deceased employee's children if those children were born outside of marriage. Using the same reasoning it had earlier applied to wrongful death actions, the Supreme Court ruled that making such a distinction was unconstitutional.[13]

States also used to treat husbands and wives differently based on assumptions about the different roles of men and women. The sex-based distinctions inherent in the program were captured in its original name: work*men*'s compensation. In 1980 the Supreme Court ruled unconstitutional a typical sex-based statute.[14] The Missouri law presumed that a widow was wholly dependent upon her deceased husband. A widower, however, had to prove that he received more than half his support from his deceased wife to obtain the benefit. The state argued that its rules properly reflected the different economic positions of working men and women and that it was cheaper to presume a wife's dependency than require proof of it in every instance. The Court ruled that administrative efficiency could not justify the sex-based classification.

In response, most states extended the benefit to both spouses without proof of dependency, but some required proof of dependency by either surviving spouse. Michigan and Maryland made this choice; every surviving spouse must prove dependency. California had declared its statute unconstitutional even before the Supreme Court ruling.[15] It, too, remedied the unconstitutionality by requiring both husbands and wives to prove dependency. California later amended its statute so that a surviving spouse who earned less than $30,000 in the year preceding the employee's death is presumed dependent upon her spouse. Those who earned more must prove their total or partial dependency.[16]

Some states award the benefit to a spouse based on relationship alone. Many states modify the rule for spouses to include only those living together at the time of the death. This condition is so consistent with common sense that one might miss its importance. The *legal relationship* of husband and wife exists whether or not the couple lives together. Spouses are eligible for many economic benefits solely based on their legal relationship. For example, a retirement-age wife separated from but still married to her retired husband is eligible for his Social Security survivors' benefits when he dies. Those statutes that award workers' comp benefits automatically only to those living with their deceased spouses demonstrate an intent to compensate only for a loss in the survivor's ability to meet expenses. It's the *function* of sharing a home that warrants the death benefit, not the legal relationship.

Unless a statute awards the death benefit based on relationship alone, a survivor must prove he was dependent on the employee. All workers' comp statutes include the concepts of *total* and *partial* dependency. In some states if someone depends wholly on the employee then partial dependents get nothing; in others the benefit is split among dependents. Many state statutes list those people eligible to prove that they were dependent on the deceased employee.

Bill Valentine was denied benefits because unmarried partners of any sex are not on the list in New York. Scott Smith received benefits because California permits someone who is "a member of the family or household of the employee" to apply for the benefit.[17] In 1979, a court ruled that a man's unmarried partner qualified under the statute.[18] In another California case, the thirteen-year-old grandson of the deceased unmarried partner was found eligible.[19]

In Maryland as well, anyone "wholly dependent"—or partially dependent if no one is wholly dependent—can receive the compensation.[20] In 1950, a woman who lived with a man for ten years was found eligible for benefits. The state's highest court cited with approval the principle that workers' compensation "is not a code of morals, but is a practical device for the economic protection of employees and those dependent upon them."[21]

The emphasis on proof of dependency in workers' compensation statutes presents a good opportunity to consider the purpose of the statutes and how to achieve that purpose without making marriage a rigid dividing line. If the purpose of the original workers' comp scheme was continued financial support of dependent wives, then the fix to the unlawful gender-based classification that made the statute gender-neutral in most states obscures that purpose. Payment to all surviving spouses based on an assumption of total dependency frustrates the purpose of supporting only those who are dependent and only to the extent of their dependency.

States like Maryland, Michigan, and California recognize this, because marriage to the deceased does not always result in payment of any, let alone total, death benefits. All spouses in Michigan and Maryland, and those in California who earn more than $30,000 a year, must prove dependency on their deceased spouses. If they were partially dependent, they receive a partial award.

So, had Bill and Joe lived in Maryland, Bill would have been eligible for death benefits as a member of Joe's household. His entitlement to any payment, however, would have depended on the degree to which he was dependent upon Joe—the same standard applicable to spouses. States have different ways of calculating partial dependency; in California, for example, the measure depends upon the amount the deceased worker contributed to the household (as opposed to his personal needs) including expenses that contributed to the standard of living.[22] Scott Smith received benefits based on his partial dependency on Harvey Milk.

The New York law does more than exclude Bill. It *includes* those not remotely dependent upon the deceased employee. For example, in one case the father of a twenty-five-year old was able to share in his son's $50,000 workers' comp death benefit even though he had abandoned the child as an infant.[23] A statute designed to protect those dependent upon the employee should not produce such a result, and would not in many states.

Larry Courtney faced the same hurdle as Bill Valentine in his quest for benefits as a result of his partner Eugene Clark's death in the September 11 attacks on the World Trade Center. But in August

2002 the New York legislature passed a law making domestic partners of those who died in the September 11 attacks eligible for workers' compensation benefits.[24] The statute extended eligibility on the same terms as spouses to same- and different-sex domestic partners. The survivor needed to show either registration as domestic partners with an employer or a governmental unit or "unilateral dependence or mutual interdependence, as evidenced by a nexus of factors including, but not limited to, common ownership of real or personal property, common householding, children in common, signs of intent to marry, shared budgeting, and the length of the personal relationship with the employee."[25]

New York does not adjust the amount of compensation paid when the survivor was not wholly dependent upon the employee. Larry received the entire spousal award. It appears that neither Eugene nor Joe had children. Spouses don't need to have children to receive a workers' comp death benefit. As Eugene's domestic partner, Larry receives $400 a week indefinitely. While this recognizes Larry and Eugene's relationship as equally valuable to that of married couples, it overlooks a larger question that applies to both types of relationships: On what basis does a nondisabled adult have a claim to financial compensation from scarce resources for the loss of an income-earning loved one?

Consider the following case, also the result of the September 11 attacks. Paul Innella died, leaving Victoria, a twenty-two-month-old child, the product of his relationship with Jennifer Novara. Jennifer received the $400 a week workers' comp death benefit on Victoria's behalf. After enactment of the statute treating the domestic partners of September 11 victims the same as spouses, Lucy Aita successfully asserted a claim as Paul's domestic partner. As a result, Lucy receives $220 per week. Victoria receives $180.[26]

Whether Lucy was Paul's wife or his domestic partner is immaterial. Preferring her over Victoria overlooks that Paul's child is an *inevitable* dependent. Lucy had a son. If Paul was supporting him, in some states he would have had a separate claim as a dependent, but not in New York.

Oregon workers' comp law has a provision for unmarried partners. It gives death benefits to the survivor of an unmarried different-sex couple who have a child together. (Given other law in Oregon, a court would likely extend this to a same-sex couple raising a child together.) In a recent case, a court ruled that an unmarried partner was not eligible because the child she had with the deceased worker was no longer a minor.[27]

This law gets it both right and wrong. It's wrong to exclude someone whose child is grown, because the *derivative* dependence caused by having raised the child remains. It's also wrong to differentiate between married and unmarried couples. If the decision is that those with children deserve the benefit and those without children do not, then marital status should be irrelevant. Where the law might get it right, however, is in withholding benefits from an adult partner who did not raise a child with the deceased worker. Even if a state does value the interdependency between adults, interdependents should not be the priority. Workers' comp benefits are a finite amount split among survivors; with scarce resources, children and disabled adults who relied on the employee should come first.

The New York workers' comp law is all wrong. It awards benefits based on formal status rather than dependency. Because of that, except for those who died on September 11, it ignores unmarried couples. In cases in which a worker has no spouse or child, it gives money to distant or estranged parents. It also places the needs of able-bodied adults over the needs of children.

By handpicking provisions in existing state laws, it would be possible to craft a workers' comp death benefit scheme that:

- compensates adults and children actually dependent upon the deceased worker regardless of formal relationship;
- recognizes children as wholly dependent upon a deceased parent and an able-bodied adult as partially dependent, thereby awarding greater benefits to a surviving child than to a surviving spouse or partner;
- acknowledges greater dependence of one adult upon another when they are raising or have raised a child together; and
- defines "dependence" to recognize the partial dependence that comes when two people are economically interdependent.

From a gay rights/marriage-discrimination perspective, the problem with workers' comp death benefits is that only married couples get them; same-sex couples can't marry, so same-sex couples can't get them. The solution is allowing same-sex couples to marry. The second-best solution is creation of an institution parallel to marriage that will give couples the state-level consequences of marriage, of which the workers' comp death benefit is one.

A valuing-all-families perspective identifies a different problem. Dependency is a functional matter. If the purpose of workers' comp is partial wage replacement for those who depended upon the employee's wages, the legal relationship between the deceased and the dependents is irrelevant. Many states assess actual total and partial dependency in workers' comp cases; more states could easily do what some do already and elevate function over form. Some states also distinguish among surviving spouses, making workers' comp in those states an excellent example of not making marriage the dividing line.

This approach is better than the gay rights approach because it incorporates better values about allocation of scarce resources. It also would meet the needs of same-sex couples who do not marry/register when a formal status is available to them, and it facilitates compensation for the full diversity of LGBT interdependent households.

Social Security

Social Security is "out of step with the modern family."[28] Its impact on same-sex couples is a small piece of a huge problem traceable to the program's origins. Social Security was designed in the 1930s, when only 15 percent of married women worked outside the home.[29] It had one family structure in mind: the wage-earning husband with a dependent wife. It also had mostly white people in mind, as it excluded domestic servants and farmworkers, two predominantly African American job categories. Until 1950, men were ineligible for benefits based on the earnings of their wives. Beginning that year, a widower became eligible, but only if he proved that he had been dependent upon his wife for at least half his support.[30]

In 1977, the Supreme Court found this sex discrimination unconstitutional.[31] Congress could have eliminated the discrimination by requiring all surviving spouses to prove dependency. It didn't. Our current sex-neutral system, therefore, rewards married recipients based on their marital status alone. (In fact, a widow receives survivors' benefits even if she and her deceased husband were married for only nine months before he died.) That wasn't the original purpose. Congress added spousal benefits as a way to meet what it thought to be the greatest need—the dependent wives of wage earners. In 1965 Congress added benefits for divorced wives if their marriage had lasted more than twenty years. As a result of feminist advocacy on behalf of "displaced homemakers," the required marriage length was reduced to ten years in 1977.[32]

The program remains true to its origin. Married couples with a single earner, or with one spouse who earns the vast majority of the family income, reap the greatest benefits today. A couple with $80,000 in average income, for example, all earned by one spouse, will receive more in Social Security benefits over their lifetimes than a couple in which each averages $40,000 a year.

In this way it is similar to the income tax rates for married couples. When law professor Dennis Ventry said that "modern tax rules governing married and single taxpayers were constructed at a time when married men made rules for the benefit of other married men and their families," he could have just as well been speaking of Social Security.[33] Married same-sex couples would benefit under income tax rates only if they approached the one-income-earner model.

Here is how Social Security benefits work: The spouse of the retired worker gets her own retirement benefit, which is half that of her husband, without ever paying into the system. The more her husband earned, the higher her benefit. If his benefit is $1,800, hers will be $900, for a total of $2,700 in household income. When her husband dies, she'll get *his* full benefit amount, $1,800, for a reduction of income to her household of only one-third.

A spouse always has this option to receive benefits calculated as 50 percent that of her spouse. But members of an equal-earning couple elect to receive benefits based on their individual earnings, because their total is more than the sum of one spouse's benefit plus the spousal benefit of 50 percent that amount. As an example, assume each is entitled to $1,350 based on his own earnings; the household will receive $2,700. The spousal benefit for someone receiving $1,350 is $675, so the household would receive only $1,925 if the second earner elected to receive the spousal benefit.

But this equal-earning couple is disadvantaged relative to a couple with a single high-income earner when the first spouse dies. In the equal-earning couple the survivor is left only with her own benefit, $1,350, causing a 50 percent cut in income.

Because same-sex couples have no access to the spousal retirement or survivors' benefit, those with significant income disparity between the two partners lose when compared with a married couple in the same situation. If the high earner is the first to die, the survivor will have only his own benefits to rely upon.

One publication on LGBT family policy uses the example of "Thorsten," who earns $44,000 a year, and "Christopher," who earns $4,000. Based on their current earnings, Thorsten's retirement benefit will be $1,527 a month and Christopher's $303. If Thorsten dies first, Christopher will be left with his $303 benefit. If Thorsten and Christopher were a married couple, they would receive Thorsten's $1,527 plus a spousal benefit of half that ($764), which is $461 a month more than Christopher's benefit alone. Regardless of who dies first, the survivor would receive the amount of Thorsten's benefit—$1,527 a month.[34]

Unmarried same- and different-sex couples with more evenly split lifetime earnings will be in a position more like that of married couples with similar incomes. Neither gets the benefit that goes to the spouse of a high-income earner. Because black married couples are far more likely than white ones to earn roughly equal amounts, they too are disadvantaged in the current system.[35]

All those who pay into Social Security subsidize the wives of high-income husbands, including multiple wives, as long as each was married to the wage earner for at least ten years. That's because the widow and each surviving divorced wife receives 100 percent of the benefit the worker was receiving while he was alive, regardless of whether she ever paid into the system herself or raised children with him. Unlike workers' compensation death benefits, which usually divide a fixed amount of money among dependents, there's no limit to the amount of money available to ex-wives, as long as each marriage lasted ten years.

Consider Newt Gingrich. He was married to Jackie for nineteen years; they had two children. He was married to Marianne for eighteen years; they had no children. When he dies, his current wife, Callista, with whom he has no children, *and* Jackie, *and* Marianne, will *each* be entitled to the full amount of his monthly Social Security checks. (If Gingrich stays married to Callista until 2010, then they divorce, and he remarries, four women will be entitled to survivors' benefits based on his earnings.) The highest benefit level in 2007 is $2,116 per month. If Gingrich's earnings entitle him to the highest benefit, that's what each former spouse will receive upon his death, every month until she dies.

On the other hand, a never-married worker, or a divorced worker whose marriage lasted less than ten years, has only her own earnings on which to base her benefits. If she raised children, she may have had less opportunity and fewer years to earn high wages. This makes a difference, because benefits are based on thirty-five years of earnings; those who take time from the full-time workforce to raise children, or who lose jobs because of their childcare obligations, can never recoup that loss. This workers' retirement benefit will likely be less than the survivors' benefit available to any one of Gingrich's former wives.

Minor children receive survivors' benefits when a worker dies. This is one of the most significant reasons why a nonbiological parent should do a second-parent adoption even if she is married or in a civil union with the child's biological parent; the federal government may not have to recognize a parent-child relationship created through a same-sex marriage or civil union, but it must recognize an adoption decree.

A widow or surviving divorced spouse caring for a child under sixteen also receives survivors' benefits. Unmarried couples lose because an unmarried different- or same-sex partner caring for the deceased worker's child can't get benefits. In 1979 the U.S. Supreme Court upheld this distinction. By then, the advances of the earlier part of the decade had met a concerted backlash. Although four justices believed this distinction unconstitutionally penalized a child born to an unmarried couple, the five-justice majority allowed Congress to make it.[36]

Right now Social Security pays benefits based on *actual dependency* on the deceased worker to two categories of survivors who are not a spouse, divorced spouse, or child: the *parent* of a deceased worker if she is at least sixty-two and not entitled on her own to a higher benefit, and the minor *stepchild* or *grandchild* of the deceased worker. Both categories of recipients must prove that they were receiving at least half their support from the worker at the time of his death. Grandchildren must meet additional requirements; they can't be receiving benefits through a parent, and their parents must usually be dead or disabled. These provisions fit well with Social Security's purpose of providing for a worker's *dependents.*

If these rules were extended to anyone who could prove the decedent provided more than half his support, marriage would matter less in distributing Social Security survivors' benefits. The stepchild rule should be extended. What matters is not that the deceased worker was married to the child's mother, but that he was supporting a child although under no obligation to do so.

Economists have developed many proposals for reforming Social Security in light of today's family demographics.[37] Some make marriage matter less, including providing a minimum benefit for everyone and assigning credits for caring for young children. Some make marriage matter differently, by, for example, crediting each spouse with half the couple's combined earnings. All try to remedy the current system's bias in favor of one-earner married couples. Advocates for same-sex couples could play a role in envisioning reforms, but the marriage-equality perspective is not the right framework for this.

Advocates for same-sex marriage ask that gay and lesbian couples be treated as married couples are now treated. But when they support their argument with evidence of some concrete *harm* from lack of access to marriage, they make a different claim—that they are entitled to what married couples now have.

This is a fair argument when invoking the survivors' benefits that go to parents with minor children. It is a problematic one, however, when invoking the current system of retirement and survivors' benefits for the elderly. The same-sex couples who stand to gain the most from marriage equality for purposes of Social Security are those whose married counterparts benefit too much from the system today—couples with a single high-income earner. Marital status alone gives them too much. Progressive reformers are urging a more just benefit distribution. A guaranteed minimum benefit for everyone would be a good start, and it would have nothing to do with marriage.

Conclusion

> We the undersigned—lesbian, gay, bisexual and transgender (LGBT) and allied activists, scholars, educators, writers, artists, lawyers, journalists, and community organizers—seek to offer friends and colleagues everywhere a new vision for securing governmental and private institutional recognition of diverse kinds of partnerships, households, kinship relationships and families. In so doing, we hope to move beyond the narrow confines of marriage politics as they exist in the United States today.

So begins a 2006 document titled "Beyond Same-Sex Marriage: A New Strategic Vision for all our Families & Relationships."[1] Written by two-dozen LGBT individuals calling for an overtly progressive framework around the goal of achieving marriage for same-sex couples, the document calls for the fight for same-sex marriage to be part of "a larger effort to strengthen the stability and security of diverse households and families." It advocates fighting against "the full scope of the conservative marriage agenda."

The foundation of that agenda is the assertion that the married heterosexual couple is the only family form worthy of legal recognition and proper for raising children. It is in furtherance of *that* claim that the marriage movement opposes LGBT parenting and marriage for same-sex couples.

The marriage-equality movement counters that aspect of conservative ideology, and this is an honest, worthy, and just cause. Once marriage for same-sex couples moved from a discussion of priorities among LGBT advocates, as exemplified in the Stoddard-Ettelbrick exchange in 1989, to a matter subject to an up or down vote in state elections, there were only two sides to choose from.

Those who oppose same-sex marriage think that we LGBT people are unworthy of equality, and that our lives are of less use than theirs to the building of strong communities. Some, especially adherents of the Religious Right, think we are sick, sinful people, dangerous to children and undeserving of protection against discrimination. I disagree with every aspect of their position.

Those who support marriage equality want a child in any part of this country to know that if he grows up to love someone of his own sex there is nothing wrong with him. They want same-sex couples to occupy public spaces just as different-sex couples do. They want lesbian, gay, bisexual, and transgender people to be safe on the streets and secure in their jobs. I agree with all of these goals.

When Evan Wolfson debates David Blankenhorn, there is no question about which side I support.

But the other positions of the marriage movement are as alarming as their condemnation of LGBT families, and that is why a broader agenda is necessary.

A law reform agenda that values all LGBT families and relationships, and by extension those of heterosexuals as well, does *not* start with the package of rights that marriage gives different-sex couples and work down from there, strategizing about how many of those rights politicians are willing to grant same-sex couples who sign up with the state in a status called civil union or domestic partnership. Instead, such an agenda starts by identifying the needs of all LGBT people and works up from there to craft legislative proposals to meet those needs.

This is a different mindset and will produce different results. For example: In 2006 the Washington Supreme Court ruled against same-sex couples seeking marriage. Gay rights activists went to the state legislature seeking domestic partnership. They were successful. The domestic partnership law begins with a statement that because same-sex couples cannot marry they lack access to certain rights accorded married couples. It continues: "The rights granted to state registered domestic partners in this act will further Washington's interest in promoting family relationships and protecting family members during life crises."

But other than benefits for partners of state employees, the law affords only the following to registered couples:

- hospital visitation;
- surrogate healthcare decision making in the absence of a directive to the contrary;
- related matters such as right to consent to organ donation and right to dispose of remains;
- the right to inherit under the state's law on intestate succession and to administer each other's estates.[2]

Existing laws assign these rights now to spouses or blood/adoptive "next of kin" unless documents such as wills or powers of attorney say otherwise. Registering eliminates the need to write these documents. The law allows same-sex couples, and different-sex couples where one partner is at least sixty-two, to register. They must live together.

But there is widespread agreement across the political spectrum that these are matters of personal autonomy. Cast in these terms, the Washington law should be open to any two unmarried people who wish to designate each other as "family" for these purposes, and it should not require that they live together.

This would help all LGBT people who need these protections—including those who are not in couples or who don't live with their partners—and many non-LGBT people as well.

Marriage-equality leader Evan Wolfson saw this very differently. After Washington's governor signed the law, Wolfson *criticized* the fact that different-sex couples could register. He said it conveyed the impression that the law was about handling legal issues rather than about recognizing same-sex couples. He claimed it diminished the rights of gay couples and called it "the right wing's way of saying... we're not legitimating gay relationships."[3]

This is the challenge for the LGBT movement and the lawyers who represent it:

Laws that value all families are not primarily about legitimating gay relationships that mirror marriage. They are about ensuring that every relationship and every family has the legal framework for economic and emotional security. Laws that value all families value same-sex couples but not only same-sex couples. Lesbian, gay, bisexual, and transgender people live in varied households and families. A valuing-all-families approach strives to meet the needs of all of them, making real the vision in the "Beyond Same-Sex Marriage" statement that "marriage is not the only worthy form of family or relationship, and it should not be legally and economically privileged above all others."

Looking Ahead

Gay rights litigators argue for marriage equality in state courts, using state constitutions. They have mined legal precedents looking for support. In Vermont, they argued that exclusion from marriage violated the state constitution's common benefits clause. The clause affirms that "government is, or ought to be, instituted for the common benefit, protection, and security of the people, nation, or community, and not for the particular emolument or advantage of any single person, family, or set of persons, who are a part only of that community." That argument resulted in civil unions for same-sex couples. It sounds like a plausible basis to argue for the needs of diverse families. It's time to see if other state constitutions might support the needs of all family structures.

The work of the marriage-equality litigators reverberates in legislatures. Successful cases—those in which the courts rule that the current laws are unconstitutional—wind up in the legislature for a remedy. Losses also can wind up in the legislature, as Washington demonstrates, when enough political support exists to address some of the problems same-sex couples experience. Even in states without marriage-equality litigation, such as Maine, New Hampshire, and Oregon, nearby efforts can prod legislators to act.

Once the issue of crafting laws to protect families is before a legislature, the constraints of making legal arguments to judges disappear. In the legislature it is possible to ask for what all families need. Even if gay rights groups see their constituency as only LGBT people and their relationships, households, and families, it is possible to ask for what *they all need,* not only those that mirror married heterosexual couples.

Models for laws that might be on such a legislative agenda include:

- the Maryland advance directive registry, with its provisions for visitation and disposition of remains;
- the District of Columbia law on surrogate healthcare decision making, which places domestic partners (registration *not* required) at the top, includes close friends, and allows close friends to challenge relatives if they know the patient better;
- the New York law on disposition of remains, which also does not require partner registration;
- the Salt Lake City "adult designee" employee benefits law;
- the Colorado "harmless error" statute, derived from the Uniform Probate Code, on wills lacking all the formalities;
- the federal Office of Personnel Management rule that allows employees to take sick leave to care for "any individual related by blood or affinity whose close association with the employee is the equivalent of a family relationship";
- the New Hampshire law that extends inheritance rights to unmarried different-sex couples who live together for three years;
- the Washington court decisions equitably dividing the property of unmarried couples when they split up or upon the death of one partner (the ALI principles would be better);
- the Family and Medical Leave Act regulation defining "child" as one for whom the employee has "day-to-day responsibilities" and provides financial support;
- the California and Maryland laws authorizing workers' compensation death benefits based on actual dependency;
- the District of Columbia definition of de facto parent as the legal equivalent of a parent; and
- second-parent adoptions and orders of parentage now available in many states.

Some of these need improvements, but they are good places to start. By matching relationships to the purpose of a law it is possible to meet the needs of today's families. It is possible to do this across the country, not only in those places with a political climate supportive of gay rights. Advocacy linked to the purpose of a law or policy bypasses antigay sentiment. It will garner support from many people who stand to gain from this approach.

Increasingly, legislators are voting to protect a wide range of families because they do not want to cast a vote in the name of "gay rights." Activists understandably find their motivations distasteful. I urge advocates to wholeheartedly embrace good proposals that help all LGBT relationships *and that include unmarried different-sex couples.* When a law excludes unmarried heterosexual couples it sends the distinct message that marriage is special, and that the law's purpose is to meet the needs of those "rightly" excluded from that status. This *is* an offensive message. When unmarried heterosexual couples are eligible for the law's benefits, then the law is not about marriage at all; it is about valuing all families. The model laws cited above all meet this standard.

Some marriage-equality advocates criticize as utopian the vision in the "Beyond Same-Sex Marriage" statement. They think that obtaining the support that all families need to thrive and prosper is a more difficult goal than obtaining marriage equality. If this is true, it is because the marriage movement and the Right have inundated the culture with the claim that what they call "family breakdown" *causes* poverty and all other social problems.

When marriage-equality advocates sidestep this false assertion and only counter right-wing claims specific to access to marriage for same-sex couples, they risk contributing to the climate that makes advocacy for diverse families difficult. I do not believe most marriage-equality advocates want to contribute to that climate. I believe it happens nonetheless.

Members of the marriage movement will hate a valuing-all-families agenda. They are committed to a privileged place for marriage. They base this privilege on their claim that family diversity is responsible for our social ills. They take every opportunity to repeat this claim. Seeking law reform that values all families will give them such an opportunity.

Repeating this claim distracts attention from real solutions to poverty, like the plan the Center for American Progress proposes —twelve steps to reduce poverty by 50 percent in ten years. Promoting marriage is *not* one of those steps. For the Right, it is the only step.

Fighting these marriage-movement claims is as important a role for organizations that represent all LGBT people as is fighting the claims they make that are specific to same-sex couples and parents. Joining with other groups that also seek to redirect for the good of the many a portion of the wealth now concentrated in the hands of the few is the only way that all lesbian, gay, bisexual, and transgender people will have both equality and justice.

The fight for laws that value all families is a fight for justice. It is not strictly a fight for equality under a set of laws enacted long ago, when families were very different, that no longer serve their original purpose or that serve a purpose discredited in an egalitarian and pluralistic society.

This vision is not new in the LGBT community. It was there at the founding of the modern gay rights movement after Stonewall. It was fundamental to radical feminism. It was intimately bound up with the changing legal and cultural norms that stripped marriage of its role in demarcating good and bad sex, good and bad motherhood, and good and bad families. It was there in the 1989 draft of the Family Bill of Rights, which advocated opening up marriage to same-sex couples in the context of urging reform of health, housing, employment, immigration, and family law to meet the needs of all families. It was there in the National Gay and Lesbian Task Force assessment of the harms in the Bush administration's "welfare reform" proposal.

It remains part of imagining the United States as a place of both equality and justice for all.

Acknowledgments

Horace Ports, my ninth-grade social studies teacher at Edgemont High School in 1965, taught me to question conventional wisdom about the Cold War, and by extension about everything, and not to believe everything I read. Judith Fetterley, my University of Pennsylvania English teacher in 1971, gave me the tools to see male supremacy, rather than a natural order, in the respective roles of men and women in both literature and society. Judith Areen, my Georgetown law school family law teacher in 1973 supported my quest to protect the relationships of lesbian mothers and their children and nurtured me as a young legal scholar. I wouldn't be who or where I am today without the contribution that each made to my development.

My thanks to Michael Bronski, who gave me the opportunity to write this book for Beacon Press and provided great input throughout the process. My Beacon editor, Gayatri Patnaik, and her assistant, Tracy Ahlquist, helped me get the book done. Lauren Taylor was indispensable as my editor and my friend.

Mary Bonauto, Jon Davidson, Shannon Minter, and Judith Stacey read individual chapters and made comments that gave me lots to think about and that improved the final product. Martha Ertman, Nan Hunter, and Jana Singer read multiple chapters; the suggestions of each have made their way into the book.

Dean Claudio Grossman provided generous financial support, and Washington College of Law (WCL) faculty members provided feedback on my ideas and shared their specialized knowledge with me. I am especially grateful to Nancy Abramowitz, Pamela Bridgewater, Mary Clark, Fernanda Nicola, Ann Shalleck, and Dennis Ventry. When I visited at the University of Arizona in 2004–5, Barbara Atwood challenged me with just the right mixture of support and skepticism. Laura Rosenbury, Gary Spitko, and Richard Storrow answered questions about fields they know more about than I do. Art Leonard keeps track of every LGBT law development and generously shares what he knows.

Numerous staff at WCL made it possible for me to do my work. My thanks to: Elma Gates, Flor Hernandez, Billie Jo Kaufman, Susan Lewis-Sommers, Jason Rauch, Rosalena Thompson, and Sharon Wolfe. I owe a special debt to librarian Adeen Postar, who found every source I needed, sometimes at a moment's notice.

Many students helped me with research, including Heather Aitken, Andrea Irwin, Fatema Merchant, Rory Pred, and Emily Stark. I want to single out Becca Levin for special thanks for her year as my Dean's Fellow and her extraordinary effort as I finalized the manuscript. Thanks also to former students Laura Astrada, Kelly Barrett, and Heather Collier, who read portions of the draft.

Many academics and advocates keep me posted on family law developments affecting marriage and LGBT families in their countries: Katherine Arnup, Graeme Austin, Bill Atkin, Nicholas Bala, Claire Bear, Daniel Borrillo, Susan Boyd, Pierre DeVos, Aeyal Gross, Rainier Hiltunen, Kathleen Lahey, Jenni Milbank, Adilson Jose Moreira, Miranda Stewart, Kees Waaldijk, Kristen Walker, Robert Wintemute, and Hans Ytterberg.

The group that wrote the "Beyond Same-Sex Marriage" vision statement gave me great ideas and the assurance that I was not alone within the LGBT community. I am especially grateful to Joseph DeFillipis of Queers for Economic Justice for bringing us together in April 2006.

I am blessed with a loving "family of origin" and "family of friends" and I thank them all for their support. As I wrote this book, my partner of almost twenty years, Cheryl Swannack, encouraged me, listened to my ideas and witnessed my agony at trying to translate those ideas to paper, kept our household going, and nurtured me with food and love. Thanks, Cheryl. I love you.

Notes

Introduction

1. Casey Charles, *The Sharon Kowalski Case: Lesbian and Gay Rights on Trial* (Lawrence: University Press of Kansas, 2003).

2. *Burns v. Burns*, 253 Ga. App. 600 (2002).

3. Sean Cahill, Mitra Ellen, and Sarah Tobias, *Family Policy: Issues Affecting Gay, Lesbian, Bisexual, and Transgender Families* (New York: Policy Institute of the National Gay and Lesbian Task Force, 2003), 21–22.

4. Cahill, Ellen, and Tobias, *Family Policy*, 149–50.

5. *Cord v. Gibb*, 219 Va. 1019 (1979).

6. *Graves v. Estabrook*, 149 N.H. 202, 204 (2003).

7. Kate Klise, "Get Married or Move Out," *People*, March 27, 2006.

8. *In re Jason C.*, 129 N.H. 762 (1987).

9. James Slack, Luke Salkeld, and Nick McDermott, "Euro-Court Denies Sisters the Same Tax Breaks as Gay Couples," *Daily Mail*, December 13, 2006.

10. *Sierotowicz v. N.Y. City Hous. Auth.*, 2006 U.S. Dist. LEXIS 19644 (E.D.N.Y. 2006).

11. "Death Benefit Voted for Homosexual's Lover," *New York Times*, November 11, 1982.

Chapter One: The Changing Meaning of Marriage

1. Leo Kanowitz, *Women and the Law: The Unfinished Revolution* (Albuquerque: University of New Mexico Press, 1969), 35–37.

2. See National Park Service, "Declaration of Sentiments," www.nps.gov/archive/wori/declaration.htm.

3. *Bradwell v. Illinois*, 83 U.S. 130, 141 (1873).

4. Nancy F. Cott, *Public Vows: A History of Marriage and the Nation* (Cambridge, Mass.: Harvard University Press, 2000), 53–55.

5. Kanowitz, *Women and the Law*, 28–31, 41, 46–47.

6. *Carlson v. Carlson*, 75 Ariz. 308, 310 (1953).

7. *McGuire v. McGuire*, 157 Neb. 226, 238 (1953).

8. *Goesaert v. Cleary*, 335 U.S. 464 (1948).

9. Maren Lockwood Carden, *The New Feminist Movement* (New York: Russell Sage Foundation, 1974), 59–60.

10. The Feminists, "Women: Do You Know the Facts about Marriage?" leaflet, 1969, in *Sisterhood Is Powerful: An Anthology of Writings from the Women's Liberation Movement*, edited by Robin Morgan (New York: Random House, 1970), 601–2.

11. Susan J. Douglas and Meredith W. Michaels, *The Mommy Myth: The Idealization of Motherhood and How It Has Undermined Women* (New York: Free Press, 2004), 38–39.

12. Ninia Baehr, *Abortion without Apology: A Radical History for the 1990s* (Boston: South End Press, 1990), 25.

13. Radicalesbians, "The Woman-Identified Woman," in *Out of the Closets: Voices of Gay Liberation*, edited by Karla Jay and Allen Young, rev. ed. (New York: New York University Press, 1992), 172–77.

14. The Handbook of Texas Online, "National Women's Conference, 1977," www.tsha.utexas.edu/handbook/online/articles/NN/pwngq.html.

15. Abzug's speech is included in the documentary film *Sisters of '77*, by Allen Mondell, Cynthia Salzman Mondell, and Brian Hockenbury (Dallas: Media Projects, 2005).

16. Ann Fessler, *The Girls Who Went Away: The Hidden History of Women Who Surrendered Children for Adoption in the Decades before Roe v. Wade* (New York: Penguin Press, 2006); Rickie Solinger, *Wake Up Little Susie* (New York: Routledge, 2000).

17. Herma Hill Kay, "From the Second Sex to the Joint Venture: An Overview of Women's Rights and Family Law in the United States during the Twentieth Century," *California Law Review* 88, no. 6 (2000): 2017–94.

18. *Reed v. Reed*, 404 U.S. 71 (1971).

19. *Frontiero v. Richardson*, 411 U.S. 677 (1973).

20. *Weinberger v. Wiesenfeld*, 420 U.S. 636 (1975).

21. *Califano v. Goldfarb*, 430 U.S. 199 (1977).

22. *Stanton v. Stanton*, 421 U.S. 7, 10 (1975).

23. *Orr v. Orr*, 440 U.S. 268 (1979).

24. *Kirchberg v. Feenstra*, 450 U.S. 455 (1981).

25. Harry D. Krause, *Illegitimacy: Law and Social Policy* (Indianapolis: Bobbs-Merrill, 1971), 25–28.

26. Harry D. Krause, "Bringing the Bastard into the Great Society: A Proposed Uniform Act on Legitimacy," *Texas Law Review* 44, no. 5 (1966): 829–59, 830.

27. Brief for the attorney general, State of Louisiana, as amicus curiae in *Levy v. Louisiana*, 391 U.S. 68 (1968).

28. *Glona v. American Guarantee & Liability Ins. Co.*, 391 U.S. 73 (1968).

29. *Weber v. Aetna Cas. & Surety Co.*, 406 U.S. 164 (1972).

30. *Stanley v. Illinois*, 405 U.S. 645 (1972).

31. *Gomez v. Perez*, 409 U.S. 535 (1973).

32. *New Jersey Welfare Rights Org. v. Cahill*, 411 U.S. 619 (1973).

33. *King v. Smith*, 392 U.S. 309 (1968).

34. *Griswold v. Connecticut*, 381 U.S. 479 (1965).

35. *Eisenstadt v. Baird*, 405 U.S. 438, 453 (1972).

36. *United States Dep't of Agric. v. Moreno*, 413 U.S. 528 (1973).

37. Herma Hill Kay, "'Making Marriage and Divorce Safe for Women' Revisited," *Hofstra Law Review* 32, no. 1 (2003): 71–92.

38. Quoted in *Families, Politics, and Public Policy: A Feminist Dialogue on Women and the State*, edited by Irene Diamond (New York: Longman, 1983), 8.

Chapter Two: Gay Rights and the Conservative Backlash

1. Karlis C. Ullis, *Sandy and Madeleine's Family* (San Francisco: Multi-Media Resource Center, 1974).

2. R. A. Basile, "Lesbian Mothers I," *Women's Rights Law Reporter* 2, no. 1 (1974): 3–25; Rhonda R. Rivera, "Our Straight-Laced Judges: The Legal Position of Homosexual Persons in the United States," *Hastings Law Journal* 30, no. 4 (1978): 799–956; Nan D. Hunter and Nancy D. Polikoff, "Custody Rights of Lesbian Mothers: Legal Theory and Litigation Strategy," *Buffalo Law Review* 25, no. 3 (1976): 691–734.

3. Ibid.

4. John D'Emilio, *Sexual Politics, Sexual Communities: The Making of a Homosexual Minority in the United States, 1940–1970* (Chicago: University of Chicago Press, 1983), 102–7.

5. Ibid., 152–57.

6. Allen Young, "Out of the Closets, Into the Streets," in *Out of the Closets: Voices of Gay Liberation*, edited by Karla Jay and Allen Young, rev. ed. (New York: New York University Press, 1992), 10.

7. Donn Teal, *The Gay Militants* (New York: Stein and Day, 1971).

8. Del Martin and Phyllis Lyon, *Lesbian/Woman* (San Francisco: Glide Publications, 1972).

9. Del Martin and Phyllis Lyon, "Lesbian Mothers," *Ms.*, October 1973.

10. *Christian v. Randall*, 516 P.2d 132 (Colo. Ct. App. 1973).

11. John Gallagher and Chris Bull, *Perfect Enemies: The Battle between the Religious Right and the Gay Movement* (Lanham, Md.: Madison Books, 2001), 16–17, 219.

12. Joan Gubbins et al., "'. . . To Establish Justice . . .': Minority Report," in National Commission on the Observance of International Women's Year, *The Spirit*

of Houston: The First National Women's Conference (Washington, D.C.: U.S. Government Printing Office, 1978), 265–72.

13. Hyde Amendment, Pub. L. No. 94–439, sec. 209, 90 Stat. 1418 (1976).

14. *Poelker v. Doe,* 432 U.S. 519 (1977).

15. *Califano v. Boles,* 443 U.S. 282 (1979).

16. "Voting against Gay Rights," *Time,* May 22, 1978, www.time.com/time/magazine/article/0,9171,919647,00.html.

17. Thomas J. Burrows, "Family Values: From the White House Conference on Families to the Family Protection Act," in *Creating Change: Sexuality, Public Policy, and Civil Rights,* edited by John D'Emilio, William B. Turner, and Urvashi Vaid (New York: St. Martin's Press, 2000), 349.

18. Burrows, "Family Values," 347.

19. NOW Legal Defense and Education Fund, *National Assembly on the Future of the Family: A Report* (New York: November 19, 1979), 23.

20. *M.P. v. S.P.,* 169 N.J. Super. Ct. 425, 438 (App. Div. 1979).

Chapter Three: Redefining Family

1. *Braschi v. Stahl Associates Co.*, 74 N.Y.2d 201, 211 (1989).

2. *In re Guardianship of Kowalski,* 478 N.W.2d 790 (Minn. Ct. App. 1991); Casey Charles, *The Sharon Kowalski Case: Lesbian and Gay Rights on Trial* (Lawrence: University Press of Kansas, 2003); Karen Thompson and Julie Andrzejewski, *Why Can't Sharon Kowalski Come Home?* (San Francisco: Spinsters/Aunt Lute, 1988).

3. *Singer v. Hara,* 11 Wn. App. 247 (Wash. Ct. App. 1974).

4. Nadine Brozan, "Parley Asserts U.S. Undercuts Family," *New York Times,* July 28, 1982.

5. Ibid.

6. Alice Rickel, "Extending Employee Benefits to Domestic Partners: Avoiding Legal Hurdles while Staying in Tune with the Changing Definition of the Family," *Whittier Law Review* 16, no. 3 (1995): 737–76, 742–45.

7. *Domestic Partner/Non-Traditional Family Recognition in Campus Benefits Policies: 1990 Survey* (Washington, D.C.: National Gay and Lesbian Task Force, 1990).

8. *Equal Opportunities Ordinance,* sec. 3.23(2), City of Madison, Wisconsin, available at www.municode.com/resources/gateway.asp?pid=50000&sid=49.

9. Barbara J. Cox, "Choosing One's Family: Can The Legal System Address the Breadth of Women's Choice of Intimate Relationship?" *Saint Louis University Public Law Review* 8, no. 2 (1989): 299–338; Barbara J. Cox, "Alternative Families: Obtaining Traditional Family Benefits through Litigation, Legislation and Collective Bargaining," *Wisconsin Women's Law Journal* 2, no. 1 (1986): 1–52.

10. Laura Benkov, *Reinventing the Family: The Emerging Story of Lesbian and*

Gay Parents (New York: Crown, 1994), 86–98; Neil Miller, *In Search of Gay America: Women and Men in a Time of Change* (New York: Atlantic Monthly Press, 1989), 121–30.

11. *In re Opinion of the Justices,* 530 A.2d 21 (N.H. 1987).

12. Angela Mae Kupenda, "Two Parents Are Better than None: Whether Two, Single, African American Adults—who are not in a traditional marriage or a romantic or sexual relationship with each other—Should be Allowed to Jointly Adopt and Co-Parent African American Children," *University of Louisville Journal of Family Law* 35, no. 4 (1997): 703–20.

13. *Bezio v. Patenaude,* 410 N.E.2d 1207 (Mass. 1980).

14. *S.N.E. v. R.L.B.*, 699 P.2d 875 (Alaska 1985).

15. *Roe v. Roe,* 324 S.E.2d 691 (Va. 1985).

16. *Daly v. Daly,* 715 P.2d 56 (Nev. 1986).

17. *Bowers v. Hardwick,* 478 U.S. 186, 192 (1986).

18. *In re Appeal in Pima County Juvenile Action B-10489,* 151 Ariz. 335, 340 (Ariz. Ct. App. 1986).

19. Los Angeles City Task Force on Family Diversity, *Final Report: Strengthening Families: A Model for Community Action* (Los Angeles, Calif., 1988).

20. Andrew Sullivan, "Here Comes The Groom: A Conservative Case for Gay Marriage," *The New Republic,* August 28, 1989.

21. Thomas B. Stoddard, "Why Gay People Should Seek the Right to Marry," and Paula L. Ettelbrick, "Since When Is Marriage a Path to Liberation?" in *Lesbian and Gay Marriage: Private Commitments, Public Ceremonies,* edited by Suzanne Sherman (Philadelphia: Temple University Press, 1992), 13–19; 20–26.

22. Family Bill of Rights; unpublished draft document, on file with author.

23. Sally Kohn, *The Domestic Partnership Organizing Manual* (Washington, D.C.: National Gay and Lesbian Task Force, 1999), 8.

24. Katrine Ames et al., "Domesticated Bliss," *Newsweek,* March 23, 1992.

25. Zachary Bromer, "Domestic Partner Benefits Becoming Mainstream," www.vault.com/nr/newsmain.jsp?nr_page=3&ch_id=401&article_id=53265&listelement=2&cat_id=1089.

Chapter Four: The Right and the Marriage Movement

1. John Gallagher and Chris Bull, *Perfect Enemies: The Battle between the Religious Right and the Gay Movement* (Lanham, Md.: Madison Books, 2001), 26.

2. Quoted in Debra J. Sanders, "Standing Firm and Whining," *San Francisco Chronicle,* September 2, 1994.

3. Andrew Rosenthal, "Quayle Attacks a 'Cultural Elite,' Saying It Mocks Nation's Values," *New York Times,* June 10, 1992.

4. "Transcript of Speech by Clinton Accepting Democratic Nomination," *New York Times,* July 17, 1992.

5. The American Presidency Project, "The Vision Shared: The Republican Platform, Uniting Our Family, Our Country, Our World," adopted August 17, 1992, www.presidency.ucsb.edu/showplatforms.php?platindex=R1992.

6. Patrick J. Buchanan, 1992 Republican National Convention Speech, Houston, Texas, August 17, 1992, available at www.buchanan.org/pa-92-0817-rnc.html.

7. Pat Robertson, "Speech, 1992 Republican Convention," www.patrobertson.com/Speeches/1992GOPConvention.asp.

8. Quoted in Kevin Sack, "The 1992 Campaign: The Vice President; Quayle Tries to Separate Family Values and 'Murphy Brown,'" *New York Times*, September 3, 1992.

9. Forerunner.com, "Remarks by William Bennett, Former Secretary of Education, at the Republican Party Convention's Nomination of Dan Quayle for U.S. Vice President on August 19, 1992," http://forerunner.com/forerunner/X0407_Remarks_by_William_B.html.

10. Quoted in Maralee Schwartz and Kenneth J. Cooper, "Equal Rights Initiative in Iowa Attacked," *Washington Post*, August 23, 1992.

11. Gallagher and Bull, *Perfect Enemies*, 98–106.

12. Quoted in Larry Tye, "Right Sees Debate of Gays as Way Back to Power," *Boston Globe*, February 25, 1993.

13. "Births to Single Moms Hit Record," *Chicago Tribune*, February 26, 1993.

14. Barbara Dafoe Whitehead, "Dan Quayle Was Right," *Atlantic Monthly* (April 1993).

15. William Galston, "Stable Families Fabric of Strong Society," *Wisconsin State Journal*, April 25, 1993.

16. Charles Murray, "The Coming White Underclass," *Wall Street Journal*, October 29, 1993.

17. Quoted in William M. Welch, "Age-Old Debate on Morality Takes New Life," *USA Today*, December 14, 1993.

18. Judith Stacey, "Scents, Scholars, and Stigma: The Revisionist Campaign for Family Values," *Social Text* 40 (autumn 1994).

19. Ibid.

20. David Blankenhorn, *Fatherless America: Confronting Our Most Urgent Social Problem* (New York: Basic Books, 1995); David Popenoe, *Life without Father: Compelling New Evidence That Fatherhood and Marriage Are Indispensable for the Good of Children and Society* (New York: Martin Kessler, 1996).

21. Blankenhorn, *Fatherless America*, 96–123.

22. Popenoe, *Life without Father*, 109–38.

23. William A. Henry, "Gay Parents: Under Fire and on the Rise," *Time*, September 20, 1993.

24. *In re M.M.D.*, 662 A.2d 837 (D.C. 1995).

25. *Personal Responsibility and Work Opportunity Reconciliation Act of 1996*, Public Law 104–193, U.S. Code 42 (1997), sec. 601.

26. Linda J. Waite and Maggie Gallagher, *The Case for Marriage: Why Married People Are Happier, Healthier, and Better Off Financially* (New York: Doubleday, 2000).

27. Quoted in Scott Coltrane, "Marketing the Marriage 'Solution': Misplaced Simplicity in the Politics of Fatherhood," *Sociological Perspectives* 44, no. 4 (2001): 389.

28. Linda C. McClain, *The Place of Families: Fostering Capacity, Equality, and Responsibility* (Cambridge, Mass.: Harvard University Press, 2006), 117–154; Kathryn Edin and Maria Kefalas, *Promises I Can Keep: Why Poor Women Put Motherhood before Marriage* (Berkeley: University of California Press, 2005); Melanie Heath, "Making Marriage Count in Law and Public Policy: Symbolic Boundaries and Gendered Anxieties" (paper presented, Annual American Studies Association Meeting, New York, 2007).

29. Sean Cahill and Kenneth T. Jones, *Leaving Our Children Behind: Welfare Reform and the Gay, Lesbian, Bisexual, and Transgender Community* (Washington, D.C.: National Gay and Lesbian Task Force, December 10, 2001) 62.

30. Heath, "Making Marriage Count."

31. Institute for American Values and Institute for Marriage and Public Policy, *Marriage and the Law: A Statement of Principles* (New York: Institute for American Values, 2006), 6–8. Also available at http://center.americanvalues.org/?p=47.

32. Ibid.; *Maynard v. Hill*, 125 U.S. 190, 210–11 (1888).

33. Nancy F. Cott, *Public Vows: A History of Marriage and the Nation* (Cambridge, Mass.: Harvard University Press, 2000); Hendrik Hartog, *Man and Wife in America: A History* (Cambridge, Mass.: Harvard University Press, 2000); Marilyn Yalom, *A History of the Wife* (New York: HarperCollins, 2001); Stephanie Coontz, *Marriage, A History: From Obedience to Intimacy, or How Love Conquered Marriage* (New York: Viking, 2005).

34. Frank Furstenberg, "Can Marriage Be Saved?" *Dissent* (summer 2005).

35. Ibid.

36. Brief for Andrew E. Cherlin et al. as amici curiae supporting appellees, *Baehr v. Miike*, No. 91–1394–05, 1996 WL 694235 (Hawaii Cir. Ct. Dec. 3, 1996), available at www.qrd.org/usa/legal/hawaii/baehr/1997/brief.doctors.of.sociology-06.02.97.

37. Louise B. Silverstein and Carl F. Auerbach, "Deconstructing the Essential Father," *American Psychologist* 54, no. 6 (June 1999).

38. *The Role of the Father in Child Development*, 2nd ed., edited by Michael E. Lamb (New York: John Wiley & Sons, 1981).

39. *Howard v. Child Welfare Agency Review Bd.*, CV 1999–9981, 2004 WL 3154530 at *5–6 (Ark. Cir. Ct., Dec. 29, 2004).

40. Michael Wald, "Adult's Sexual Orientation and State Determinations Regarding Placement of Children," *Family Law Quarterly* 40, no. 3 (2006): 381–434, footnote 56.

41. Ibid., 389–90.

42. Ibid., 404.

43. Ibid., 405.

44. David Fein and Theodora Ooms, "What Do We Know about Couples and Marriage in Disadvantaged Populations?: Reflections from a Researcher and a Policy Analyst" (paper presented, Annual Research Conference of the Association for Public Policy Analysis and Management, Washington, D.C., November 3–5, 2005).

45. Wendy D. Manning and Susan L. Brown, "Children's Economic Well-Being in Married and Cohabiting Parent Families," *Journal of Marriage and Family* 68, no. 2 (2006).

46. See Paula Roberts, "Out of Order? Factors Influencing the Sequence of Marriage and Childbirth among Disadvantaged Americans" (Policy Brief no. 9, Washington, D.C.: Center for Law and Social Policy, January 2007), 5.

47. Bella DePaulo, *Singled Out: How Singles are Stereotyped, Stigmatized, and Ignored and Still Live Happily Ever After* (New York: St. Martin's Press, 2006), 55–56.

48. Fein and Ooms, "What Do We Know about Couples and Marriage?" 2–3.

49. Lawrence R. Mishel, Jared Bernstein, and Sylvia Allegretto, *The State of Working America 2006/2007* (Ithaca, N.Y: Cornell University Press, 2007), 302–4.

50. Avis Jones-DeWeever, "Marriage Promotion and Low-Income Communities: An Examination of Real Needs and Real Solutions" (briefing paper, Institute for Women's Policy Research, Washington, D.C., June 2002).

51. Janie Peterson, Xue Song, and Avis Jones-DeWeever, "Life after Welfare Reform: Low-Income Single Parent Families, Pre- and Post-TANF" (Research in Brief, Institute for Women's Policy Research, Washington, D.C., May 2002).

52. Economic Policy Institute, *The State of Working America 2006/2007*, "Inequality" and "International Comparisons" fact sheets, www.stateofworkingamerica.org/facts.html.

53. Ibid., "Income" fact sheet.

54. David Cay Johnston, "Income Gap Is Widening, Data Shows," *New York Times*, March 29, 2007.

55. Economic Policy Institute, *The State of Working America*, "Inequality" and "Income" fact sheets.

56. Ibid., "Poverty" fact sheet.

57. Institute for American Values and Institute for Marriage and Public Policy, *Marriage and the Law*.

58. Vivian Hamilton, "Mistaking Marriage for Social Policy," *Virginia Journal of Social Policy and the Law* 11, no. 3 (2004): 307–72, 368.

59. Coltrane, "Marketing the Marriage 'Solution,'" 394.

60. See Steven K. Wisendale, "Think Tanks and Family Values," *Dissent* (spring 2005).

61. Joel F. Handler and Yeheskel Hasenfeld, *Blame Welfare, Ignore Poverty and Inequality* (New York: Cambridge University Press, 2007).

62. Ibid., 316–48.

63. Center for American Progress, *From Poverty to Prosperity: A National Strategy to Cut Poverty in Half* (Washington, D.C.: Center for American Progress, April 2007), 2–5.

64. Brief for Andrew E. Cherlin et al., *Baehr v. Miike.*

65. Sheila B. Kamerman, "Gender Role and Family Structure Changes in the Advanced Industrialized West: Implications for Social Policy," in *Poverty, Inequality and the Future of Social Policy,* edited by Katherine McFate, Roger Lawson, and William Julius Wilson (New York: Russell Sage Foundation, 1995), 243.

66. Mishel, Bernstein, Allegretto, *The State of Working America,* 348–51; Sylvia A. Allegretto, with Rob Gray, "Economic Snapshots," Economic Policy Institute, www.epi.org/content.cfm/webfeatures_snapshots_20060719.

67. Institute for American Values and Institute for Marriage and Public Policy, *Marriage and the Law.*

68. Russell Shorto, "What's Their Real Problem with Gay Marriage? It's the Gay Part," *New York Times Magazine,* June 19, 2005.

69. Brief for Legal and Family Scholars as amici curiae supporting appellants, *Conaway v. Deane,* No. 24-C-04–005390 (Md. Ct. App. 2006), available at www.aclu.org/lgbt/relationships/27251lgl20061019.html.

70. UNICEF, *Child Poverty in Perspective: An Overview of Child Well-Being in Rich Counties* (Report Card 7, Innocenti Research Centre, Florence, Italy, 2007), 42; Organisation for Economic Co-operation and Development, *Society at a Glance: OECD Social Indicators,* 2006 edition, www.oecd.org/els/social/indicators/SAG; United Nation Statistics Division, *Social Indicators,* http://unstats.un.org/unsd/demographic/products/socind/default.htm.

71. Lynn D. Wardle, "Is Marriage Obsolete?" *Michigan Journal of Gender and the Law* 10, no. 1 (2003): 189–236, 219.

72. Maggie Gallagher, "What is Marriage For? The Public Purposes of Marriage Law," *Louisiana Law Review* 62, no. 3 (2002): 773–92, 780.

73. National Marriage Project, *The State of Our Unions 2003: The Social Health of Marriage in America* (Piscataway, N.J.: National Marriage Project, 2003), 4.

74. Focus on the Family, "Same-Sex 'Marriage' and Civil Unions," www.family.org/socialissues/A000000464.cfm.

75. Southern Baptist Convention, "The Baptist Faith and Message," www.sbc.net/bfm/bfm2000.asp.

76. Bob Schwarz, "Promise Keepers Meeting Opens Friday, Group Encourages Better Husbands, But Critics See Right-Wing Agenda," *Charleston Gazette*, July 8, 2004.

77. Carlos A. Ball, "Lesbian and Gay Families: Gender Nonconformity and the Implications of Difference," *Capital University Law Review* 31, no. 4 (2003): 691–750.

78. Nan D. Hunter, "Marriage, Law, and Gender: A Feminist Inquiry," *Law & Sexuality* 1, no. 1 (1991): 9–30.

Chapter Five: LGBT Families and the Marriage-Equality Movement

1. Bruce Bawer, *A Place at the Table: The Gay Individual in American Society* (New York: Poseidon Press, 1993).

2. *Baehr v. Lewin*, 852 P.2d 44 (Hawaii 1993).

3. Andrew Sullivan, *Virtually Normal: An Argument about Homosexuality* (New York: Alfred A. Knopf, 1995).

4. Jonathan Rauch, *Gay Marriage: Why It Is Good for Gays, Good for Straights, and Good for America* (New York: Henry Holt, 2004).

5. Lovegevity, "The Marriage Movement: A Statement of Principles," http://web.archive.org/web/20010104041400/www.marriagemovement.org/html/report.html.

6. Human Rights Campaign Foundation, "Employers That Offer Domestic Partner Health Benefits," www.hrc.org/Template.cfm?Section=Search_the_Database&Template=/CustomSource/WorkNet/srch.cfm&searchtypeid=3&searchSubTypeID=1.

7. *Lawrence v. Texas*, 539 U.S. 558 (2003).

8. *Romer v. Evans*, 517 U.S. 620 (1996).

9. *In re Adoption of Minor T.*, 17 Fam. L. Rptr. 1523 (D.C. Super. Ct. 1991). The author was Laura and Victoria's attorney.

10. See Leslie Cooper and Paul Cates, *Too High a Price: The Case against Restricting Gay Parenting*, 2nd ed. (New York: American Civil Liberties Union Foundation, 2006), 16–24. Examples of these statements of support follow. *The Child Welfare League of America:* Evidence shows that children's optimal development is influenced more by the nature of the relationships and interactions within the family unit than by its particular structural form. *American Psychological Association:* There is no scientific basis for concluding that lesbian mothers or gay fathers are unfit parents on the basis of their sexual orientation. On the contrary, results of research suggest that lesbian and gay parents are as likely as heterosexual parents to provide supportive and healthy environments for their

children. *American Academy of Pediatrics:* Denying legal parent status through adoption to co-parents or second parents prevents . . . children from enjoying the psychological and legal security that comes from having 2 willing, capable, loving parents. *American Medical Association:* Our AMA will support legislative efforts to allow the adoption of a child by the same-sex partner, or opposite sex non-married partner, who functions as a second parent or co-parent to that child. *American Psychiatric Association:* Second parent adoptions, which grant full parental rights to a second unrelated adult (usually an unmarried partner of a legal parent), are often in the best interest of the child(ren) and should not be prohibited solely because both adults are of the same gender. *American Academy of Child and Adolescent Psychiatry:* There is no evidence to suggest or support that parents with a gay, lesbian, or bisexual orientation are per se different or deficient in parenting skills, child-centered concerns and parent-child attachments, when compared to parents with a heterosexual orientation. *National Association of Social Workers:* The literature . . . undermines negative assumptions about gay men and lesbians as parents. The most striking feature of the research on lesbian mothers, gay fathers, and their children is the absence of pathological findings. The second most striking feature is how similar the groups of gay and lesbian parents and their children are to the heterosexual parents and their children that were included in the studies. *North American Council of Adoptable Children:* Children should not be denied a permanent family because of the sexual orientation of their potential parents. *American Academy of Family Physicians:* The AAFP established a policy to be "supportive of legislation which promotes a safe and nurturing environment, including psychological and legal security, for all children, including those of adoptive parents, regardless of the parents' sexual orientation."

11. The National Gay and Lesbian Task Force, "Second-Parent Adoption in the U.S., as of May 2007," http://www.thetaskforce.org/reports_and_research/second_parent_adoption_laws.

12. *Elisa B. v. Superior Court*, 37 Cal. 4th 108 (2005); *In re Parentage of Robinson*, 383 N.J. Super. Ct. 165 (Ch. Div. 2005).

13. American Law Institute, *Principles of the Law of Family Dissolution: Analysis and Recommendations*, sec. 2.18 (c) (2000).

14. Council on Family Law, *The Future of Family Law: Law and the Marriage Crisis in North America* (New York: Institute for American Values, June 2005).

15. District of Columbia Code, sec. 16–801 (1) and 16–803 (2007).

16. *Solomon v. District of Columbia*, Civ. Action 94–2709, Order April 27, 1995.

17. *Langan v. St. Vincent's Hosp. of New York*, 850 N.E.2d 672 (2006).

18. *Graves v. Estabrook*, 818 A.2d 1255 (N.H. 2003); *Dunphy v. Gregor*, 642 A.2d 372 (N.J. 1994); *Lozoya v. Sanchez*, 66 P.3d 948 (N.M. 2003).

19. *Reep v. Commissioner of Dep't of Employment & Training,* 412 Mass. 845 (1992).

20. *Gormley v. Robertson,* 83 P.3d 1042 (Wash. Ct. App. 2004).

21. *Vasquez v. Hawthorne,* 33 P.3d 735 (Wash. 2001) (en banc).

22. *Irizarry v. Bd. of Educ. of City of Chicago,* 251 F.3d 604 (7th Cir. 2001).

23. *In re Jacob, In re Dana,* 660 N.E.2.d 397 (N.Y. 1995).

24. *Baehr v. Lewin,* 852 P.2d 44 (Hawaii 1993).

25. *Hawaii Revised Statutes,* sec. 572C-1–7.

26. Alaska Const. art. I, sec. 25; *Brause v. Dep't of Health & Soc. Servs.,* 21 P.3d 357 (Alaska 2001).

27. *Baker v. State,* 170 Vt. 194 (1999).

28. *Vermont Statutes Annotated,* title 15, sec. 1204 (2007); David Moats, *Civil Wars: The Battle for Gay Marriage* (New York: Harcourt, 2004).

29. *Goodridge v. Dept. of Public Health,* 798 N.E.2d 941 (Mass. 2003).

30. Human Rights Campaign, "Relationship Recognition in the U.S.," www.hrc.org/Template.cfm?Section=Your_Community&Template=/ContentManagement/ContentDisplay.cfm&ContentID=16305.

31. National Gay and Lesbian Task Force, "Marriage Map," www.thetaskforce.org/reports_and_research/marriage_map; Human Rights Campaign, "Marriage/Relationship Recognition," http://hrc.org/Template.cfm?Section=Center&Template=/TaggedPage/TaggedPageDisplay.cfm&TPLID=63&ContentID=17353.

32. *State v. Carswell,* 2007 Ohio 3723 (2007).

33. *Nat'l Pride at Work, Inc. v. Governor of Mich.*, 2007 Mich. App. LEXIS 240 (Mich. Ct. App. 2007).

34. Deborah Bulkeley, "Funds to Ban Gay Unions 92% In-State," *Deseret Morning News,* February 9, 2006.

35. Quoted in Paul Egan, "Court Rejects Same-Sex Benefits; Gays Working for Michigan Government, Colleges Lose Health Coverage for Partners; Appeal Planned," *Detroit News,* February 3, 2007.

36. Kent Burbank, "The Anatomy of a Movement: Dissecting Arizona's Victory Against Proposition 107," *Peacework* (April 2007).

37. John D'Emilio, "The Marriage Fight Is Setting Us Back," *The Gay and Lesbian Review* 13, no. 6 (2006).

38. Carlos Ball, "The Backlash Thesis and Same-Sex Marriage: Learning from *Brown v. Board of Education* and Its Aftermath," *William and Mary Bill of Rights Journal* 14, no. 4 (2006): 1493–1538.

39. Gregory M. Herek, "Legal Recognition of Same-Sex Relationships in the United States: A Social Science Perspective," *American Psychologist* 61, no. 6 (2006).

40. Gilbert Herdt and Robert Kertzner, "I Do, But I Can't: The Impact of Mar-

riage Denial on the Mental Health and Sexual Citizenship of Lesbians and Gay Men in the United States," *Sexuality Research and Social Policy: Journal of NSRC* 3, no. 1 (2006).

41. Ellen Lewin, "Commodifying Same-Sex Marriage in the United States: Medicalization, Morality and Mental Health" (faculty working paper, Department of Women's Studies, University of Iowa, 2006).

42. Gay & Lesbian Advocates & Defenders, "Why Marriage Matters," www.glad.org/rights/OP1-whymarriagematters.shtml.

43. William N. Eskridge Jr. and Darren R. Spedale, *Gay Marriage: For Better or Worse?: What We've Learned from the Evidence* (Oxford, U.K., and New York: Oxford University Press, 2006).

44. National Gay and Lesbian Task Force, "How Unequal Are Civil Unions?" (italics added), available at www.thetaskforce.org/reports_and_research/how-unequal.

45. Lisa Bennett and Gary J. Gates, *The Cost of Marriage Inequality to Children and Their Same-Sex Parents,* www.hrc.org/content/contentgroups/publi cations1/kids_doc_final.pdf.

46. Gay & Lesbian Advocates & Defenders, "Why Marriage Matters."

47. Brief for American Psychological Association and New Jersey Psychological Association as amici curiae in support of plaintiffs-appellants at 51–52, *Lewis v. Harris,* 875 A.2d 259 (N.J. Super. Ct. 2005) (No. A-2244–03T5), available at www.lambdalegal.org/our-work/in-court/briefs/lewis-v-harris-brief-13.html.

48. Brief for National Association of Social Workers as amici curiae in support of plaintiffs-appellants at 8, 12, *Lewis v. Harris,* 875 A.2d 259 (N.J. Super. Ct. 2005) (No. A-2244-03T5), available at www.lambdalegal.org/our-work/in-court/briefs/lewis-v-harris-brief-7.html.

49. Herdt and Kertzner, "I Do, But I Can't."

50. Evan Wolfson, *Why Marriage Matters: America, Equality, and Gay People's Right to Marry* (New York: Simon & Schuster, 2004).

51. Lambda Legal, "Denying Access to Marriage Harms Families," http://familyequality.org/dmhf.pdf.

52. *Family and Medical Leave Act,* U.S. Code 29 (2007), sec. 2601.

53. U.S. Office of Personnel Management, "Sick Leave to Care for a Family Member with a Serious Health Condition," https://www.opm.gov./oca/leave/HTML/12week.asp.

54. See Kath Weston, *Families We Choose: Lesbians, Gays, Kinship* (New York: Columbia University Press, 1991).

55. *District of Columbia Code,* sec. 32–501(4) (2007).

56. *DeWolf and Watts v. Countrywide,* complaint and press release available at www.lambdalegal.org/our-work/in-court/cases/dewolf-and-watts.html.

57. Gay & Lesbian Advocates & Defenders, "GLAD's Marriage-Related Cases," www.glad.org/marriage.

58. American Civil Liberties Union, "*Deane and Polyak v. Conaway*—Meet the Plaintiffs," http://aclu.org/lgbt/relationships/12376res20040713.html.

59. Lambda Legal, "Beyond Dispute: The Breadth of Lambda Legal's Relationship Work," www.lambdalegal.org/our-work/issues/marriage-relationships-family/marriage/beyond-dispute-the-breadth.html.

60. Judith Stacey, "Legal Recognition of Same-Sex Couples: The Impact on Children and Families," *Quinnipiac Law Review* 23, no. 2 (2004): 529–41, 539–40.

Chapter Six: Countries Where Marriage Matters Less

1. *Miron v. Trudel,* [1995] 2 S.C.R. 418, 420.

2. Kathleen A. Lahey, *Are We Persons Yet?: Law and Sexuality in Canada* (Toronto: University of Toronto Press, 1999), 15, n. 58–59.

3. Ibid.

4. *M v. H* [1999] 2 S.C.R 3.

5. *Modernization of Benefits and Obligations Act,* c. 12 (2000).

6. Nicholas Bala, "The Debates about Same-Sex Marriage in Canada and the United States: Controversy Over the Evolution of a Fundamental Social Institution," *Brigham Young University Journal of Public Law* 20, no. 2 (2006): 195–231, 212.

7. *Ross v. Reaney,* [2003] O.J. No. 2366 (ON.C. 2003).

8. Law Commission of Canada, *Beyond Conjugality: Recognizing and Supporting Close Personal Adult Relationships* (Ottawa: Law Commission of Canada, 2001).

9. Leo Pare, "Alberta Against the Wall," *Lloydminster Meridian Booster,* A1, December 12, 2004; Leo Pare, "Referendum Rejected," *Lloydminster Meridian Booster,* December 15, 2004.

10. *Adult Interdependent Relationships Act,* SA 2002, c. A-4.5.

11. Jenni Millbank, "The Changing Meaning of 'De Facto' Relationships," *Current Family Law* 12, no. 82 (2006): 1–11; Jenni Millbank, "The Recognition of Lesbian and Gay Families in Australian Law: Part 1, Couples," *Federal Law Review* 34, no. 1 (2006): 1–44; Jenni Millbank, "The Recognition of Lesbian and Gay Families in Australian Law: Part 2, Children" *Federal Law Review* 34, no. 2 (2006): 205–260.

12. Reg Graycar and Jenni Millbank, "From Functional Family to Spinster Sisters: Australia's Distinctive Path to Relationship Recognition," *Washington University Journal of Law and Policy* 24 (July 2007).

13. Millbank, "The Recognition of Lesbian and Gay Families in Australian Law: Part 1, Couples."

14. Ibid.

15. Bill Atkin, "The Challenge of Unmarried Cohabitation—The New Zealand Response," *Family Law Quarterly* 37, no. 2 (2003): 303–26, 304.

16. *More or Less Together: Levels of Legal Consequences of Marriage, Cohabitation and Registered Partnerships for Different-Sex and Same-Sex Partners,* edited by Kees Waaldijk (Paris: Institut National D'etudes Demographiques, 2005); International Lesbian and Gay Association (ILGA)-Europe, "Same-Sex Marriage and Partnership: Country by Country," www.ilga-europe.org/europe/issues/marriage_and_partnership/same_sex_marriage_and_partnership_country_by_country.

17. Waaldijk, *More or Less Together*; The Supreme Court of Appeal of South Africa, *Fourie v. Minister of Home Affairs,* Case no: 232/2003 (2004), www.law.wits.ac.za/sca/summary.php?case_id=12942); International Lesbian and Gay Association (ILGA)-Europe, "Same-Sex Marriage and Partnership: Country by Country."

18. Adilson Jose Moreira, "Equality for Same-Sex Couples: Brazilian Courts and Social Inclusiveness," *Harvard Review of Latin America* 6, no. 3 (2007): 46–48. Additional information from Adilson Jose Moreira, "From De Facto Partnerships to Stable Unions: The Construction of Equality in the Brazilian Same-Sex Union Jurisprudence," 2006, unpublished manuscript.

19. Ibid.

20. Shahar Lifshitz, *Cohabitation Law in Israel: In Light of Civil Law Theory of the Family* (Haifa, Israel: Haifa University, 2005), 23–30; Tal Rosner, "New Regulation: Gays Can Inherit Partners' Assets," *YNetNews,* www.ynetnews.com/articles/0,7340,L-3248122,00.html.

21. United Nations Economic Commission for Europe, "Trends in Births outside Marriage, 1980 and 2001," www.unece.org/stats/trends/ch2/2.11.xls; UNICEF, *Child Poverty in Perspective: An Overview of Child Well-Being in Rich Counties* (Report Card 7, Innocenti Research Centre, Florence, Italy, 2007), 42.

22. Human Rights Watch and Immigration Equality, *Family, Unvalued: Discrimination, Denial, and the Fate of Binational Same-Sex Couples under U.S. Law* (New York: 2006), available at www.hrw.org/doc/?t=pubs.

23. International Conference on LGBT Human Rights, "Declaration of Montreal," 2006, www.declarationofmontreal.org/DeclarationofMontreal.pdf.

Chapter Seven: Valuing All Families

1. United States Government Accountability Office, *Defense of Marriage Act: Update to Prior Report* (Washington, D.C.: U.S. Government Accountability Office, January 23, 2004).

2. Equality Maryland, *Marriage Inequality in the State of Maryland* (Silver Spring, Md.: Equality Maryland, 2006).

3. Martha Albertson Fineman, *The Neutered Mother, the Sexual Family, and Other Twentieth Century Tragedies* (New York: Routledge, 1995).

4. Martha Albertson Fineman, *The Autonomy Myth: A Theory of Dependency* (New York: New Press, 2004).

5. Grace Ganz Blumberg, "Cohabitation without Marriage: A Different Perspective," *UCLA Law Review* 28, no. 6 (1981): 1125–81, 1128.

6. Grace Ganz Blumberg, "Legal Recognition of Same-Sex Conjugal Relationships: The 2003 California Domestic Partner Rights and Responsibilities Act in Comparative Civil Rights and Family Law Perspective," *UCLA Law Review* 51, no. 6 (2004): 1555–1618, 1555.

7. Law Commission of Canada, *Beyond Conjugality: Recognizing and Supporting Close Personal Adult Relationships* (Ottawa: Law Commission of Canada, 2001), 17.

8. D. Kelly Weisberg and Susan Frelich Appleton, *Modern Family Law: Cases and Materials,* 3rd ed. (New York: Aspen Publishers, 2006), 262–65.

9. Homer H. Clark Jr., *The Law of Domestic Relations in the United States,* 2nd ed. (St. Paul, Minn.: West, 1988).

10. Ibid.

11. Women's Law Center of Maryland, Inc., *Families in Transition: A Follow-Up Study Exploring Family Law Issues in Maryland* (Towson, Md.: Women's Law Center of Maryland, December 2006).

12. John DeWitt Gregory, Peter N. Swisher, and Sheryl L. Wolf, *Understanding Family Law,* 2nd ed. (New York: Matthew Bender, 2001), 310–12.

13. *Stroud v. Stroud,* 49 Va. App. 359 (2007).

14. Weisberg and Appleton, *Modern Family Law,* 234–44.

15. *Stanley v. Illinois,* 405 U.S. 645, 656 (1972).

16. *Reed v. Reed,* 404 U.S. 71, 76 (1971).

17. *Arthur v. Milstein,* 949 So. 2d 1163 (Fla. 4th DCA 2007).

18. *New York Public Health,* sec. 4201(1)(c)(iii) (Lexis 2007).

19. *Barbee v. Barbee,* 311 Md. 620 (1988).

20. David S. Buckel, "Unequal Justice for Gays in Hostile Court Room," *National Law Journal,* August 18, 1997.

21. Catherine F. Klein and Leslye E. Orloff, "Providing Legal Protection for Battered Women: An Analysis of State Statutes and Case Law," *Hofstra Law Review* 21, no. 4 (1993): 801–1190.

22. *People v. Williams,* 24 N.Y.2d 274 (1969).

23. See Elizabeth M. Schneider, *Battered Women and Feminist Lawmaking* (New Haven, Conn.: Yale University Press, 2002); Susan Schechter, *Women and Male Violence: The Visions and Struggles of the Battered Women's Movement* (Boston: South End Press, 1982).

24. Klein and Orloff, "Providing Legal Protection."

25. Ibid.

26. Donna St. George, "The Forgotten Families; Grandparents Raising Slain Soldiers' Children Are Denied a Government Benefit Intended to Sustain the Bereaved," *Washington Post,* February 16, 2007.

27. Ibid.

28. Code of Federal Regulations, Title 29 Part 825.113(c)(3).

29. This couple is an example from the caseload of Jay Toole, shelter organizer for Queers for Economic Justice. Bella and Fran are not their real names.

30. New York City Department of Homeless Services, "Family Services," http://home2.nyc.gov/html/dhs/html/homeless/famserv.shtml.

31. *Sierotowicz v. N.Y. City Hous. Auth.*, 2006 U.S. Dist. LEXIS 19644 (E.D.N.Y. 2006).

32. Frank S. Alexander, "The Housing of America's Families," *Emory Law Journal* 54, no. 3 (2005): 1231–70.

33. *Mychal Judge Police and Fire Chaplains Public Safety Officers' Benefit Act of 2002,* Public Law No: 107–196, 107th Cong., 2d. sess. (June 24, 2002).

Chapter Eight: Domestic Partner Benefits for All Families

1. American Civil Liberties Union, "*Deane and Polyak v. Conaway*: About the Plaintiffs," http://aclu.org/lgbt/relationships/12376res20040713.html.

2. Northwestern Women's Law Center, "Our Clients' Statement," www.nwwlc.org/publications/client_statements/subramaniam.htm.

3. U.S. Census Bureau, "Income Stable, Poverty Rate Increases, Percentage of Americans without Health Insurance Unchanged," press release, August 30, 2005, www.census.gov/Press-Release/www/releases/archives/income_wealth/005647.html.

4. Michael A. Ash. and M. V. Lee Badgett, "Separate and Unequal: The Effect of Unequal Access to Employment-Based Health Insurance on Same-Sex and Unmarried Different Sex-Couples," *Contemporary Economic Policy* 24, no. 4 (2006).

5. M.V. Lee Badgett, *Money, Myths, and Change: The Economic Lives of Lesbians and Gay Men* (Chicago: University of Chicago Press, 2001), 77.

6. Alice Kessler-Harris, *A Woman's Wage: Historical Meanings and Social Consequences* (Lexington: University of Kentucky Press, 1990), 23–25.

7. Centers for Disease Control and Prevention, "Table 1–1. Live Births, Birth Rates, and Fertility Rates, by Race: United States, 1909–2000," www.cdc.gov/nchs/data/statab/t001x01.pdf; U.S. Census Bureau, "Table MS-2. Estimated Median Age at First Marriage, by Sex: 1890 to the Present," www.census.gov/population/socdemo/hh-fam/ms2.pdf.

8. U.S. Census Bureau, "Measuring 50 years of Economic Change," www.census.gov/prod/3/98pubs/p60–203.pdf; Center for Women and Work, "Women in the Workforce: Facts about Working Women," www.cww.rutgers.edu/dataPages/FactSheet1.pdf.

9. Frank S. Alexander, "Of Families and Housing Laws," *Emory Report* 58, no. 18 (February 6, 2006).

10. Jason Fields, *America's Families and Living Arrangements: 2003* (Washington, D.C.: U.S. Census Bureau, November 2004).

11. Stacy Sneeringer, "Normalizing the Alternative: The U.S. Census and Societal Views of Alternative Families" (working paper, University of California, Berkeley Faculty of Economics Department, Berkeley, 2004).

12. Tavia Simmons and Martin O'Connell, *Married-Couple and Unmarried Partner Households: 2000* (Washington, D.C.: U.S. Census Bureau, February 2000); U.S. Census Bureau, "General Demographic Characteristics: 2005," http://factfinder.census.gov/servlet/ADPTable?_bm=y&-geo_id=01000US&-qr_name=ACS_2005_EST_G00_DP1&-ds_name=&-redoLog=false.

13. Ash and Badgett, "Separate and Unequal."

14. Ibid. (Recent research demonstrates that covering domestic partners does not entail significant additional expenditures.)

15. U.S. Department of Health and Human Services, "Insure Kids Now!" www.insurekidsnow.gov.

16. Code of Federal Regulations, Title 29, Part 825.113(c)(3).

17. Alaska Civil Liberties Union v. State, 122 P.3d 781 (Alaska 2005); Snetsinger v. Mont. Univ. Sys., 104 P.3 445 (Mont. 2005); Order, *Bedford and Breen v. N.H. Tech. Coll. Sys.,* Nos. 04-E-299 and 04-E-0230 (N.H. Super. Ct. 2005), available at www.glad.org/GLAD_Cases/bedford_breen_documents.html; *Tanner v. Oregon Health Sci. Univ.,* 971 P.2d 435 (Or. Ct. App. 1998).

18. National Gay and Lesbian Task Force, "State Nondiscrimination Laws in the U.S. Map," www.thetaskforce.org/reports_and_research/nondiscrimination_laws.

19. Suzanne Hoholik, "Some Eager for City to Expand Health Plan," *Columbus Dispatch,* April 28, 2002.

20. Derek P. Jensen, "Partner Benefits Turned Down," *Salt Lake Tribune,* July 13, 2005; Holly Mullen, "Fear Drove County Vote on Benefits," *Salt Lake Tribune,* July 14, 2005.

21. Heather May, "SLC Will Offer Health Care to Unwed Couples; Executive Order: Gay Advocates Hail the Mayor's Decision to take the Unilateral Action Wednesday," *Salt Lake Tribune,* September 20, 2005.

22. Ibid.

23. Salt Lake City Ordinance, *Benefits for Dependents of Employees,* sec.

2.52.100 (2006), http://66.113.195.234/UT/Salt%20Lake%20City/index.htm and www.slcgov.com/council/newsreleases/Household-Benefits-Revised.pdf.

24. Heather May, "Rocky Vetoes Council's Benefit Plan," *Salt Lake Tribune,* February 21, 2006.

25. Salt Lake City Council, *Minutes of Meeting,* February 7, 2006, www.slcgov.com/search/search.asp

26. *In Re Utah State Retirement Board's Trustee Duties and Salt Lake City Ordinance No. 4 of 2006,* Civ. No. 050916879; Jason Bergreen, "SLC Benefits Plan OK'd," *Salt Lake Tribune,* May 14, 2006.

27. Leigh Dethman, "County Revisiting Partner Perks," *Deseret Morning News,* April 9, 2007.

28. Stephanie Simon, "The Nation; Conservative's Bill Offers Some Rights to Gay Couples," *Los Angeles Times,* February 12, 2006.

29. Simon, "The Nation"; "Focus on the Family Issues Statement on Reciprocal Beneficiary Bill," *Dakota Voice,* February 8, 2006, www.dakotavoice.com/200602/20060208_2.html.

30. Sean Cahill, "Welfare Moms and the Two Grooms: The Concurrent Promotion and Restriction of Marriage in US Public Policy," *Sexualities* 8, no. 2 (2005).

31. *Tax Equity for Health Plan Beneficiaries Act of 2007,* HR 1820, 110th Cong., 1st sess. (March 29, 2007).

Chapter Nine: Coping with Illness: Medical Care and Family and Medical Leave

1. Lambda Legal, "University of Maryland Medical System to Be Sued Wednesday by Gay Man Prevented from Visiting His Dying Partner at Shock Trauma Center in Baltimore," February 27, 2002, www.lambdalegal.org/news/pr/university-of-maryland.html.

2. "Poster Couple; Lesbians Lend Their Name to Groundbreaking Court Ruling," *Grand Rapid Press,* April 4, 2004.

3. Gay & Lesbian Advocates & Defenders, "Carol Conklin and Janet Peck," www.glad.org/marriage/Kerrigan-Mock/Janet&Carol.html.

4. *Whitman v. Mercy-Memorial Hospital,* 128 Mich. App. 155 (1983).

5. Lambda Legal, "University of Maryland Medical System."

6. *Federal Patient Self Determination Act 1990,* Public Law 101–508, codified at *U.S. Code* 42 (1990), sec. 1395 cc (a).

7. K. Michael Lipkin, M.D., "Brief Report: Identifying a Proxy for Health Care as Part of a Routine Medical Inquiry," *Journal of General Internal Medicine* 21, no. 11 (November 2006): 1188–91.

8. Ibid.

9. National Conference of Commissioners on Uniform State Laws, *Uniform Health-Care Decisions Act,* approved by the American Bar Association, February 7, 1994 in Kansas City, Missouri.

10. Last Acts, *Means to a Better End: A Report on Dying in America Today* (Washington, D.C.: Last Acts National Program Office, 2002), 10.

11. American Association for Single People, "2000 Census—AASP Report," www.unmarriedamerica.org/Census%202000/marital-status-adults-trends.htm.

12. *District of Columbia Code,* sec., 21–2202 (2007).

13. *Annotated Statutes of New Mexico,* sec. 24–7A-5.

14. National Conference of Commissioners on Uniform State Laws, *Uniform Health-Care Decisions Act,* approved by the American Bar Association, February 7, 1994 in Kansas City, Missouri.

15. American Bar Association, "Surrogate Consent in the Absence of an Advance Directive," www.abanet.org/aging/legislativeupdates/docs/Famcon04.pdf.

16. Last Acts, *Means to a Better End.*

17. *Colorado Revised Statutes,* sec. 15–18.5–103 (2006).

18. *District of Columbia Code Annotated,* sec. 21–2210(2)(f).

19. Amy Gardner, "Surprising Unity on Va. Hospital Visit Bill; Conservatives Support Right That Includes Gays," *Washington Post,* February 19, 2007.

20. *New York Public Health Law,* sec 2805-q.

21. *Maryland Medical Decision Making Act of 2005,* HB 1021/SB 796.

22. Governor Robert L. Ehrlich Jr. to the Honorable Thomas V. Mike Miller Jr., President of the Senate, State House, 20 May 2005, vetoing Senate Bill 796—Medical Decision Making Act of 2005.

23. Health—Advance Directives—Registry—Drivers' Licenses and Identification Cards, HB 319/ SB 236, 421st Session of the Maryland General Assembly, codified at *Maryland Transportation Code Annotated,* sec. 12–303.1.

24. Dan Furmansky, e-mail message to author, April 9, 2007.

25. Kimberly Menashe Glassman, "Balancing the Demands of the Workplace with the Needs of the Modern Family: Expanding Family and Medical Leave to Protect Domestic Partners," *University of Michigan Journal of Law Reform* 37, no. 3 (2004): 837–80, 853.

26. *Ross v. Denver Dep't of Health & Hosps.,* 883 P.2d 516 (Colo. Ct. App. 1994).

27. Ronald D. Elving, *Conflict and Compromise: How Congress Makes the Law* (New York: Simon & Schuster, 1995).

28. Jody Heymann, Alison Earle, and Jeffrey Hayes, *The Work, Family, and Equity Index: How Does the United States Measure Up?* (Montreal: Project on Global Working Families and the Institute for Health and Social Policy, 2007).

29. Judy Greenwald, "Low Take-Up Reported for California's Paid Leave Law;

But Year-Old Program Expected to Increase in Popularity," *Business Insurance,* July 11, 2005.

30. *Code of Federal Regulations,* Title 29, Part 825.113(c)(3).

31. *District of Columbia Family and Medical Leave Act of 1990,* D.C. Law 8–181, (3 October 1990), codified at *District of Columbia Code,* sec. 32–501 et seq.

32. United States Department of Labor, "Administering Family and Medical Leave by Covered Establishments," www.dol.gov/esa/whd/fmla/fmla/chapter6.htm.

33. *Healthy Families Act,* 110th Cong., 1st sess., S910/ HR 1542.

34. Code of Federal Regulations, Title 5, Parts 630.201: https://www.opm.gov/oca/leave/html/12week.asp.

35. Jody Heymann, "The Healthy Families Act: The Importance to Americans' Livelihoods, Families, and Health," (testimony, U.S. Senate Committee on Health, Education, Labor, and Pensions, Hearing on The Healthy Families Act, February 13, 2007), available at www.mcgill.ca/newsroom/news/?ItemID=23823.

Chapter Ten: When a Relationship Ends through Dissolution or Death: Distributing Assets and Providing for Children

1. *L. S. K. v. H. A. N.,* 813 A.2d 872 (Pa. Super. Ct. 2002).

2. *Norris v. Norris,* 16 Ill. App. 3d 879 (1974).

3. *Marvin v. Marvin,* 18 Cal. 3d 660 (1976).

4. *Cyrton v. Malinowitz,* 831 N.Y.S.2d 347 (N.Y. Super. Ct. 2006).

5. In *Hewitt v. Hewitt* a couple had lived together for fifteen years and had three children. The court ruled it would not enforce any agreement between them because to do so would undermine marriage. 77 Ill. 2d 49 (Ill. 1979).

6. Dianna B. Elliott and Jane Lawler Dye, "Unmarried Partner Households in the United States: Descriptions and Trends 2000 to 2003," www.census.gov/acs/www/Downloads/PAA-up_poster4.ppt.

7. *Connell v. Francisco,* 127 Wn.2d 339 (1995).

8. *Gormley v. Robertson,* 120 Wn. App. 31 (2004).

9. American Law Institute, *Principles of the Law of Family Dissolution: Analysis and Recommendations,* sec. 6.02, Comment (2000).

10. Ibid., sec. 6.03(1).

11. Ibid., sec 6.03(7).

12. Quoted in Nancy D. Polikoff, "Making Marriage Matter Less: The ALI Domestic Partner Principles Are One Step in the Right Direction," *2004 University of Chicago Legal Forum,* no. 1 (2004): 358–80, 358.

13. Quoted in Unmarried America, "American Law Institute Report Triggers Debate on the Beleaguered Institution of Marriage," www.unmarriedamerica

.org/members/news/2003/January-News/ALI_report_triggers_debate_on_the_beleaguered_institution_of_marriage_Jan_14,2003.html.

14. Quoted in Cheryl Wetzstein, "Splitting Up and the Law; Book's Affirmation of 'Family Diversity' Stirs Debate," *Washington Times*, September 14, 2006.

15. Polikoff, "Making Marriage Matter Less," 366–72.

16. Jenni Millbank, "The Changing Meaning of "De Facto" Relationships," *Current Family Law* 12, no. 82 (2006): 4.

17. Virginia Grainer, "What's Yours Is Mine: Reform of the Property Division Regime for Unmarried Couples in New Zealand," *Pacific Rim Law and Policy Journal Association* 11, no. 2 (2002): 285–318.

18. Lambda Legal, "*Miller-Jenkins v. Miller-Jenkins*," www.lambdalegal.org/our-work/in-court/cases/miller-jenkins.html.

19. American Law Institute, *Principles of the Law of Family Dissolution*, sec. 2.03(b) (2000).

20. For example, *In re Parentage of L.B.*, 155 Wn.2d 679 (2005) and *Holtzman v. Knott (In re H.S.H-K)*, 193 Wis. 2d 649 (1995).

21. American Civil Liberties Union, "Don't Fence Him Out: Gay Rancher Loses His Home of 23 years," www.aclu.org/lgbt/relationships/23927res20060125.html.

22. *Rex v. Tovrea (In re Estate of Wiltfong)*, 148 P.3d 465 (Colo. Ct. App. 2006).

23. *Colorado Revised Statutes, Colorado Probate Code*, title 15, articles 10–17 (Lexis 2006).

24. American Law Institute, *Restatement (Third) of Property: Wills and Other Donative Transfers*, sec. 3.3 (1999).

25. *In re Estate of Peters*, 210 N.J. Super. Ct. 295 (App. Div. 1986) affirmed by *In re Estate of Peters*, 107 N.J. 263 (1987).

26. *Donati v. Office of Personnel Management*, 2006 M.S.P.B. 321 (MSPB 2006) stayed by *Donati v. Office of Personnel Management*, 2007 M.S.P.B. 44 (MSPB 2007).

27. *New Hampshire Revised Statutes Annotated*, sec. 457:39 (Lexis 2007).

28. E. Gary Spitko, "An Accrual/Multi-Factor Approach to Intestate Inheritance Rights for Unmarried Committed Partners," *Oregon Law Review* 81, no. 2 (2002): 255–350; Lawrence W. Waggoner, "Marital Property Rights in Transition," *Missouri Law Review* 59, no. 1 (1994): 21–104.

29. Olinka Koster, "Sisters Take Their Case to Europe over the 'Gay Bias' on Death Tax; We deserve equal treatment say spinsters who share their family home," *2006 Associated Newspapers Ltd.*, September 13, 2006.

30. "Lambda Legal Pens Bill to Protect Surviving Domestic Partners from Unequal Tax Assessment," www.lambdalegal.org/news/pr/lambda-legal-pens-bill-to.html.

31. *Deering's California Codes Annotated, Revenue and Taxation Code*, sec. 62 (2007).

32. Jane Gross, "Older Women Team Up to Face Future Together," *New York Times*, February 27, 2004.

33. Anna Muraco, "Intentional Families: Fictive Kin Ties between Cross-Gender, Different Sexual Orientation Friends," *Journal of Marriage and Family* 68, no. 5 (2006).

34. *Burden and Burden v. the United Kingdom*, no. 13378/05, ECHR 2006.

35. *Pension Protection Act of 2006*, HR 4, 109th Congress, 2nd sess. (August 17, 2006).

36. Quoted in Human Rights Campaign, "Pension Law Includes Important Protection for Same-Sex Couples Under Federal Law," www.hrc.org/Template.cfm?Section=Press_Room&CONTENTID=33607&TEMPLATE=/ContentManagement/ContentDisplay.cfm.

Chapter Eleven: Losing an Economic Provider: Wrongful Death, Workers' Compensation, and Social Security

1. Evelyn Nieves, "Couple Guilty of All Charges In Fatal Attack by Their Dog," *New York Times*, March 22, 2002.

2. T. A. Smedley, "Some Order Out of Chaos in Wrongful Death Law," *Vanderbilt Law Review* 37, no. 2 (1984): 273–300.

3. *Levy v. Louisiana*, 391 U.S. 68 (1968); *Glona v. American Guarantee & Liability Ins. Co.*, 391 U.S. 73 (1968).

4. *Levy*, 71.

5. *Glona*, 75.

6. Cited in John G. Cullhane, "Even More Wrongful Death: Statutes Divorced from Reality" *Fordham Urban Law Journal* 32, no. 2 (2004): 171–95, 178–79.

7. *Arizona Revised Statutes*, sec. 12–612 (Lexis 2007), *Michie's West Virginia Code Annotated*, sec. 55–7-6 (Lexis 2007); *Michigan Compiled Laws Service*, sec. 600.2922(3)(c) (Lexis 2007); Nancy J. Knauer, "The September 11 Attacks and Surviving Same-Sex Partners: Defining Family through Tragedy," *Temple Law Review* 75, no. 1 (2002): 31–99, 61–64, 72–73.

8. *California Civil Procedure Code*, sec. 377.60 (b) and (c) (2007).

9. *Graves v. Estabrook*, 149 N.H. 202 (2003).

10. *Lozoya v. Sanchez*, 133 N.M. 579 (2003); *Fernandez v. Walgreen Hastings Co.*, 126 N.M. 263 (1998).

11. *Valentine v. Am. Airlines*, 17 A.D.3d 38 (N.Y. App. Div. 2005).

12. "Death Benefit Voted for Homosexual's Lover," *New York Times*, November 11, 1982.

13. *Weber v. Aetna Casualty & Surety Co.*, 406 U.S. 164 (1972).

14. *Wengler v. Druggists Mut. Ins. Co.*, 446 U.S. 142 (1980).

15. *Arp v. Workers' Comp. Appeals Bd.*, 19 Cal. 3d 395 (1977).

16. *Deering's California Codes Annotated, California Labor Code,* sec. 3501 (2007).

17. Ibid., sec. 3503.

18. *Department of Industrial Relations v. Workers' Comp. Appeals Bd.*, 94 Cal. App. 3d 72 (1979).

19. *Associated Indem. Corp. v. Industrial Acci. Com.*, 132 Cal. App. 2d 564 (Cal. Ct. App. 1955).

20. *Maryland Labor and Employment Code Annotated,* sec. 9–681(a). (2007).

21. *Kendall v. Housing Authority of Baltimore City,* 196 Md. 370, 379 (1950).

22. *Atlantic Richfield Co. v. Workers' Comp. Appeals Bd.*, 31 Cal. 3d 715 (1982).

23. *Crisman v. Marsh & McLennan Cos.*, 6 A.D.3d 899 (N.Y. App. Div. 2004).

24. Lambda Legal, "New NY State Law Giving Spousal Benefits to Gay Partners of 9/11 Victims Is a 'Significant Step Forward,' But Gay Families Still Unprotected in Tragedies," www.lambdalegal.org/news/pr/new-york-911-september-11-benefits-domestic-partner-spouse.html.

25. *New York Workers' Compensation Law,* sec. 4.

26. *Novara ex rel. Jones v. Cantor Fitzgerald,* 20 A.D.3d 103 (N.Y. App. Div. 2005).

27. *Cato v. Alcoa-Reynolds Metals Co. (In re Sworden),* 210 Ore. App. 721 (2007).

28. Rochelle Stanfield and Corinna Nicolaou, *Social Security: Out of Step with the Modern Family* (Washington, D.C.: Urban Institute, 2000).

29. Melissa M. Favreault, Frank J. Sammartino, and C. Eugene Steuerle, eds., *Social Security and the Family: Addressing the Unmet Need in an Underfunded System* (Washington, D.C.: Urban Institute, 2002), 26.

30. Ibid., 32.

31. *Califano v. Goldfarb,* 430 U.S. 199 (1977).

32. Favreault, Sammartino, and Steuerle, *Social Security and the Family,* 28.

33. Dennis Ventry, "For Richer, For Poorer: How Tax Policymakers Protected and Punished American Families, 1948–2007" (unpublished manuscript).

34. Sean Cahill and Sarah Tobias, *Policy Issues Affecting Lesbian, Gay, Bisexual and Transgender Families* (Ann Arbor: University of Michigan Press, 2007), 34–35.

35. Dorothy A. Brown, "Social Security and Fairness: Impact on Minorities, Low-Income Persons, and Nontraditional Families: Social Security and Marriage in Black and White," *Ohio State Law Journal* 65 (2004): 111–44.

36. *Califano v. Boles,* 443 U.S. 282 (1979).

37. Melissa M. Favreault and C. Eugene Steuerle, *Social Security and Survivor Benefits for the Modern Family* (Washington, D.C.: Urban Institute, 2007).

Conclusion

1. The full statement is at www.beyondmarriage.org.

2. An Act relating to protecting individuals in domestic partnerships by granting certain rights and benefits, SHB 1351, State of Washington, 60th Legislature, 2007 Regular Session (February 9, 2007).

3. Quoted in Lisa Keen, "Wash. Gov. Signs DP Law," *Bay Area Reporter* 37, no. 19, April 26, 2007.

Index